BEYOND
BULLET POINTS

4TH EDITION

Cliff Atkinson

BEYOND
BULLET POINTS

4TH EDITION

 Microsoft

BEYOND BULLET POINTS

Published with the authorization of Microsoft Corporation by:
Pearson Education, Inc.

ISBN-13: 978-1509-30553-7
ISBN-10: 1-5093-0553-X

Library of Congress Control Number: 2018934573

1 18

TRADEMARKS

WARNING AND DISCLAIMER

SPECIAL SALES

For information about buying this title in bulk quantities, or for special sales opportunities (which may include electronic versions; custom cover designs; and content particular to your business, training goals, marketing focus, or branding interests), please contact our corporate sales department at corpsales@pearsoned.com or (800) 382-3419.

For government sales inquiries, please contact governmentsales@pearsoned.com.

For questions about sales outside the U.S., please contact intlcs@pearson.com.

CREDITS

EDITOR-IN-CHIEF
Greg Wiegand

SENIOR ACQUISITIONS EDITOR
Laura Norman

DEVELOPMENT EDITOR
Rick Kughen

MANAGING EDITOR
Sandra Schroeder

SENIOR PROJECT EDITOR
Tracey Croom

COPY EDITOR
Wordsmithery

INDEXER
Valerie Perry

PROOFREADER
Scout Festa

TECHNICAL EDITOR
Echo Swinford

EDITORIAL ASSISTANT
Cindy J. Teeters

INTERIOR DESIGNER
Maureen Forys,
Happenstance Type-O-Rama

COVER DESIGNER
Twist Creative, Seattle

COMPOSITOR
Maureen Forys,
Happenstance Type-O-Rama

To my good friend, Jaine.
—CLIFF ATKINSON

ACKNOWLEDGMENTS

My thanks to Laura Norman at Pearson for shepherding this book to completion, to Rick Kughen and Echo Swinford for their expert editorial insight, and to the Pearson production team for transforming words and pictures into the book you hold in your hands.

CONTENTS AT GLANCE

CONTENTS

ABOUT THE AUTHOR

CLIFF ATKINSON is an acclaimed writer, popular keynote speaker, and an independent communications consultant to leading attorneys and Fortune 500 companies.

He crafted the presentation that persuaded a jury to award a $253 million verdict to the plaintiff in the nation's first Vioxx trial in 2005, which *Fortune* magazine called "frighteningly powerful."

Cliff's bestselling book *Beyond Bullet Points* (published by Microsoft Press) was named a Best Book of 2007 by the editors of Amazon.com, and has been published in four editions and translated into a dozen languages including Chinese, Korean, and Russian.

This book expands on a communications approach he has taught internationally at top law firms, government agencies, business schools and corporations, including Sony, SC Johnson, Chevron, Toyota, Del Monte, Nestlé, Deloitte, BBDO, The NPD Group, Ipsos, Facebook, Amgen, Bristol-Myers Squibb, Intel, Microsoft, the American Bar Association and the United Nations International Criminal Tribunal.

Cliff's work has been featured in *The New York Times, Los Angeles Times, Wall Street Journal, and Fox News.*

Cliff received his B.A. in English and journalism from Baylor University in Texas and his M.B.A. from Richmond, The American International University in London. After serving as a captain in the U.S. Air Force, he held marketing positions for start-up companies and then launched his own business as a full-time communications consultant in 2001. He currently resides in New York City.

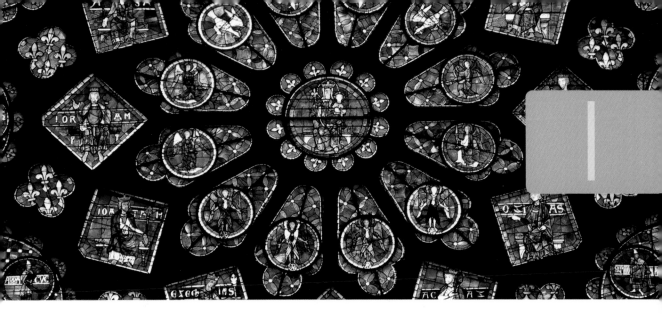

INTRODUCTION: A CANVAS OF LIGHT

Sometimes, when you least expect it, a story can change your life.

I was 24 and a lieutenant in the Air Force stationed in Spain. It was my first big job, chief of public affairs, overseeing the base newspaper and relationships with the media and the local community. I had dreamed of living in Europe while I was growing up in Texas, and this job was a perfect fit for a college English and Journalism major.

Whenever I could, I took vacation time to tour the cities of Europe. One rainy summer day on a trip through France, I drove an hour south of Paris, to a town called Chartres. When I arrived at the front steps of the cathedral, it looked like every other one I had seen in Europe—the walls a depressing gray, the streets quiet, and the cavernous interior empty.

I joined a group of other tourists who were waiting for a guide, and up walked a tall man with a shock of thick, gray hair, wearing a tweed jacket and speaking a perfect gentleman's English. "I'm Malcolm Miller," he said. "Welcome to Chartres—my home for the past 30 years." Malcolm was the author of several books on the cathedral, and the recipient of the highest civilian honor in France for his in-depth knowledge of Chartres.

"Chartres is shrouded in mystery," he began. "We don't know who built it—not a single architect, artisan, laborer, sculptor, glassmaker, or painter took credit for the work you see here. It was a true labor of love."

Malcolm pointed to the empty streets around the cathedral and explained that in the 12th century, they would have been packed with pilgrims who had traveled hundreds of miles by foot to see the Cathedral of Our Lady of Chartres. "The outside of the cathedral would have been buzzing with activity," he said. He gestured to the walls. "These were jam-packed with the stalls of merchants selling meat, fruit, vegetables, and fabrics. Over there are the benches where moneychangers conducted their business."

The gray exterior walls were impressive, adorned with intricate carvings and flying buttresses, but Malcolm said the surfaces were once painted in bright colors, making them even more spectacular. "Imagine pilgrims arriving, their mouths agape in wonder as they marveled at the canopies of color above them."

I was swept away by Malcolm's storytelling. I felt like a wide-eyed pilgrim at the end of a long journey, too, walking in wonder through the front doors of the cathedral for the first time, toward the cavernous space inside.

"Here inside the nave," Malcolm said, "you would have been immersed in a great scene of a throng of unwashed pilgrims, the smell of incense, the sound of hymns, the shadows of flickering candles, and the voices of merchants selling wine." He gazed up the soaring walls at the still-colorful ceiling. "Above it all is still the world's largest collection of stained glass—176 windows, ablaze with rays of sunlight shining through."

He gave us a moment to take in the vast array of scenes embedded in the glass as shown in Figure 1. "This is a like a library, except the books are written in stained glass and sculpture," Malcolm said. He led us to stand in front of a glittering rose window, some 30 feet across.

"These stained-glass windows were not just decorative," he said. "Their purpose was to teach, at all levels." In its day, Chartres was a world-class center of learning, home to a famous school that re-introduced Greek manuscripts to Europe and inspired a 12th-century renaissance. "Parents taught their children by pointing to the glass, and telling them stories," he said. "Clergy taught doctrine as they paused before the windows. The educated taught each other through symbols and allegories."

Malcolm turned and pointed to the interior walls, now covered with colored light from the rays of sun shining through the windows. "What you see echoes an inspiring vision of a new city coming down out of heaven," he said, "shining with glory and brilliance like that of a very precious jewel. Imagine we're getting a preview of paradise!"

Figure 1

The North Rose Window at Chartres Cathedral is a 12th-century visual aid packed with meaning embedded in the shapes and colors of the stained glass. Visitors pointed to the figures and symbols as they told stories about them, teaching others and creating a shared sense of purpose.

As the tour ended, I stood transfixed, digesting what had just happened. In the space of an hour-long tour, Malcolm had used his storytelling skills to expand the imagination of a military officer like me, transforming a gray building into a vision of paradise. Through his masterful telling, he awoke my imagination, bringing to life the smells, sounds, sights, and sensations of life in the 12th century. He described how compelling visuals—the stained-glass windows—could effectively transfer knowledge, shift perceptions, and create a shared sense of purpose among people.

That day, I realized that sharing a story fulfills a deep human desire to express ourselves and to connect with each other. But it would take years before I would fully appreciate Malcolm's other lesson about storytelling—the power of images and light.

The next year, I attended Squadron Officers School in Montgomery, Alabama, a professional development course for newly minted captains. We ran obstacle courses, played simulated war games—and had to give presentations. Although I was in the communications field, storytelling did not come naturally to me, and I shared with many a fear of public speaking. I thought it would be easier to give a talk if I created visual aids to help me remember what I wanted to say.

The military did not yet have slide software, which had been invented only five years before. The state-of-the-art technology for visual aids was overhead projectors, so I pulled out a sheet of clear acetate and a thin-tipped black marker to create the images I would project on the screen.

On the first overhead transparency shown in Figure 2, I sketched a crude graphic to help tell a story about the challenges that military officers face in peacetime, such as bad press, protests, and occasional accidents. On the second overhead, I created a bulleted list of text that spelled out the principles of information that I applied in my profession.

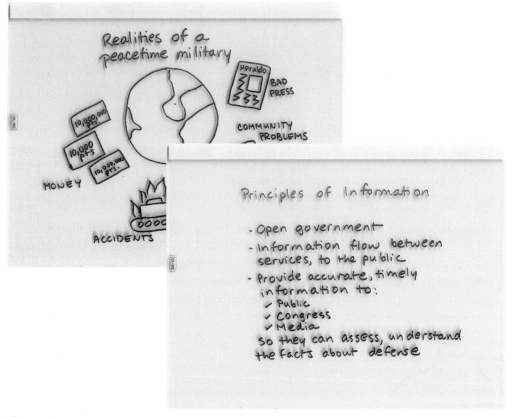

Figure 2

This is how I told a story in 1991, like the rest of the world, by sketching a graphic and writing out a list of bullet points on an overhead transparency.

The visual aids helped guide my talk along and made me feel more comfortable with public speaking. But they were a far cry from the visual storytellers of Chartres. In fact, I had not even told a story that the audience could connect with.

The Air Force major with a buzz cut was not impressed. "Cliff, I liked your creativity," he said. "But you never answered the question of *what's in it for me*? Why should I care about your topic?"

I learned another important lesson: I needed to pay attention to what the audience needed, not what I needed.

After my next assignment in Europe, I left the military for the civilian world and held various communications jobs until I enrolled in business school in London to study for a master's degree in business administration.

I wrote a paper on entertainment industry economics for my statistics class, and my assignment was to present the results to the class. I wanted to create some visual aids, so I opened a software program called PowerPoint for the first time. PowerPoint had been invented to make the process of creating and presenting visual aids easier and faster than the previous technology of overhead transparencies, placing control directly into the hands of anyone who had a personal computer. It was already quickly spreading throughout the business and academic worlds.

The first thing I did was choose the most beautiful background I could find for my slides—a blue and white pattern that vaguely looked like water or stained glass. I used the default template to create my first slide, already preformatted with a heading and a bulleted list of text.

Like everyone else at the time, I used PowerPoint as a typewriter; I tapped in bullet point lists of text, slide after slide, as shown in Figure 3. Although I added an occasional chart to spice things up, every slide looked pretty much the same. I later learned that this default template was based on a survey of the most popular formats for overhead transparencies in the 1980s—long before storytelling became the norm in communication.

When I delivered my presentation, I clicked through the slides one by one, reading the bullet points to my audience. As a presenter, I felt constrained because I had to read the slides as I had created them, list of text after list of text. Worse, my statistics professor, Jon, looked bored. "Cliff, it looks like you covered everything you wanted to cover," he said. "But I'm still not clear; what are the three most important points you want to make?"

Again, I hadn't told a story. I learned another lesson: distill complicated information to its essence. A quick way to do that is to ask yourself: *After this presentation is over, what are the three most important things I want an audience member to tell someone else that it was about?*

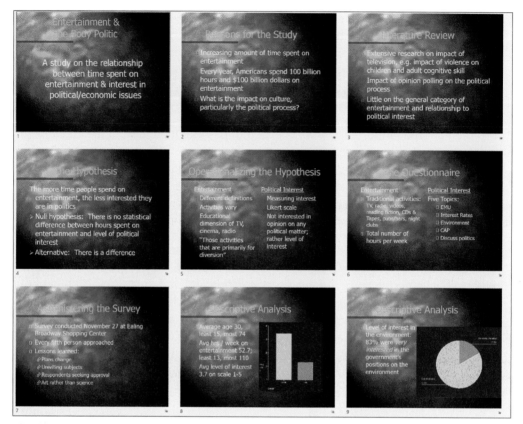

Figure 3

When I first used PowerPoint, my storytelling looked like this; I used the default template to create my slides in business school, just like everybody else.

After I graduated with an MBA, I moved to San Francisco and struggled to find my niche as a communicator. I continued to be fascinated by ways that projected images could be used to tell a story and to prompt people to engage in conversation that leads to action.

One day, I was browsing the news online and saw the stunning photographs that the Hubble Space Telescope sent back on its mission to probe the origins of our universe. One image stood out for me—a spiral nebula—so I downloaded a copy. I wanted to display the image, but I didn't know how to use image-editing software; I opened PowerPoint because the software made it so easy to work with graphics. I inserted the image on a blank slide and scaled it up to fill the slide.

The shape and colors of the nebula reminded me of a rose window at Chartres, so I downloaded an image of the stained glass, inserted it on the slide, and cropped the two images to match at their centers.

Something clicked. When I looked at the images side by side, as in Figure 4, I realized that even though the two images were created 800 years apart, they were both telling the most important stories of their time—the origin stories that shaped the understanding of the cosmos and our place within it.

I gathered a group of my friends to see if I could use the images to prompt a discussion about storytelling. I set up a projector and screen connected to my laptop with the photograph of the rose window on the slide, and with the image on the large screen behind me. "A medieval storyteller once stood before a stained-glass window and used the images as prompts to tell stories that helped people find meaning and direction in their everyday lives," I told them.

Figure 4

I realized that both a stained-glass window and a photo of a nebula were visual prompts to tell important stories to audiences.

I clicked a remote-control device to make the image of the nebula appear and continued, "Today, scientists use images to tell us stories about the origin of the stars and give us a sense of our place in the universe." The two photos in this surprising juxtaposition prompted a lively discussion among my friends about storytelling, and how we could use visuals to inform and persuade our audiences. Through my experiment, I realized that PowerPoint was not the first technology to project light on a wall and use it to tell important stories; humans had been doing that for quite a long time.

However, there still was one missing piece: every story has a beginning, middle, and end, which meant I would need more slides. When I returned home, I created a new PowerPoint file, which opens by default with a text-based slide in Normal view. Then I switched to Slide Sorter view and added blank slides until they filled the entire screen as in Figure 5.

Like my colleagues from 800 years ago, I was now a multimedia storyteller. However, now I had the benefit of presentation software and projectors at my fingertips (Figure 6) to do what they had done—tell stories, awaken emotion, build community, and make each other smarter.

I now saw PowerPoint as a canvas of light.

Figure 5

I created a set of blank slides and realized that it is a storyboard, with unlimited potential to tell a story in creative, interesting, and effective ways.

Figure 6

A laptop and projector were tools to create a canvas of light and prompt stories that move people to action.

The style of my slides dramatically changed (Figure 7), as I started each visual story with a blank slate and chose simple images and animation to bring an idea to life, make complex ideas understandable, and prompt dialogue.

I knew I was on to something, but now I had to make a connection between this new perspective and the way everyone around me was continuing to use PowerPoint the usual way in their everyday work lives. At the time, I was a lone wolf, excited about the new possibilities for smart, clear, and engaging storytelling. I was convinced that many people could benefit from what I had to say and that I could someday make a living doing what I loved. My only problem was that at the moment, I had no clients and no leads.

I volunteered to write free articles for a website for marketers called MarketingProfs, with headlines like "Bullet Points Kill (Effective Communication)," "How to Addict Your Audience to Your PowerPoint," and "Turn Hollywood Secrets into Blockbuster Sales." I became an evangelist for shifting the way we use slides from a book to a storyboard. Unbeknownst to me, while I realized the power of visual storytelling, so too did my future clients.

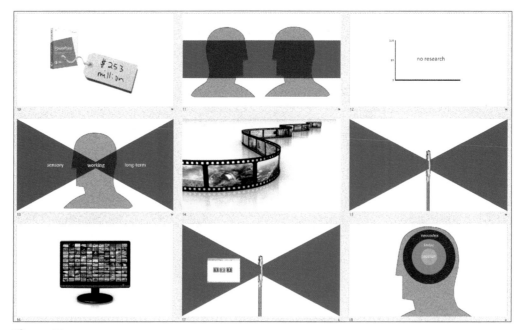

Figure 7

The style of my presentations changed, as I used simple images and photographs to prompt a visual story.

One sunny summer morning in Los Angeles, as a warm breeze blew the scents of exotic flowers through the open windows of my home office, I was reading my email when the phone rang. I thought it was a telemarketer.

"Is this Cliff Atkinson?" the voice on the other end of the line said. I answered yes, and the voice said, "My name is David, and you might have heard of the company I work for."

Yes, like everyone else, I had heard of the company—it was a household name with the largest market capitalization in the world and more than 300,000 employees. This company would be the dream client for consultants who had spent years in the trenches, slowly working their way from small clients to medium-sized and eventually, if they were lucky, to the board of directors of this huge and famous company. Here I was in shorts and a t-shirt, and out of the blue, my dream client was calling me. I silently cheered and listened carefully to what David had to say.

"Cliff, if we engage you we have to ask that you don't reveal the name of my company," he said, and I agreed. "So here's the situation," he continued. "A while ago, the board decided that we wanted all of our communications to be clear and simple, so we launched a re-branding campaign that successfully accomplished that goal." He described the rollout of an initiative that changed the global look of the company and introduced a new tagline. However, there was one problem with the rollout.

"The campaign worked great everywhere through the company, except for our slide presentations here in the boardroom. The top leaders want slides to help them make clearer, smarter, and faster decisions. But we see now that the slides themselves have become a problem standing in the way. We've been reading your articles about visual storytelling. Would you be willing to help us?"

Figure 8

The board of directors of one of the world's largest companies called me because the slides they saw were standing in the way of making decisions.

It took a little time for my mind to wrap around what David was asking. Until recently, most people looked at slides from the vantage point of the presenter, concerned with their own *outbound* message and how to shape it to be persuasive to their audiences. However, in this case, the board members (Figure 8) were looking at slides from the view of an audience, which viewed many *inbound* messages on a regular basis. This particular audience comprised the most powerful people in one of the largest organizations in the world. And now, the audience was staging a revolt.

This was my opportunity to put storytelling into practice. It took a millisecond to say yes, and we agreed that I would write a white paper to analyze the situation and address the problem.

I asked to see examples of presentations that the board was seeing at this data-driven engineering company. As was my practice by now, I opened the file in Slide Sorter view so I could get a sense of the big picture of all the slides before getting into the details of any single slide.

I saw that the slides were filled with massive amounts of technical information, which I am confident represented the top-level thinking of the brightest and best analysts and executives at the organization. However, they were dense with information, difficult to read and interpret.

"How did the slides come to be made this way?" I asked David.

"We've always run into the problem of having too much information to present," he said. At first, the company's presentations had dozens, and sometimes hundreds, of slides. Then they tried to solve the problem by limiting the number of slides to ten, five, or three.

What happened was predictable: the presenters took the same amount of information and squeezed it into fewer slides by reducing the font size and making the graphics smaller. Then the board decided to limit presentations to one slide. "Presenters shrank the font size, diagrams, and visuals so small that we needed a microscope to read them!" David said.

I agreed that these slides contained an overwhelming amount of information (like the ones in Figure 9). I also saw many things missing. First and foremost, there was no story. Instead of a coherent framework to tie the information together with a beginning, middle, and end, these slides were a series of fragmented, disjointed thoughts that were hard to link from one slide to the next.

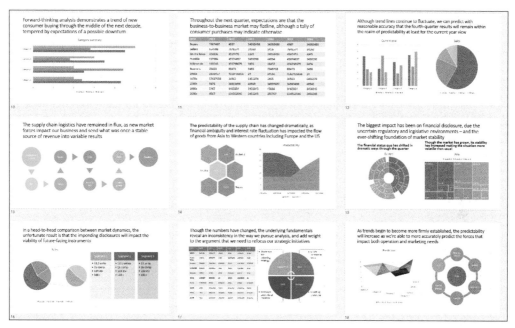

Figure 9

The typical slides that I saw were overloaded with information and were lacking in story and persuasive strategy, and the solution I recommended became the basis for this book.

The first few slides made no emotional connection with the audience, and didn't answer the viewer's question: *What's in it for me?* The slides did not present a problem the audience was facing, nor propose a course of action. They did not persuasively frame the topic to increase the likelihood of getting approval for a course of action. The three most important ideas were nowhere to be seen.

The individual slides were so complicated that a viewer had no idea where to look, which made them confusing and overwhelming, and there was a breakdown in interpersonal connection. When these slides were presented in person to an audience, they would interfere with eye contact between presenter and audience, diminish spontaneity, detract from the credibility and personality of the presenter, and shut down dialogue completely.

My solution was to apply what I had learned: step away from the slides and focus on your audience and what you want to accomplish, reformat your information for decision-making, frame your case from your audience's perspective, and tell a persuasive story.

Later I realized I was simply applying the lessons I had learned from others in my life:

- ■ The importance of telling a story from Malcolm.
- ■ Knowing your audience from the Air Force major at Squadron Officers School.
- ■ Distilling your message from my MBA statistics professor.

I delivered the white paper, and then the company hired me for a new project to create a set of user guides to train them to apply some of these core lessons to their presentations.

Shortly after completing the project, I spoke about my experience at a conference, and someone from Microsoft asked me if I would be interested in writing a book about what I was doing. That conversation became the first edition of this book that arrived in bookstores in 2005; then I updated the book in a second edition in 2007, a third edition in 2011, and now this fourth edition in 2018. Over the years, *Beyond Bullet Points* has sold more than 100,000 copies, was named a Best Book of 2007 by the editors of Amazon, and has been translated into more than a dozen languages including Chinese, Korean, and Russian.

Through the editions, I've continued to incorporate improvements based on experience and feedback from workshops and training at organizations large and small. What you hold in your hands is the distilled wisdom of years of visual storytelling and the step-by-step instructions that show you how to apply it to your message and help you engage, inform, and persuade others.

At the core of the message is the power of a story. Because after all, when you least expect it, a story really can change your life.

WHO THIS BOOK IS FOR

If you find yourself needing to persuade, educate, or inspire other people, this book is for you. As the volume of information grows and the pace of decision-making increases, it's more important than ever that we all develop and hone our communication abilities. These days, the most crucial skills are the ability to cut through the clutter, establish what's most relevant, and make our thoughts accessible through crisp words and clear pictures. This book is designed to help you do just that—to tap into the power of visual storytelling to present your best case and achieve the results you want.

Assumptions

This book assumes you already have a working knowledge of Microsoft Office Word and PowerPoint and that you have already prepared and delivered basic presentations. You'll get the most out of the book if you have in mind a real-world presentation that you will have to deliver at some point.

HOW THIS BOOK IS ORGANIZED

This book shows you step-by-step how to craft a visual story from start to finish, beginning with the first few chapters that introduce the approach in the book and provide an overview of the road ahead. Chapter 1 tells a real-world story of how someone used the approach in this book to achieve headline-making results. Chapter 2 aims to bust a few core myths that stand in the way of using slides effectively. Chapter 3 provides an overview of the process along with core principles and building blocks for visual storytelling.

Using a real-world presentation as an example, the next section focuses on preparing your information for visual storytelling. Chapter 4 introduces a way to craft your core story structure and set up your first few slides, while Chapter 5 guides you through the process of distilling your information to the most important points you want your audience to remember.

Once you've gotten your script written, the next chapters guide you through the process of turning your story into a storyboard. Chapter 6 shows you how to turn your outline into slides, Chapter 7 introduces sketching as a powerful planning method, and Chapter 8 shows you how find and add graphics to your storyboard.

The book ends with tips on how to deliver your visual story in Chapter 9. Chapter 10 introduces a range of different examples that complement the core example used in the majority of the book.

WHERE TO GET THE COMPANION CONTENT

The companion content Web page for this book includes copies of key tools described in the book; which can be downloaded from *www.beyondbulletpoints.com* or the following page:

https://aka.ms/BeyondBulletPts4E/downloads

ERRATA, UPDATES, & BOOK SUPPORT

We've made every effort to ensure the accuracy of this book and its companion content. You can access updates to this book—in the form of a list of submitted errata and their related corrections—at:

https://aka.ms/BeyondBulletPts4E/errata

If you discover an error that is not already listed, please submit it to us at the same page.

If you need additional support, email Microsoft Press Book Support at *mspinput @microsoft.com*.

Please note that product support for Microsoft software and hardware is not offered through the previous addresses. For help with Microsoft software or hardware, go to *http://support.microsoft.com*.

A THEATER OF PERSUASION

In this chapter, you will:

- Learn how one presenter achieved remarkable results by using the visual storytelling approach described in this book.
- View specific visual examples of visual storytelling at work.
- Recognize the potential of what you can do with your own presentations.

Only a few months after the first edition of *Beyond Bullet Points* arrived in bookstores, I received an unexpected phone call.

"This is Dara, and I work for a lawyer in Texas named Mark Lanier." Dara explained that Mark had a big case coming up, representing a client who was suing a pharmaceutical company for selling a painkiller that caused her husband's fatal heart attack.

"In every case that Mark brings to trial, he likes to take a skill set to the next level," she explained, "and this time it's his PowerPoint."

"I had no idea that lawyers used PowerPoint in courtrooms," I said.

"They sure do," she said. "And to get Mark ready for trial, we bought him a stack of books on PowerPoint to read while he was on vacation in Greece."

I thought I was the only one nerdy enough to read those kinds of books on vacation.

"Mark says he read book after book on PowerPoint, and they all talked about how to make bullet points prettier," she went on. "But then he found your book, and liked what you had to say about how to tell a persuasive story using PowerPoint."

I still couldn't figure out why Dara was calling me.

"Mark wants to know; can we fly you out here to Houston to help us create the opening statement for the trial?"

I had no idea how to create an opening statement for a trial. I asked Dara to tell Mark that I was honored that he liked my book, but it didn't seem like the job for me. "I've never even stepped foot in a courtroom. I don't have any training in law. How in the world could I help Mark prepare his case?"

"Don't worry about that," Dara replied. "We'll take care of the law. You just help us with the visual story."

Dara sent a first-class airline ticket, and a week later I was on a flight to Houston.

I arrived at Mark's office already sweating at 9 a.m. on the hot and humid July day, and the chilly air conditioning was a welcome relief. Up walked Mark, a young guy with thick brown hair, stubble, and designer glasses—not my image of a lawyer.

"Cliff, welcome!" he boomed. "We're so glad to have you here!"

I'd done a little research on Mark and learned that he specialized in representing plaintiffs in personal injury trials, and had a long string of mind-boggling big wins for his clients. He was so accomplished that I kept wondering why he'd called me.

Mark led me to a conference room, where he introduced me to his team of world-class lawyers, experts, and psychologists who specialize in understanding the minds of jurors.

"Cliff, here's our challenge," Mark said. "We've got three million documents in this case. Hundreds of hours of video depositions. And the science is seriously complicated behind the drug and how it works on the body. We've got to take all that and make it all easy for an average juror here in Texas to understand. How would you approach that?"

I gave it some quick thought. It didn't seem so daunting if I approached it the way I did everything else. "Like any presentation," I said. "Tell me more about your typical juror so we can get into their minds and frame this from their perspective. Then let's format the information in a way that will help them make a decision. And then let's distill the case into three crisp points, and we'll apply a compelling story theme to that."

Mark agreed, and we got to work, using the principles described in this book to write an outline and create the storyboard for trial.

A few weeks later, I returned for the trial. I arrived in Angleton, Texas, a quiet town of 18,000 people on the Gulf Coast near Houston. The doors of the old gray county courthouse in the town square opened to a flood of television crews that crowded the hallways. A group of newspaper reporters surged into the main courtroom, squeezing into uncomfortable wooden benches and tapping updates on their laptops to the newsrooms of the *New York Times,* the *Wall Street Journal,* the Associated Press, *Fortune,* and Reuters. They were there to cover a major news event: the opening statements kicking-off a high-stakes pharmaceutical company trial.

Everyone in the courtroom stood when the jurors filed into the room and settled into their seats. The room was silent when Mark stood up to face the jurors. He turned to his client, the plaintiff, who was sitting in the first row with her family. "Your Honor," Mark said, "if I may begin by introducing my client to the jury and to the Court." As Carol Ernst stood, Mark introduced her and her daughter. Carol's husband, Bob, had died of a heart attack, and she suspected that a painkiller her husband had taken was a cause of the heart attack. She'd filed a lawsuit against the defendant, the drug's manufacturer.

As Carol sat down, Mark walked toward the jury box, past the row of lawyers sitting at the defense table. The defense attorneys were from two internationally recognized law firms; with billions of dollars in their war chest, the company could afford the best. Facing such a formidable opponent with deep pockets, Mark knew he would need to be at the top of his game and use the tools and techniques he had to the best of his ability to make the greatest impact.

Mark paused at the jury box and made eye contact with each of the 12 jurors. Before the jurors arrived, Mark had wheeled the lawyers' podium to the side of the courtroom because he didn't want a piece of furniture, or anything else, to stand between him and his audience. Mark had a folksy style when he talked to jurors, speaking with a Texas drawl, in colorful language, and a conversational manner. But by now, Mark's legal opponents knew because of his strong track record of successful verdicts in jury trials, interpreting his simple style as unsophisticated would be a big and expensive mistake.

The judge had explained to the jurors earlier that when they took their oath, they had become court officials like himself and the lawyers. The jurors were charged with administering justice in this case, by listening to all the evidence in open court and making a decision based on the facts, the judge's instructions, and reading of the law. Like any audience, they sat ready to hear what the presenter would say.

KNOW YOUR AUDIENCE
Get to know your audience well before you start planning your presentations. Mark knew several things about his audience—the legal teams from both sides had prepared a written questionnaire for the jurors, in which they found that the jurors were in their 20s and 40s, high-school educated, and from a range of professions, including an electrician, a college student, a construction worker, a product technician, a homemaker, a secretary, and a government employee. The lawyers also had an opportunity to ask jurors questions in person during a Q&A session called *voir dire*. In your own presentations, the better you know your audience, the better you'll be able to customize your material to them.

Even the most experienced speakers get nervous before a big presentation, and Mark was no exception. Mark must have felt nervous not just because the jurors were watching him closely, but because plaintiffs' attorneys like Mark can spend upward of $1 million to bring a case to trial on behalf of their clients, and if they lose, they lose everything they put into the case. The defendant had a great deal to lose as well because this was the first case related to this drug to go to trial against the pharmaceutical company. Beyond any negative media coverage the case might bring, a negative verdict could have a big impact on the company's bottom line. It could lose millions of dollars in the case itself, and possibly billions of dollars in market value if its stock price dropped with the news. This presentation was about as high-stakes as any presentation can get.

STEPPING ONTO THE MEDIA STAGE

Mark glanced down at his laptop computer, which sat facing him on a small table below the jury box, out of sight of the jurors. What he saw on his laptop screen was a feature in PowerPoint called Presenter vew, which gave Mark a special view of the presentation that only he could see. Like the teleprompter that broadcasters use to present their speaking notes, this sometimes-overlooked PowerPoint feature gives you the ability to see additional information that does not appear on the screen the audience sees.

As he began speaking, Mark's thumb pressed the button on a remote-control device which he cupped in his hand at his side where the audience would not notice it. This remote would be his constant companion for the next couple of hours as he used it to advance the PowerPoint slides while he spoke, giving him flexibility to slow down or speed up to match his narration and ensure that the experience appeared seamless to the jurors.

Mark began his presentation. "It's extremely important to me that you hear what this case is about," he said. "So I've put together different exhibits to try and help it stick in your brain and help you focus on what we think are critical points." Mark clicked the remote-control button, signaling his laptop to advance to the first slide. An image of Carol and Bob appeared on the 10-foot screen directly behind Mark. From where the jurors sat, it appeared that Mark was in a giant television set as the images on the screen would soon start dissolving and changing behind him in a seamlessly choreographed media experience.

The projected colors, images, and words were so thoroughly integrated into the presentation experience that turning off the projector would have been like eliminating the set of a theater production or the screen in a movie theater. Never breaking eye contact with the jurors or looking back at the screen, Mark now began to tell a gripping story that would lay out the evidence of the plaintiff's case through the next two and a half hours of the presentation.

A SINGULAR STORY

What was notable about Mark's first slide, similar to the one shown in Figure 1-1, was not so much what was on it, but rather what was not on it. You would expect the slides of a PowerPoint presentation to be filled with bullet points, but here the jurors saw only a single, simple—and powerful—photograph. Such full-screen images were rare at the time in PowerPoint presentations, but this image fit in perfectly with what Mark would do next.

FIGURE 1-1

A family photo of Bob and Carol similar to this showed the happy couple after they were married.

With a photograph of the couple on the screen as his backdrop, Mark began telling an anecdote to introduce Bob and Carol to the jurors. "Let me tell you a little bit about Bob," Mark said. "Bob was a great fellow who always took [Carol] to wonderful, interesting places. They went to the kite festival in Washington State. They went to the balloon launch in Albuquerque. They had a lot of fun. He got her into tandem bike racing. They weren't the winning kind of athletes. They just did it to be together, and it was a good, fun way for them to live together."

Mark knew that telling specific details of a story, as in this anecdote about Bob and Carol, is an effective way to introduce a new and complicated topic to an audience. With a simple story of a bike race, the jurors could quickly imagine what Carol and Bob's relationship and lives were like. Seeing the family photograph would make it easier for jurors to relate to the plaintiff, perhaps reminding the jurors of similar photos they have taken or seen in their own families. The photo and details of the couple's life together would work powerfully to quickly introduce Carol and Bob to the jury and make an emotional connection with them. This slide worked much more effectively than a list of bullet points ever could because we don't live our lives in bullet points—we live in images and stories.

"They did get married after being together for a number of years," Mark explained. "They were introduced over exercise. And you'll hear Carol talk about her daughter being the matchmaker between Carol and Bob." Here, Mark noted that the jurors would hear from Carol herself on the stand, establishing a sense of anticipation that they would get to hear from her firsthand. Mark knew that hinting at events to come is an effective way to grab any audience's interest.

Mark clicked the remote control again and displayed the same photograph, except now the background behind the photograph had disappeared, as shown in Figure 1-2. As the new photograph appeared, Mark said, "They had a wonderful time together. But ultimately, the picture starts to fade, and things start to go differently. And let me tell you why." People are not used to seeing family photographs where the background suddenly disappears, so this visually set the stage that something unexpected was about to happen to Carol and Bob. The audience emotions that Mark had associated with the photograph were suddenly stripped away.

Clicking again, Mark displayed a new version of the photograph, except in this one, Bob was missing. In his place was a thick black line, like the chalk outline from a crime scene, as shown in Figure 1-3. "You see, Bob Ernst is dead today," Mark said. "One of my witnesses that I want to bring in the case I cannot bring you. Bob Ernst cannot come in here today. He is no longer here. He didn't know he was going to need to be here. He didn't leave us anything in video. He didn't leave us anything in writing that would talk about the issues that we need to talk about."

FIGURE 1-2

The next slide shows the same photograph with the background stripped away to indicate that something unexpected had happened.

FIGURE 1-3

This slide shows Bob missing from the photograph, with only a thick black line to indicate where he once was.

This striking photograph visually communicated to the jurors that the worst had happened—that Bob and Carol's happiness ended abruptly and unexpectedly when Bob died of a heart attack. The black outline around where Bob had been in the photo visually brought home the point that Bob's death had suddenly left a hole in Carol's life, and in her heart.

Mark knew that his audience came from a part of Texas that was growing increasingly conservative and that the jurors might not be predisposed to award a big verdict to a plaintiff in a product liability case like this. But with the thick black outline that indicated where Bob had been, Mark also introduced a powerful new outline for his presentation. If the jurors were not going to be friendly toward a product liability case, Mark was now visually reframing his opening statement to a new storyline that the conservative jurors would find more engaging—a murder mystery. In this third photograph, the black outline subtly but powerfully communicated a familiar story setting that the jurors immediately would understand—a crime scene from a television show. This unexpected use of a familiar convention from TV would surprise the jurors and make the idea stick in their minds. This slide would then thematically transition to the next, pivotal, slide in the presentation.

Mark clicked the remote again, and this time a black slide appeared with the phrase CSI: Angleton on it, like the slide shown in Figure 1-4. "If we were going to put it into a TV show, this would be 'CSI: Angleton.'" He said. "What you're going to do is follow the evidence, like any good detective would."

Figure 1-4

Next the words "CSI: Angleton" appeared on the screen as Mark told jurors that they would be like crime scene investigators, sorting through the evidence to figure out what caused Bob's death.

In an entertaining fictional story, the main character is someone an audience observes from a distance. But Mark knew that in a nonfiction presentation, making the audience the center of the action would dramatically increase their sense of involvement.

In keeping with classical storytelling form, Mark's next step would be to present the main characters with a problem they would have to face.

THE HEART OF THE PROBLEM

Mark clicked the remote control to advance to the next slide, showing an image of a headquarters building, like Figure 1-5, as he said, "The evidence is going to lead you to one place—the front steps of one of the largest pharmaceutical companies in the world." Mark explained that he would show a great deal of evidence from many sources that all proved the company's drug was a cause of Bob's heart attack. Then he added, "There are lots of different ways it can be painted," and jurors would have to eventually weigh the evidence against everything else they would hear.

FIGURE 1-5

Next, Mark showed a photo of the headquarters building of the pharmaceutical company, like this, and told jurors that the evidence in the case would lead to the company's doorstep.

Mark clicked the remote button to show the next slide, a photograph of a gavel and flag, like Figure 1-6, as he said, "You're going to hear all of this evidence because your job to do is to get us to justice. Nobody else has this power. A judge can't do it. Politicians can't do it. Nobody else can do it. This is where you can make a difference in the world."

FIGURE 1-6

With a gavel and flag displayed on the screen, Mark explained that the jurors could bring the situation to justice.

The image of the gavel along with Mark's narration reinforced the problem the jurors faced: they will see the evidence against the company, and they will have to sort through it and make a decision that delivers justice.

Next, as Mark began to click to a slide like Figure 1-7, he said, "How are you going to do it? My suggestion to you is, again, you've got to follow the evidence. First of all, I'm going to show you a motive." The word *motive* appeared on the screen (left) along with a picture of a stack of money. "I'm going to show you the means," he said, as the word *means* and an image of pills similar to this one appeared on the screen (middle). "I'm going to show you the death," he said, as the word *death* and the familiar outline of Bob appeared next to Carol on the screen (right).

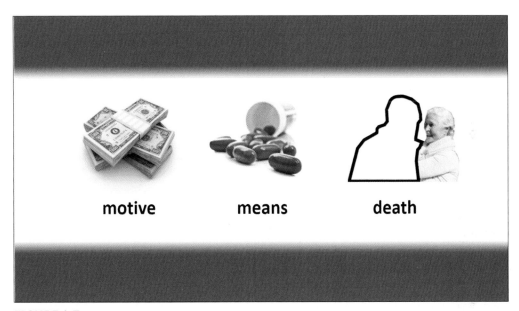

FIGURE 1-7

This summary slide visually distills the entire case into a single image. The horizontal bars above and below the icons are red to indicate that this slide stands out as the most important in the presentation.

With these slides, Mark asked the jurors to follow the simple formula that underlies every murder-mystery story: motive + means = death. Even jurors who don't watch TV would know this familiar structure from books, board games, or stories in the news. Earlier, Mark hinted at a murder-mystery motif with the black outline and again with the CSI reference, and now at the most important part of the presentation, he fully established the murder-mystery motif as the structure for the entire presentation to come.

Although the slide appears simple, it is sophisticated in its effect because it reduces a complex case into something easy to understand and follow.

DISTILLING TO THE ESSENCE

On top of the vast amount of information he needed to communicate, Mark faced the constraints of a limited amount of time to talk to his audience. In a couple of hours, he had to present the jurors with an overview of the case, educate them about key concepts, and equip them with a framework to understand the six weeks of testimony to come. And he had to do all this while keeping jurors interested and engaged.

Mark solved the problem of potentially overwhelming his audience by distilling his presentation into three parts that he would spend equal amounts of time explaining. Using the murder-mystery motif as a familiar structure, Mark verbally and visually introduced the enormously complex case to jurors as being "as easy as 1, 2, 3" to understand, using this summary slide as he spoke.

Next, Mark clicked the remote to show the slides containing his key points, like the images shown in Figure 1-8, as he introduced each of the three sections of the presentation. Instead of overwhelming jurors with three million documents, Mark guided them along what appeared to be a very simple story as he introduced the three most important parts of the case, which he would explain in more detail as his presentation moved forward.

Now the jurors could relax as they listened and watched the story unfold.

Mark knew that an audience couldn't possibly remember all the information they see and hear, but it helps if you give them graphical cues to the presentation's organization and the slides' relative importance. The look of these three slides was based on the style of the earlier summary slide, carrying forward the story visually to complement Mark's verbal explanation. The simple split-screen layout of the slides, the use of the striking red color, and the consistent graphical style ensured that when these slides appeared, they would stand out as the most important among all the slides.

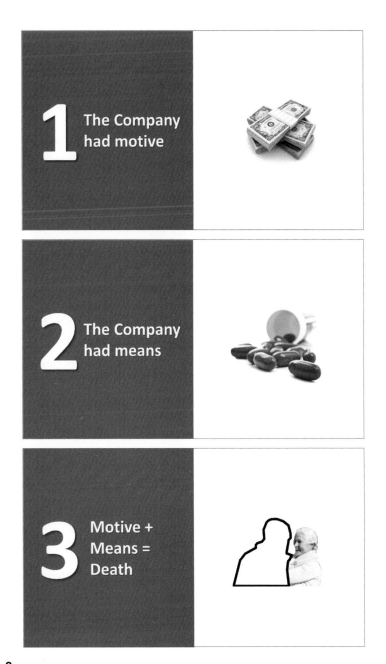

FIGURE 1-8

As he introduced each of the three sections of the opening statement, Mark displayed slides that carried forward the theme from the earlier summary slide, including the red backgrounds on the left half of each slide.

MIXING MEDIUMS

With this simple yet clear and engaging introduction to his opening statement, Mark had succeeded in presenting a framework that would be easy for jurors to follow. He continued to integrate the story seamlessly through the remaining slides over the rest of his presentation.

As Mark continued the presentation, many slides looked like the ones shown in Figure 1-9. The slides were designed so that the jurors' attention would first go to the most important information at the top of the screen—a headline that summarized the main point at hand, like a newspaper headline. Next, the jurors would see a simple graphic that illustrated the specific headline. Last, the jurors' attention would shift from the screen to Mark, who explained the point of the slide in more detail. The range of visuals used on the slides included a wide variety of photographs, medical illustrations, documents, screen captures, timelines, and more.

Mark clicked through the 153 slides of this presentation at a pace of about 45 seconds per slide, which allowed his audience to digest the information on the screen and in his narration before moving forward to the next slide and the next part of the story. This pace kept the jurors visually interested and showed them only what they needed to know when they needed to know it.

Conventional PowerPoint slides can overwhelm audiences with too much information on the screen, but Mark's presentation contained only one idea per slide. Instead of reading bullet points from the screen, Mark used his slides as visual cues to prompt him on the next point he would make, allowing him to speak with a natural and spontaneous style that came from the depth of his knowledge and authority on his topic. And instead of looking at the screen to see what was on it, Mark kept his attention focused on the jurors, making eye contact with each person throughout the presentation.

Beyond the slides, Mark used other media and physical props to engage with the audience over the course of the presentation. At times, he switched the screen to a document projector, where he displayed physical paper documents and highlighted passages on the pages with a yellow marker as he explained the significance of the evidence. Later he used a large paper flip chart that he calls a "doublewide," where he wrote out key terms and concepts with large markers. Sometimes he switched from the slides to a brief video that illustrated a point. Other times, he used physical props such as a plastic model of a heart held up in his hand to teach jurors the science behind heart attacks.

Mark used these different types of media to keep things varied and interesting throughout the presentation and to keep the experience from feeling too slick and produced. And after using each type of media, Mark always returned to the PowerPoint presentation on the 10-foot screen because it was a visually unifying tool he could use to move the story forward. The shifting and dissolving images holding the audience's interest on the large screen seamlessly came together with Mark's physical presence, and his voice filled in the details while remaining consistent with the visual presentation.

That day in Angleton, Mark used PowerPoint to create a theater of persuasion that would influence and persuade jurors to see the situation his way.

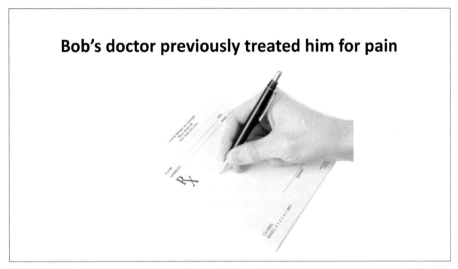

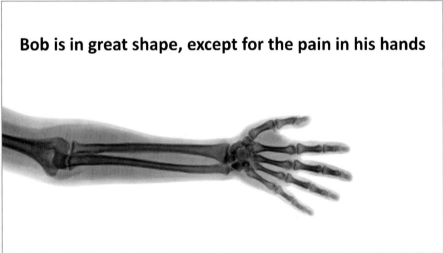

FIGURE 1-9

The slides within each section of the presentation used a similar layout style, which helped the jurors quickly understand the information.

FADE TO GRAY

After Mark finished his presentation, the judge allowed a break, and the jurors left the courtroom. Now it was the defense team's turn to present its opening statement. They got their PowerPoint presentation ready on its own laptop computer and rolled back the podium to where it had been before Mark moved it, in front of the jury box. When the jurors returned, the defense lawyer walked up to the podium, looked down at his printed notes, and began to read the text of his opening statement to the jurors.

In the crucial first few minutes of the presentation, when it is essential to make an audience feel like the presentation is all about them, the lawyer recited details about the admirable history of the pharmaceutical company. Instead of making the presentation human by telling an anecdote about a real person, he cited dry data about the millions of people the company aims to reach with its various drugs. As he read the prepared script in formal and impersonal language, someone else on his team advanced the slides forward on the computer, sometimes missing a cue and leaving a disconnect between what the attorney said and what the jurors saw on the screen. The lawyer occasionally turned back to look at the screen behind him to robotically point at a complicated chart or a long passage of text.

Rather than immerse the jurors in a dynamic and engaging visual experience, the attorney next showed a slide with a photograph of the company's former CEO in a coat and tie as he talked about the CEO and his family, his biography, his public service, and his civic involvement. Missing the chance to connect with the everyday people in the jury with color and character, the defense attorney continued with slides that showed formal photographs of other corporate executives, and he talked about their Ivy League educations, detailed biographies, and long lists of accomplishments. Missing the point that less is more, later the lawyer displayed the familiar bullet points, charts, and long passages of text that the jurors strained to read.

The jurors never warmed up to the chilly and formal tone of the defense attorney's prepared talk. The podium that was now in front of the jurors had erected a wall between the presenter and his audience, the prepared script took away the lawyer's natural voice and spontaneity, and the slides on the screen became a 10-foot distraction from the lawyer who was speaking.

At the end of the defense's presentation, everyone stood as the jurors left the courtroom, and then the court adjourned for the day. If what attorneys believe is true, the two presentations the jurors had just experienced would play a significant role in the verdict they would reach at the end of the trial. Whatever the jurors thought that day, the journalists in the room wasted no time in pronouncing their verdict about how they thought the two presentations had gone.

STARK CHOICES

The news media often cover opening statements of legal trials, but it's rare when the topic of the coverage is the presentation style itself. According to the coverage of this opening statement the next day, something exceptional had happened in the Angleton courtroom. By *Fortune* magazine's account, Mark "gave a frighteningly powerful and skillful opening statement," speaking "without notes and in gloriously plain English" and taking on the defendant "with merciless, spellbinding savagery." The reporter had not noticed that Mark did have notes—his PowerPoint presentation in Presenter view on his laptop below the jury box. The *New York Times* reported that in comparison with Mark's opening, the defense lawyer's presentation was "staid" and that "he read portions of his statement and illustrated his talk mostly using blue-and-yellow PowerPoint pie charts and long excerpts of letters from the Food and Drug Administration."

Fortune went on: "The trial offers jurors a stark choice between accepting (Mark) Lanier's invitation to believe simple, alluring and emotionally cathartic stories" and the defense's "appeals to colorless, heavy-going soporific Reason. Lanier is inviting the jurors to join him on a bracing mission to catch a wrongdoer and bring him to justice." In contrast, the *Fortune* article continued, the defense "is asking the jurors to do some-thing difficult and unpleasant like—well—taking medicine."

Six weeks later, the trial ended, and the jurors entered the jury room to deliberate. After a day and a half of discussion, the jurors made their decision, and the journal-ists and lawyers filled the courtroom again to hear what they would say. The jurors awarded Mark's client Carol a stunning $253 million verdict. Amid the storm of international headline news, the pharmaceutical company's market capitalization fell $5 billion.

After the verdict was announced, the *Wall Street Journal* reported one juror as say-ing, "'Whenever [the defense] was up there, it was like wah, wah, wah,' ... imitating the sounds Charlie Brown's teacher makes in the television cartoon. 'We didn't know what the heck they were talking about.'"

The impact of the PowerPoint presentation in Mark's opening statement proved to last long after the trial. Six months later, Mark met with the Angleton jurors during a focus group session to see what they remembered about the trial, and the jurors vividly recalled the specific story and images that Mark presented in his opening statement.

Although using PowerPoint in a new way helped win the day in Angleton for the plaintiff, the story didn't end there; many more cases involving the same drug went to trial in other courtrooms around the U.S. Later, the pharmaceutical company's market capitalization recovered, and the company agreed to settle all Vioxx claims in 2007 with a $4.85 billion settlement fund.

WINDS OF CHANGE

Aside from the verdict against the pharmaceutical company, that July day demonstrated the dramatic results an effective approach can have on a single presentation in a single room with a single audience.

The *Beyond Bullet Points* approach had never been used in a courtroom before the Angleton trial, but since that day, its impact is still reverberating through the legal profession. Today, if a legal team faces a courtroom opponent who is using the approach, they know they have to respond somehow and raise the bar of their own presentations.

Legal teams that have faced opponents using this approach in the courtroom have started to adopt the story themes and graphics that the other side uses. For example, in trials against the pharmaceutical company that followed the Angleton verdict, the defense lawyers began using the "CSI" theme in their presentations. When Mark faced them again, he used techniques to counter what the defense lawyers did, raising the bar even higher.

The same sorts of impacts are being felt in other professions as well, as visual storytelling begins to transform the status quo for presenters everywhere. Beyond lawyers and law firms, people in many other professions and organizations are accomplishing significant results with this approach, including presenters in major corporations, nonprofit organizations, universities, research firms, and government agencies. They use the approach for a wide range of functions, such as marketing, sales, training, and education. In this book, you'll find examples of presentations from different fields and for different purposes so that you see how to apply BBP to your own situation.

Everything Mark and many others have accomplished using the BBP approach is explained in detail in this book, and by the end, you should be well equipped with the knowledge and tools you need to start applying *Beyond Bullet Points* approach to your own presentations.

BUSTING THE TOP 3 MYTHS ABOUT POWERPOINT

In this chapter, you will:

- Learn the top myths that stand in the way of effective visual storytelling.
- Review key research principles that every presenter needs to know.
- Compare the research principles with BBP and the conventional approach.

The presentation in Chapter 1 showed how one person with software and a projector could transform a room into a theater of persuasion, and tell a compelling visual story that gets results measured in millions—and billions—of dollars.

Yet it's not just courtrooms where the power of visual storytelling is getting big results these days; it's also happening in boardrooms and meeting spaces, large and small, around the world, across every profession.

This rapid rise of visual stories is directly related to our more visual, engaged culture, which is the product of a vast new communications infrastructure that's centered on screens—from desktop monitors to projectors, to tablets and smartphones. In this age of TED Talks and social media built around images and brief text, every communicator must master the fundamentals of story, structure, storyboarding. Yet, most of us struggle when we face a daunting amount of information we need to present and the prospect of somehow turning it into a compelling visual story that will help us get the results we want.

Beyond learning the new core skills of turning words into pictures, many leaders also face formidable obstacles in their organizations where creating bullet point slides and overloaded presentations is a rite of passage. Such organizations have deeply entrenched cultures where doing anything creative or outside the box of the bullet point template is frowned upon. Fortunately, the tides of the culture are slowly changing the communications landscape and demanding that everyone become a visual storyteller. And the moments when things change most dramatically are when leaders see for themselves how creativity and storytelling can get them the results they're seeking

THE STATE OF THE ART OF PRESENTATIONS

Sometime after the attorney's victory in the courtroom, I received a call from the chief operating officer of a $1 billion private transportation company.

"Cliff, we need to win a new project that we're bidding on," he said. "It's worth a lot of money to us—$25 million annually—and it's very important to my company and me. We're not completely convinced our slides are the best they could be. Do you think you could help?"

I asked him to show me his slides so I could look at what I could do. I opened the file in Slide Sorter view so I could see all the slides at once and saw something similar to the slides in Figure 2-1.

Figure 2-1

Many presentations today are similar to this example, using the same background, category headings, and bulleted lists of text.

He had told me his audience was a small group of high-level executives who would decide on which company to choose for the project, and it was crucial to persuade them to see things his way so his team would win the bid.

The look of the slides was the same as what I see in most organizations, in most functional areas, and across most industries. They were created using the default template installed in the original version of PowerPoint in 1986, featuring a title at the top, lines of text below, and an occasional visual added throughout the presentation.

Whenever I show similar slides to workshop participants and ask how they would feel if they were about to experience these slides as an audience member, the most common responses are that the slides are overwhelming, lack focus, and are boring. This is hardly what any presenter would want to hear when her objectives are to make a positive impression and to persuade an audience to think or do something differently.

Like many presentations, the first slides were all about the company, describing its history, its achievements, and its members. This is all important information, but it's hardly a compelling start to a persuasive story. The three most important persuasive points were impossible to locate amid the busy slides. The headlines lacked meaningful information about what the slide was about, and it wasn't possible to read the story across headlines from one slide to the next.

THE TOP 10 REASONS THAT SLIDE PRESENTATIONS DON'T WORK

1. Appears overwhelming
2. Looks canned, like a one-size-fits-all presentation
3. Visually boring
4. Has a weak start
5. Appears cold, and has no emotional connection
6. All about the presenter rather than the audience
7. No clear roadmap
8. Meanders without a story
9. No dramatic tension
10. Lacks personality and authenticity

It was clear that these slides would not be much help in making a persuasive case for such an important meeting. In fact, the slides would stand in the way of effective communication by shutting down dialogue, creating a feeling of frustration, and producing a feeling that the presenter is more concerned about his company than about the audience. The hard truth is that many presentations continue to mire presenters and audiences in confusion, overwhelm, boredom, and frustration.

I assured the chief operating officer that we would transform this default approach to using slides into an effective visual story to get the results he wanted. You'll see the results in the next chapter. First, however, because this way of creating slides is so common, it's worth taking a step back and examining how we got to this default way of presenting, what the research says about how it's working, and how we can move forward into a new world of visual storytelling.

THE OLD STORY ABOUT POWERPOINT

Before presentation software and personal computers began to be widely adopted in the 1980s, leaders communicated their most important thinking and analysis in the form of written reports and memos. When they needed to communicate their ideas to others inside or outside the organization, they sent a written document or delivered an oral presentation during a meeting.

Then along came visual aids for presentations, in the form of overhead transparencies and 35mm slides that usually featured a title at the top and a bulleted list of text or a graph or chart. Visual aids broke up long-form ideas into smaller, more digestible chunks. They communicated key strategic messages to customers and the rest of the organization quickly, widely, consistently, and accurately. Putting these ideas on a screen guided a presenter's talk and promised to deliver better results by increasing persuasiveness, differentiating the presenter from the crowd, speeding up decision-making, reducing meeting times, and raising retention of information.

At the time, leaders invested large amounts of money for labor, equipment, and production costs to produce these basic 35mm slides and overhead transparencies. Then along came the personal computer revolution that put a desktop on most office workers' desktops, including a copy of a brand-new software called PowerPoint.

The original proposal for PowerPoint software described a single product that could be used by anyone and everyone to create their own slides and handouts, using three primary views, as shown in Figure 2-2:

- Normal view
- Notes Page view
- Slide Sorter view

The software promised that a leader could accomplish the objectives of visual aids, except now do it faster, easier, cheaper, and more consistently. The inventors created the default slide template to mimic the most popular formats for overhead transparencies—a title at the top, a bulleted list below, and an occasional chart or graph.

Slide Sorter view

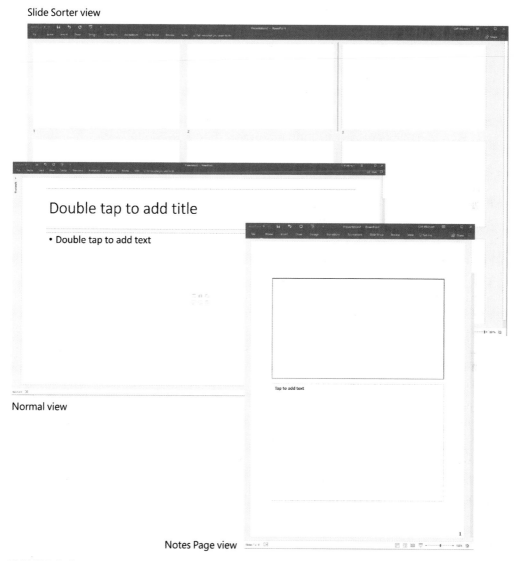

Normal view

Notes Page view

FIGURE 2-2

The three working views in PowerPoint: Slide Sorter, Normal and Notes Page.

Right out of the gate, the default template was a smashing success, and leaders in all types of organizations and professions adopted the tool as a new way to create visual aids. The tool influenced an entire new style of communication. As leaders became accustomed to using PowerPoint, an entire culture formed around its use, which created expectations for everyone to use default templates, styles, and formats in a particular way.

And like any technology, PowerPoint would have effects that no one could have predicted. Gradually, slides began to replace long-form reports, and at some organizations, slides replaced written documents altogether. Yet PowerPoint was never designed to create lengthy written reports, and soon, people began to fill slides with more and more text in smaller and smaller fonts to squeeze all the information that was once in multiple pages of a long report in a short PowerPoint deck. The result was overloaded slides that didn't work well as slides during a live presentation, nor as a comprehensive written document.

And over time, the world changed. The rapid adoption of personal computers and the growing complexity of the world led to a dramatic increase in the volume of information, as well as easy access to it. As visuals became more common, graphic design was more widely practiced.

Top-down hierarchies flattened within organizations, and audiences came to prefer formal to informal presentation styles. Even the architecture of meeting rooms changed as they reoriented to the large screens and projectors.

And we changed collectively as audiences and presenters. In the face of huge volumes of abstract data, we wanted an emotional human connection and story. Instead of a sea of text, we wanted images. Instead of overload, we wanted curation and customization. Instead of an encyclopedia of information, we wanted the *CliffsNotes*.

Empowered by social media, audiences began to assert their power and created a formidable backlash to the text- and data-filled slides that serve the presenter, but not the audience. Instead of slides that were all about the presenter, they wanted a story that was all about the audience.

With so many changes underway, it was no surprise that the default way of presenting information would begin to fail. However, the most significant blow to the prevailing bullet point approach would come from a surprising source—from researchers who were discovering words and pictures were the most effective way for people to learn. In short order, they managed to dispel three bedrock myths about PowerPoint and pave the way to more creative and effective uses of the tool.

MYTH 1: YOUR AUDIENCE WILL "GET" WHATEVER YOU SHOW THEM

In many conversations about PowerPoint, the discussion often focuses on which size font to use, how to insert a video clip, and whether the background of a PowerPoint template should be blue, black, or another color. One thing you never hear is a conversation about any research related to PowerPoint presentations. Despite the widespread use and influence of PowerPoint software in many professions, you would be hard-pressed to find research that demonstrates that the underlying theory, impact, or effectiveness of the conventional bullet point approach is better than any other approach.

For example, you won't find research indicating that presenting with bullet points on a PowerPoint slide is more effective than presenting without them. You also won't find studies showing that using a PowerPoint design template produces better learning than not using a design template. You won't find quantitative justification and rationale for commonly accepted PowerPoint design guidelines, such as the 6-by-6 rule, which states that every slide should have six lines of text with six words per line.

This lack of comparative studies on PowerPoint approaches has created a void regarding research-based guidelines on how best to use the software, and this void has been quickly filled with popular myths and cultural habits. In other words, the main reason we approach PowerPoint the way we do is simply because that's the way that we've always done it—and not because any research says it's better than any other way.

Although there is little research specifically comparing PowerPoint approaches, there is a significant body of research that has direct relevance to those who use spoken words and projected images to communicate. For decades, researchers in the fields of cognitive science and educational psychology have been studying the best ways to help people learn new information using narration and images. Their work is a treasure trove of information that is directly relevant and applicable to you when you use PowerPoint to create presentations.

RESEARCH ON MULTIMEDIA LEARNING

This chapter is informed by the work of Richard E. Mayer, Ph.D., a professor of psychology at the University of California, Santa Barbara. Ranked as the most prolific researcher in the field of educational psychology, Mayer is the author of more than 500 publications (including 30 books) and has been researching multimedia learning and problem-solving for almost 30 years. In his books and related articles and papers, Mayer proposes a way to understand the use of multimedia that promotes meaningful learning and lays out a set of principles for designing any multimedia experience based on his own research and that of others. For more information about the research on multimedia learning and its implications for PowerPoint presentations, see Richard E. Mayer, Ed., *The Cambridge Handbook of Multimedia Learning* (Cambridge University Press, 2005).

RESEARCH SHOWS THAT WORKING MEMORY IS LIMITED

Whether you think about it consciously, you probably accept fundamental assumptions about communication that shape your thinking in ways large and small. If you commonly talk about communication in terms of a sender who transmits a message to a receiver, you might assume that you send information through an unobstructed channel, like a pipeline, and the audience will receive it, fully intact, at the other end of the pipeline, as shown in Figure 2-3.

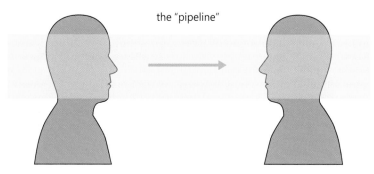

FIGURE 2-3

The pipeline concept assumes that there is an unobstructed channel between you and your audience.

With the pipeline in mind, you assume that you can produce a set of slides in whatever way you like, shown on the left in Figure 2-4. After you send the slides through the pipeline, you assume that its receivers will receive it on the other side, as shown on the right. Under this assumption, your work is then done. The only criterion for success is that you delivered the slides through the pipeline. If for some reason the audience didn't receive what you delivered, of course, it's not your fault as a presenter—after all, you delivered the slides, and what they did with the slides is their problem, not yours.

The pipeline assumption is at work when people make statements like, "We showed them the facts, but they just didn't get it," or "The presentation went right over their heads." When a verdict in a legal trial goes against one party, it is common for people to say the jury just didn't "get" the evidence, or when a sales presentation does not succeed, the presenter might say the audience just didn't "get" the benefits of the product or service. It is hard to separate the pipeline metaphor from our thinking because it is woven into the words and expressions we use commonly every day.

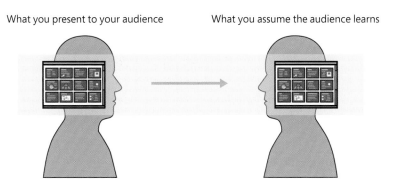

FIGURE 2-4

With the pipeline in mind, you assume that your audience will "get" whatever you "deliver" to them.

Although the pipeline metaphor is convenient, in practice, it does not deliver what you might assume it does. According to leading educational psychologist Richard E. Mayer, if you give a multimedia presentation to an audience, there are three possible outcomes, as shown in Figure 2-5.

1. The first possible outcome is that your audience experienced no learning (upper right). This is the worst-case scenario—in spite of your work in preparing your presentation and your audience's time and effort in showing up and paying attention, no learning happened to make the experience worthwhile.

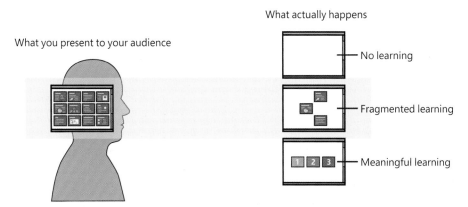

FIGURE 2-5

In reality, audiences do not automatically get what you send through the pipeline.

2 A second possible outcome is that your audience remembered perhaps the bullet points on slides 12 and 33 and the diagram on slide 26—but that's all they remembered. In this scenario, they remember only bits and pieces of the presentation because they experienced fragmented learning (middle right). In fragmented learning, the audience remembers at least some things, but from a presenter's perspective, you have no control over what they learned because the fragments could be any pieces of information among many, and you don't know which ones.

3. The third possible outcome is that the audience remembered exactly what the presenter intended—they experienced meaningful learning (lower right). Meaningful learning is what any group wants to achieve in their time together—the people in the audience understand what the presenter intended, and they can apply the information after the meeting.

Audiences routinely report that slides today are "Forgettable!" and they will often ask, "What's the point?" It's rare to hear an audience and a presenter agree that meaningful learning has occurred. To turn the situation around, you need to change the shape of the metaphor that guides the way you think about human communication.

During a presentation, the memory of an audience member is the critical human element that determines how well new information is received, processed, and stored in the human mind. Researchers who study the mind generally accept that there are three types of human memory, as shown in Figure 2-6.

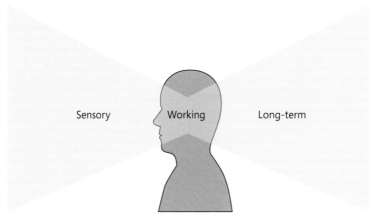

Sensory   Working   Long-term

FIGURE 2-6

The three types of human memory: sensory memory, long-term memory, and working memory.

1. **Sensory memory**—Sensory memory is the part of the mind where your audience members briefly store the initial impressions of sights and sounds as they look at and listen to the environment around them. Sensory memory is potentially unlimited in capacity, although sights and sounds might persist in sensory memory for less than a second.

2. **Long-term memory**—Long-term memory is the part of the mind where your audience members store information over an extended period, from as little as 30 seconds to as long as a lifetime. In a presentation context, this is where you would like your audience to store the new information you intend to communicate to them. Beyond just remembering the new information, you also would like them to be able to access and apply the information from long-term memory when needed. Like sensory memory, long-term memory is also potentially unlimited in its capacity.

3. **Working memory**—Sometimes called short-term memory, working memory is the part of the mind where your audience members hold their attention. The theories underlying working memory are complex, but essentially, working memory is a temporary holding area for information. As sensory memory briefly holds sights or sounds, working memory then pays attention to some of them and holds them for a matter of seconds while it works to integrate them into long-term memory.

While sensory memory and long-term memory each have unlimited capacity, working memory is severely limited in its capacity to process new information. In a seminal paper published in 1956, George A. Miller observed that people could hold a small number of "chunks" that they mentally form in what we now understand as working memory. Miller believed the number of chunks a person could remember was about seven. However, depending on the type of information, working memory expert Nelson Cowan recently revisited Miller's classic work and now estimates the capacity of working memory for new information at three or four chunks.

MORE ON WORKING MEMORY For more information about the capacity of working memory, see:

George A. Miller, "The Magical Number Seven, Plus or Minus Two: Some Limits on Our Capacity for Processing Information," *Psychological Review* 63, 81–97 (1956).

Although the limits of working memory have been acknowledged for 50 years, the concept has never been fully absorbed or integrated into our day-to-day practice and understanding of human communication. The pipeline metaphor has such a strong grip on our collective consciousness that we have effectively resisted the adoption of the research that contradicts it. However, as much as we might want to believe that there is an unobstructed pipeline between sender and receiver, the reality is that the limits of working memory put a major crimp in that metaphor.

To align our assumptions about communication with what researchers accept about the way human memory works, we must drop the old pipeline metaphor and pick up a new metaphor—the eye of the needle, as shown in Figure 2-7.

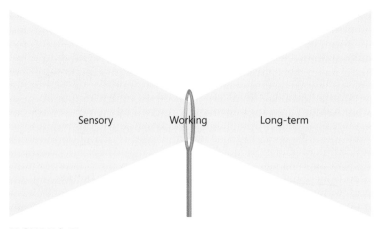

Sensory   Working   Long-term

FIGURE 2-7

The limited capacity of working memory to process new information creates a narrow passage—much like the eye of a needle—that stands between the information you present to sensory memory and the information that is integrated into long-term memory.

Keeping this new metaphor in mind when you create presentations, you know that you have a potentially unlimited amount of new information that you could show someone's sensory memory (left). You want the new information to be retained in long-term memory (right). However, working memory is so constrained in its capacity to process new information that it creates a narrow passage, much like the eye of a needle (center). This extremely small space of the "eye" of working memory constitutes the most formidable challenge you face as a presenter.

This new metaphor visually explains why audiences report either no learning or fragmented learning. If you present working memory with more new information than it can handle, as shown on the left in Figure 2-8, the eye of the needle is easily overloaded and will process and integrate into long-term memory what it can—only bits and pieces out of the entire presentation, as shown on the right. As much as you might want your audience to learn the new information you present, they will never be able to learn it unless you help that information properly pass through the eye of the needle.

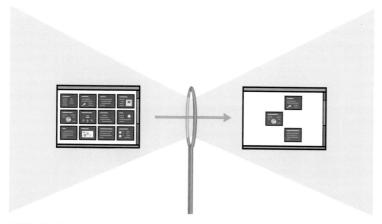

FIGURE 2-8

When you show more information than working memory can handle, audience members remember only bits and pieces.

The effect of reducing the excess load on working memory has been documented by researchers including Mayer, who conducted a study using two multimedia presentations. The first presentation featured interesting but irrelevant graphics, and the second presentation provided the same information, but without the interesting but irrelevant graphics.

Mayer measured the impact of the two approaches on audiences using two criteria:

1. Retention—the ability of the audience to simply recall the information.

2. Transfer—the ability to apply the new information creatively.

Audiences who experienced the second presentation retained 69 percent more information and were able to apply 105 percent more creative solutions using the information than those who experienced the first presentation. This study offers research-based evidence to support the saying "Less is more"—the less you overload working memory with extraneous information, the more learning improves.

THE OLD WAY IGNORES THE LIMITS OF WORKING MEMORY

With the eye of the needle metaphor in mind, take a look at a conventional PowerPoint presentation in Slide Sorter view, as shown in Figure 2-9. Audiences might not know about the limited capacity of working memory, but they do know what they're talking about when they say presentations like this are a "Data dump!" and "Overwhelming!" They've been down the road to overload before, and Slide Sorter view shows exactly how the conventional approach takes them there. The new information is clearly not presented in bite-size pieces; instead, it fills every slide, slide after slide, with overwhelming detail.

There is no visual guidance to help the viewer understand the structure.

There are no visible signals to indicate which slides are most important.

Information is not presented in bite-sized pieces.

FIGURE 2-9

Slide Sorter view of a conventional PowerPoint presentation reveals no digestible pieces and no cues about the presentation's structure or organization.

What you see here is visual overwhelm rather than visual organization. Using the same predesigned background for all of the slides gives them a uniform look, but doing so also prevents you from using a range of design techniques to visually highlight the most important information on single slides or across slides. Using the same background also makes the overall presentation appear visually repetitive, which causes visual boredom that quickly shuts down attention.

Looking at this big-picture view of the presentation, you can't see immediately the location of the most important slides. Instead, every idea has equal visual weight, and there are no cues given by the slide backgrounds about the relative importance of ideas. Working memory—with its limited capacity to process new information—must sort things out on its own and is presented here with the impossible task of holding all this new information while it figures out what's most important to know.

You also see that there is no structure that ties each of the individual slides together into a coherent whole—this presentation is just a series of bulleted lists and diagrams, slide after slide. There is no familiar framework that the audience already has in long-term memory that can guide working memory to make sense of the new information.

SETTING THE RECORD STRAIGHT   **Misconception:** People will
learn more if I show more.

Reality: Research shows that people learn better when information is presented in bite-size pieces.

VISUAL STORYTELLING RESPECTS THE LIMITS OF WORKING MEMORY

With the eye of the needle metaphor in mind, take a look at how a visual story appears in Slide Sorter view, as shown in Figure 2-10. Studies have found that people learn better when information is broken up into digestible pieces. In Slide Sorter view, you see each specific digestible piece—in the form of a single slide that contains only one main idea that is clearly summarized by a headline. This eases your audience through your story and explanation frame by frame, one piece at a time.

In the Slide Sorter view of a visual story, your eye immediately goes to the most important slides because you use layouts and backgrounds to cue your audience to where they are. This approach draws from the hard work you do when you distill your complex ideas to the essence and identify your key points. These visual cues also indicate the slides in the presentation that explain your key points and provide backup detail.

You'll use consistent layouts and backgrounds on related slides to create visual and verbal continuity among them, but when you reach a different type of slide, the layouts and backgrounds change. This orients both presenter and audience to where they are in the story, and the changing slide layouts and backgrounds offer your audience visual variety to keep their interest.

A clear structure guides the viewer on what to expect.

Extraneous information has been removed from the slides.

Information is presented in bite-sized segments, with one idea per slide.

FIGURE 2-10

Slide Sorter view shows a presentation that is broken up into digestible chunks for easier handling by working memory.

You also see from Slide Sorter view a visual story theme or motif. Researchers have found that you improve the ability of working memory to process new information by applying familiar organizing structures. This works because an important quality of working memory is that it is a two-way street. Although working memory has only limited capacity to handle new information as that information arrives, as shown on the left in Figure 2-11, it also has unlimited capacity to pull in existing information from long-term memory, as shown on the right.

This plays out in the following classic test of working memory: a researcher presents someone with new information in the form of a series of unrelated numbers, such as 2 1 2 5 5 5 1 2 3 4. The number of these individual chunks of information that someone can recall is considered the capacity of that person's working memory.

However, people can remember more of the same set of numbers when working memory pulls a structure they already know from long-term memory. For example, if 2 1 2 5 5 5 1 2 3 4 is reorganized into a familiar phone number style—212-555-1234—the information is much easier to recall.

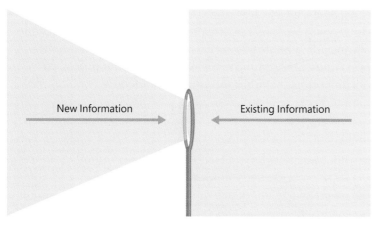

FIGURE 2-11

Working memory is limited in its capacity to process new information (left), but it is unlimited in its capacity to process existing information from long-term memory (right).

Thus a "chunk" is defined by the audience as they apply a meaningful structure from their long-term memory to new information. You help your audience accelerate understanding of new information by introducing a familiar "chunking" structure to new information you present.

MYTH 2: THE SAME SLIDE WORKS EQUALLY WELL AS BOTH A VISUAL ON A SCREEN AND AS A PRINTED HANDOUT

Now that you've busted the myth that you can show information to an audience any way you want, and they'll get it, it's time to move on to the next core myth about PowerPoint. Many think a slide works equally well as both an on-screen visual during a live presentation and as it does on a printed handout. It doesn't.

RESEARCH SHOWS YOU MUST ADDRESS BOTH VISUAL AND VERBAL CHANNELS

The concept of dual channels states that people receive and process new visual and verbal information in not one, but two separate, but related channels. The psychologist Allan Paivio described his theory of dual coding in the 1970s, and during the same decade, Alan Baddeley and Graham Hitch described a similar two-channel structure in working memory.

Today, the concept has become a widely accepted standard among researchers. In the dual-channel model, the images someone sees are processed through a visual channel—the images domain, including photographs, illustrations, charts, and graphs—as illustrated conceptually in Figure 2-12 (top). The speaker's narration is processed through the verbal channel (bottom), which is the language domain.

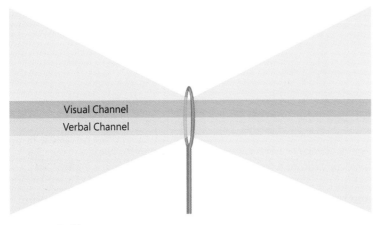

FIGURE 2-12

Working memory receives information through two channels—a visual channel and a verbal channel.

Although text on a screen is a visual element, working memory quickly verbalizes the words and sends them through the verbal channel. Research over the years has found that the way information is presented to these two channels has a big impact on the effectiveness of working memory.

MORE ON DUAL CHANNELS For more information about the dual-channels concept, see:

Alan D. Baddeley and Graham Hitch, "Working Memory," in *The Psychology of Learning and Motivation: Advances in Research and Theory*, G. H. Bower, Ed., Vol. 8, pp. 47–89 (Academic Press, 1974).

Allan Paivio, "Mind and Its Evolution" (Lawrence Erlbaum Associates, 2007).

USING NOTES PAGES ADDRESSES THE TWO CHANNELS

Using the Notes Page feature of PowerPoint addresses the reality of dual channels. As shown in Figure 2-13, a clear headline at the top of the page always summarizes the point. The off-screen text box in the bottom half of the page contains what you will say aloud while the slide is on screen. And a simple graphic on the slide area that you see in the top half of the page complements the headline and the verbal narration.

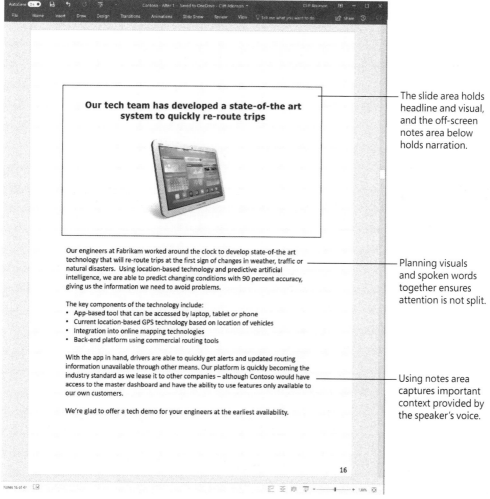

FIGURE 2-13

Using Notes Page View manages the visual channel in the on-screen slide area above and the verbal channel in the off-screen text box below.

Writing out the spoken information in the off-screen text box before you add a graphic significantly reduces the amount of information you otherwise would place in the slide area and instead keeps the slide area simple and clear. This helps working memory focus attention on the single point that you explain verbally during this slide. Instead of reading the headline verbatim, you let the audience quickly read and digest it on their own.

Using Notes Page view to tightly integrate screen and narration makes the most efficient use of the two channels of working memory. Looking at the visual and verbal areas together in Notes Page view is like looking at a single frame in a filmstrip, which is made up of a sequence of connected visual frames, each with a corresponding chunk of audio.

AN EFFECTIVE SCREEN AND HANDOUT By viewing your
slides in Notes Page view like the frames in a filmstrip, you align your approach with the dual channels—the information that is presented to the visual channel is in the on-screen slide area, and the information presented to the verbal channel is in the off-screen text box. This approach also creates a well-balanced handout that you print in paper or PDF in Notes Page format, as shown in Figure 2-13. By using PowerPoint this way, you ensure that you produce both an effective live presentation and an effective printed document.

It is no accident that the structure of a filmstrip is conspicuously similar to the dual-channels concept. When you watch a film with sound, your mind coordinates the different information from the soundtrack and the visual frames on the screen.

For almost a century, filmmakers have managed to communicate complex ideas to audiences around the world with synchronized images and sound, with little, if any, text on the screen. Likewise, working memory can easily coordinate visual and verbal channels if they are properly coordinated and presented.

With the screen behind the speaker, the audience sees and quickly digests the slide and then pays attention to the speaker and his or her verbal explanation. The entire experience appears seamless to the audience.

Using the off-screen notes area in Notes Page view also takes into account the fact that the speaker has a voice during a presentation, which offers a critical source of information that has to be planned and integrated into the experience.

This approach fundamentally changes the media model for PowerPoint from paper to a filmstrip. But the difference between a filmstrip and the visual storytelling is pacing. In film and television, you commonly view 24 to 60 frames per second. A good visual story runs at the speed of conversation—about one frame per 30-60 seconds—allowing time for the audience to digest the new information and then focus next on the presenter. This even and appropriate pacing ensures that your audience experiences only the right things at the right times.

THE OLD WAY ADDRESSES ONLY ONE CHANNEL

If you choose not to address both the visual and verbal channels, you load up the slide area at the top with all of the information you want to communicate both visually and verbally. See the Notes Page view of a conventional slide shown in Figure 2-14; because half of the available real estate available for information in Notes Page view is not used, the off-screen text box below is empty, and the slide area becomes the single place to hold both spoken words and projected images.

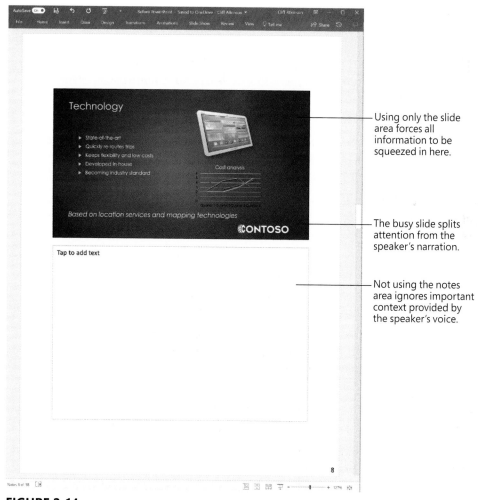

Using only the slide area forces all information to be squeezed in here.

The busy slide splits attention from the speaker's narration.

Not using the notes area ignores important context provided by the speaker's voice.

FIGURE 2-14

The conventional approach does not incorporate the dual-channels concept and instead places both visual and verbal information in the slide area only.

Ignoring the off-screen text box creates a scarcity of resources in the slide area, which predictably produces overloaded slides. Words will usually take priority over visuals, so you will tend to see slides filled with text. Visuals added to these already crowded slides are usually reduced to the size of postage stamps so they can be squeezed between the boxes of text. These dynamics produce slides that are overly complex and difficult to understand.

When this type of slide is displayed during a presentation, the audience tries to make sense of the overloaded slide instead of paying attention to the speaker. When they do shift attention to the speaker, they soon look back at the slide and work hard to try to synchronize the two sources of information. Researchers call this the split-attention effect, which creates excess cognitive load and reduces the effectiveness of learning. You can observe similar dynamics when you're watching a film or TV show, and the sound is slightly out of sync; this incongruence is very noticeable because your working memory has to do the extra work of continually trying to synchronize the mismatched images and narration.

SETTING THE RECORD STRAIGHT   Misconception: I don't
need to worry if what I say doesn't match up with my slide.

Reality: Research shows that people understand a multimedia presentation better when they do not have to split their attention between, and mentally integrate, multiple sources of information.

Another problem with ignoring the off-screen text box in Notes Page view is that you do not recognize and plan for a primary source of information during PowerPoint presentations—your own voice. The result is that the relationship between your spoken words and projected visuals is not fully addressed. You might assume that the information on your slide can stand alone, without verbal explanation, but a PowerPoint slide does not exist in a vacuum—you are standing there speaking to your audience while you project the slide.

Audiences might not know about dual-channels theory, but they do know how they feel when presenters don't integrate the concept into their PowerPoint approach. When presenters read bulleted text from the screen, audiences complain that the presenter should "E-mail it to me!" or "Just give me the handout!" This frustration has a research basis—writing out the text of your presentation on your slides and then reading it to your audience contradicts the widely accepted theory of dual channels.

You might assume that presenting the same information in multiple ways will reinforce your point. However, if you present the same information to the two channels, you reduce the capacity of working memory and in turn reduce learning by creating what researchers call the redundancy effect.

When someone speaks, you process the verbal information at one speed. When the speaker also displays the text of the speech, you process the same information at a different speed—your mind first takes in the text visually and then verbalizes it for processing in the verbal channel.

Because the same information is arriving through the same channel at different speeds, working memory has to split attention between the two sources of information as it works hard to reconcile them. This redundancy quickly overloads working memory and impairs learning.

AN INEFFECTIVE SCREEN AND HANDOUT

By addressing only one channel in your presentation, as shown earlier in Figure 2-14, you create both split attention and redundancy in a live presentation. And by not capturing what is said verbally in the off-screen notes area, you also miss the chance to use PowerPoint to create an effective handout by printing the slides in notes page format.

Redundancy also happens when the same information is presented both visually and in the text because the same information is entering through two channels and the mind must exert more effort to reconcile them. This reduces the efficiency of working memory and can lead to the cognitive overload that so frustrates audiences.

SETTING THE RECORD STRAIGHT

Misconception: It's okay to read my bullet points from the screen.

Reality: Research shows that people understand a multimedia presentation better when the words are presented as verbal narration alone, instead of both verbally and as on-screen text.

To explore the redundancy effect, Mayer conducted experiments using two multimedia presentations. The first presentation included the same material both narrated and displayed with text on the screen, and the second presentation included the narration with the text on the screen removed. Audiences who experienced the second presentation retained 28 percent more information and could apply 79 percent more creative solutions using the information than those who experienced the first presentation.

Thus, the dual-channel concept turns one of our core assumptions about PowerPoint upside-down. Contrary to conventional wisdom and common practice, reading bullet points from a screen reduces learning rather than increases it. Research shows that when you subtract the redundant text from the screen that you are narrating, you improve learning.

MYTH 3: MAKING A LIST IS AN EFFECTIVE WAY TO PRESENT INFORMATION

Now that you've busted two of the core myths about PowerPoint, it's time to take aim at the third core myth: typing a list is an effective way to present information.

RESEARCH SHOWS THAT YOU MUST GUIDE ATTENTION

In the pipeline metaphor described earlier in this chapter, a presentation exists by itself, independent of the people who receive it; you simply pour information into the passive minds of the audience.

Yet, researchers have long known that the mind is not a passive vessel, but rather, it is an active participant in the process of learning. It is the minds of your audience who have to create understanding out of the new information they process in working memory.

You play an important role in helping your audience create understanding by designing slides in specific ways that guide the attention of working memory to the most important visual and verbal information, as illustrated in Figure 2-15.

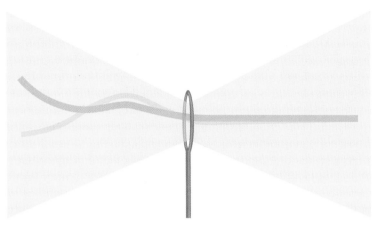

FIGURE 2-15

You must guide the attention of working memory to improve the ability of people to learn new information.

THE OLD WAY DOES NOT GUIDE ATTENTION

In the conventional PowerPoint slide shown in Figure 2-16, it's not easy to see where the presenter intends to guide attention. Such a busy slide assumes that viewers have the working memory capacity to read through all the material as they might with a written document—all while they are listening to you speak. As described earlier in the discussion of the dual-channels theory, it is easy for too much material on this slide to split the attention of the audience between screen and presenter or to impair learning by using both on-screen text and narration to explain the same information.

If you grew up writing essays and reports on paper or as Microsoft Office Word documents, it's a natural transition to think of a PowerPoint slide as a piece of paper where you start writing out your thoughts. But one of the fundamental assumptions about a piece of paper is that it can stand alone—a presenter normally does not need to be there to explain it. The only problem is that this example slide is accompanied by the narration of a live presenter—yet the slide does not take that fact into account.

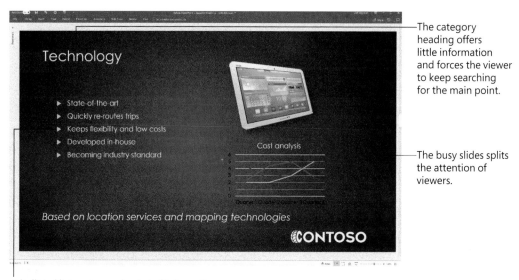

The category heading offers little information and forces the viewer to keep searching for the main point.

The busy slides splits the attention of viewers.

A bulleted list captures a bucket of information but doesn't highlight what's most important.

FIGURE 2-16

The conventional PowerPoint approach does not help working memory to select the most important information on a slide.

Another problem with thinking of the slide area as a piece of paper is that you are much more likely to fill it with text instead of a graphic. Although text on a screen is initially processed through the visual channel, as described earlier, text is quickly verbalized and sent through the verbal channel. That means text-filled slides essentially ignore the capacity of the visual channel to efficiently process information in sync with the verbal channel.

SETTING THE RECORD STRAIGHT **Misconception:** Graphics

are nice to have, but they're not essential.

Reality: Research shows that people learn better from words and pictures than from words alone. This applies when the pictures illustrate what the words say, not when pictures are added for decorative effect.

One of the reasons the example slide does not guide attention is that it uses a category heading, like those you commonly see on many slides. A category heading like "Focus Areas" can help you quickly brainstorm a list of information, but as you see here, it does nothing to guide you to a quick understanding of what is the most important information on the slide. Simply categorizing and listing information does not entail the critical thinking it takes to determine the point of the lists in the first place.

Category headings don't say anything specific, and to uncover the mystery of what you are trying to communicate when you use them, your audience members need to invest extra capacity of working memory they don't have to connect all the dots of the bullet points below the headings. And these headings put an extra burden on you and your audience as you both struggle to see the focus of your ideas through the sequence of slides in your presentation. As your audience views these headings and their corresponding stacks of bulleted lists, slide after slide, it's no wonder that they find the presentation unfocused, hard to understand, and overwhelmed with unnecessary details.

Although the slide includes a photograph, it does not illustrate the specific point of the slide and was likely added for visual decoration to "spice it up." This runs counter to the research that shows that the less you overload working memory with extraneous information, the more people learn.

SETTING THE RECORD STRAIGHT **Misconception:** People learn more when I wow them with special effects and spice up my presentations with razzle-dazzle.

Reality: Research shows that people learn better when extraneous information is removed from a presentation.

Audiences might not know about the research that indicates that you need to guide their attention, but they do know what they are talking about when they frequently say conventional presentations are "incoherent lists" with "no direction" and "a jumble." Instead of guiding working memory through the experience, this example slide creates unnecessary work by not quickly getting to the clear point, by not tapping into the visual channel, and by creating split attention and redundancy with the narration of a live presenter.

VISUAL STORYTELLING GUIDES ATTENTION

In an effective visual storytelling approach, you begin with a headline that makes your point in a complete thought. Next, you write out what you will say verbally in the off-screen text box in Notes Page view and then add a simple graphic in Normal view to produce a slide, as shown in Figure 2-17.

Our tech team has developed a state-of-the art system to quickly re-route trips — The headline clearly summarizes the main point.

— The simple slide is easy to quickly process.

— The slide features one main idea, which is easy to see and understand while the speaker continues narrating.

FIGURE 2-17

This slide guides the attention of working memory from the headline to the graphic to the person speaking.

The simplicity of this slide belies the sophisticated impact it has as it effectively guides the attention of working memory. It is crystal clear where working memory should focus first—on the headline at the top of the slide. People are used to reading newspaper headlines that summarize the main point of a story in a single sentence, and here the complete sentence headline serves the same function.

The audience doesn't have to work hard to figure out the point you want to make—instead, you have cleared the way for them to focus on the idea at hand rather than be distracted by unnecessary cognitive work.

SOME HEADLINE-MAKING RESEARCH Michael Alley,

author of "The Craft of Scientific Presentations: Critical Steps to Succeed and Critical Errors to Avoid" (Springer, 2005), conducted a study using two PowerPoint presentations, each with a different headline format. One presentation included only sentence fragments at the top of each slide, and the second presentation included a complete sentence at the top that summarized the most important point of the slide. In tests to measure the knowledge and comprehension of the information in the presentations, the audiences who experienced the slides with the complete sentence headlines saw an average improvement in test scores of 11 percentage points over the audiences who saw the slides with the sentence fragments. When you use the title area of the slide to summarize your point for your audience members, you properly guide their attention, and in the process, you ease the burden on their working memory to figure out your point.

Research has found that visuals can improve learning, but only if they illustrate the point you are making. Then the graphics tell a major part of the story as they communicate information through the visual channel in sync with your verbal explanation. This makes effective use of working memory by using both the visual and verbal channels, rather than just the verbal channel alone. It also ensures that working memory is not distracted by graphics that don't relate specifically to the information at hand. Likewise, the slide background contains no extraneous information that would add more cognitive load.

The simple elements of a clear slide work together to guide the complete presentation experience. First, the audience members quickly digest the headline, then they view the simple graphic that illustrates the headline, and then they turn their attention to the verbal explanation of the speaker. The result is an engaging multimedia experience that balances visual and verbal elements and contributes to meaningful understanding.

THE MISALIGNED TEMPLATE Many organizations create a corpo-

rate PowerPoint template to ensure that every presentation created in the organization has a similar graphical style. Although these templates can ensure a similar look across presentations, if they ignore the research realities described in this chapter, they also diminish the effectiveness of presentations of all the presenters who use them. Every organization should invest in hiring a professional who can design research-based templates that help presenters rather than hurt them.

THE OPPORTUNITY: USING POWERPOINT TO TELL A PERSUASIVE STORY THAT GETS RESULTS

Forget the old ways of using PowerPoint, because as you saw in this chapter, when you ignore the research realities, you use an approach that is broken, ineffective, and frustrating for audiences. Instead, when you choose an approach that fixes the problems, you produce experiences that audiences find engaging and meaningful.

That's because you have now reoriented the three fundamental views of PowerPoint to align with the research, and with these new ideas in mind, you are ready to unlock the power of BBP in your own presentations as you turn now to Chapter 3.

THE 5 PRINCIPLES AND 10 BUILDING BLOCKS OF PERSUASIVE VISUAL STORYTELLING

In this chapter, you will:

- Review step-by-step how the Beyond Bullet Points (BBP) Story Template creates the foundation for your presentation that you will build upon with your narration and graphics.

- Review the 5 Principles and 10 Building Blocks of persuasive visual storytelling.

- Prepare the BBP Story Template for your next presentation, and review three guidelines for writing headlines.

The toughest part of preparing a persuasive visual story is knowing where to begin. As each of us faces the prospect of transforming a mountain of information into an easily understood story that gets results, we have our work cut out for us. The challenging road ahead includes finding the right story structure to engage our audiences, making tough choices about what information to leave in—and what to leave out—as well as creating the visuals to go along with the story.

If you recall, Chapter 2 began with the story of an executive who aimed to persuade an important audience to decide to choose his company for a high-value project. But his current presentation was loaded with text and was less than persuasive. As demonstrated in this chapter, we took his message step by step through the clarifying

process that's summarized in this chapter and described in the rest of the book, and created a persuasive visual story similar to the "after" presentation in Figure 3-1.

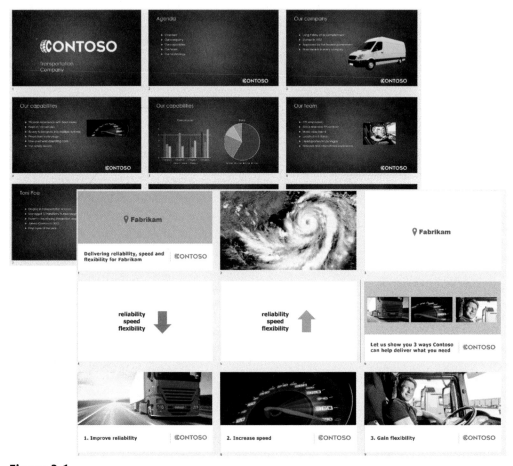

Figure 3-1

The before and after versions of the original presentation shown in Chapter 2.

After the team delivered this compelling visual story, the COO immediately wrote the CEO an email saying, "This was the best presentation we've given in 5+ years, and I'm confident we're going to win." *And they did*.

I'm convinced that every presentation can be transformed in this way, making what would otherwise be a dull and boring experience into a persuasive visual story that gets results. This book will show you how.

Many methods and approaches provide a way to outline ideas or to turn a script into a storyboard. However, the two activities are often separate, and presenters today want the efficiency of both outlining their story and creating effective slides in one fell swoop. In this chapter, you'll learn about a powerful story outlining tool that will make that efficiency possible. Along the way, you'll also learn a set of principles and story elements that can guide you from start to finish to ensure you craft a story that works for you and your audience.

INTRODUCING THE BBP STORY TEMPLATE

With the lessons of the dual-channels theory from Chapter 2 in mind, filmmaking is an appropriate model for designing multimedia presentations because it plans and manages both visual and verbal information simultaneously. Filmmakers know that the best way to start planning a film is with the written word, in the form of a script. A script is much shorter and less detailed than a novel because it assumes that the visuals and dialogue will play a major role in telling the story. The best scripts distill stories to their essence and strip away anything that does not contribute to a story's singular focus.

When a writer completes a script, the document then becomes a powerful organizing tool that puts everyone on the same page. The script is the starting point for planning and producing visuals and dialogue, and it serves as a way for everyone involved in the project to be clear on what everyone else is saying and doing. If you were a filmmaker and you started filming before you had a script, you would waste time and resources while you changed your focus and figured out the story along the way.

WHAT TOOLS DO I NEED? This book includes most of what you need to get started with BBP. Of course, you'll also need a computer with Microsoft Office 365 with Word and PowerPoint installed. Be sure to visit the companion website at www.beyond-bulletpoints.com to download a copy of the story template and find additional resources.

When you begin writing your script or outline for your presentation, you won't have to start with an empty page, because you can use the Beyond Bullet Points Story Template shown in Figure 3-2 to guide you every step of the way. The story template serves as a central organizing tool for the entire presentation. On a single page or two, you'll see the big picture of your story before you commit to adding a visual and verbal track to individual slides.

Title and Byline		
Act I – The Compelling Setup		
The Hook		
The Relevance		
The Challenge		
The Desire		
The Map		
Act II – The Engaging Action		
The Anchors (5 minutes)	**The Explanation** (15 minutes)	**The Backup** (45 minutes)
1		
2		
3		
Act III – The Thrilling Conclusion		

FIGURE 3-2

The BBP Story Template, which you can complete in a Word document.

I encourage you to give the BBP Story Template a try on your next presentation, to:

■ See how it can help you to find a compelling structure for your visual story.

■ Orient your information to the needs of your audience.

■ Distill your information to its essence.

■ Decide what to include or exclude from your message.

THE FIVE PRINCIPLES OF VISUAL STORYTELLING

Although persuasive visual storytelling is a relatively new development in presentations, a set of core principles derived from extensive theory and practical application can help you quickly get up to speed. These principles guide clear communication no matter what tool or technology you use to express it. Each of these five principles has been addressed and incorporated into the story template, so you don't have to reinvent the wheel when you start planning your next presentation.

PRINCIPLE 1: NAIL DOWN THE STORY BEFORE THE SLIDES

In the conventional way of creating slides, you open a blank slide, write in the heading, and start making a list of bullet points. Then you repeat the process again and again as you continue to build out the presentation. Because it's so easy to create slides and so hard to craft a story, the best way to begin crafting a visual story is to do something that might be difficult for veteran users of PowerPoint—to step away from the slides altogether. When you focus first on nailing down the story—the initial impression you make, the sequence of ideas, the persuasiveness of your case, and what to include and exclude—your slides will be simpler and easier to create.

Countless books have been written about the story, and the topic has seen an upsurge in many professions. Of the many types of stories you could craft, this book focuses first on your strategic story—the singular top-level story that ties together your message from beginning to middle and end. As your story is seamlessly designed into your slides and delivery, the slides themselves become your strategy, which will achieve the big-picture results you want. Later in this book, you'll also use anecdotes, which are brief stories that make a quick emotional connection or help you illustrate your point in a very relatable way.

The strategic story template you'll use in this book includes three sections, or acts, that form a classic story structure and correspond to the beginning, middle, and end of your presentation. Each act in the template is delineated by a horizontal bar extending across the page, as shown in Figure 3-3.

Act I begins your story by setting up all of the essential elements that compose every story, including the setting, the main character, an unresolved state of affairs, and the desired outcome. Act II drives the story forward by picking up on the unresolved state of affairs in Act I and developing it through the actions and reactions of the main character in response to changing conditions. Act III ends the story by framing a climax and a decision that the main character must face to resolve the situation, revealing something about his or her character. This time-tested structure keeps your audience interested in your presentation and eager to find out what happens next.

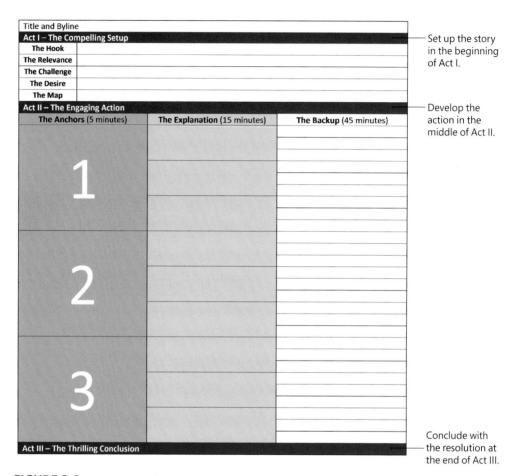

Title and Byline

Act I – The Compelling Setup — Set up the story in the beginning of Act I.

The Hook	
The Relevance	
The Challenge	
The Desire	
The Map	

Act II – The Engaging Action — Develop the action in the middle of Act II.

The Anchors (5 minutes)	The Explanation (15 minutes)	The Backup (45 minutes)
1		
2		
3		

Act III – The Thrilling Conclusion — Conclude with the resolution at the end of Act III.

FIGURE 3-3

The BBP Story Template incorporates a classic three-act story structure.

This three-part story structure follows natural patterns that underlie the way we think and understand. No one needs special training or technology to understand a classic story structure because it's the way humans have been communicating with one another throughout history. A story structure frames the context for communication and focuses attention by making information specific and relevant to an audience.

A VERSATILE OUTLINE
Many readers have reported that the BBP Story Template has proven to be an effective tool for structuring ideas for many purposes—including emails, executive summaries, and written reports.

The idea of bringing together a story and slides is a big shift from the way we tend to use PowerPoint. For years, when we had a great deal of information to present, the default template made it easy for us to make list after list, slide after slide until we ran out of information. The problem with that approach is that when we aim to persuade, information alone doesn't cut it—people want to know why they should care, what's in it for them, and who they are connecting with.

And as we created lists of information, we didn't always connect the dots between the pieces of information, forgetting the essential art of tying everything together in a single coherent message that runs from beginning to middle to end. A story structure solves the problem by tying together scattered pieces of information into a meaningful presentation.

THE ONE THING THAT WILL MAKE THE MOST DIFFERENCE IN YOUR PRESENTATIONS
The single thing you can do to dramatically improve your presentations is to define the singular story thread that carries your message from the beginning, through the middle, and to the end.

The research principles described in Chapter 2 have been around more than 50 years and the idea of a story structure thousands of years longer. These are proven ideas and techniques that work—the present challenge is how to make the concepts practical as you work on your next presentation. The fundamentals of classic story structure and the screenwriting process have already been incorporated into the story template to help get your job done quickly and efficiently.

PRINCIPLE 2: REFORMAT YOUR INFORMATION FOR A YES-NO DECISION

In addition to a classic story structure, your story template incorporates persuasive techniques that are useful for many types of presentations in different contexts. These include using Aristotle's concept that to persuade, you must appeal to emotion, reason, and personal credibility. Even if you intend to simply inform an audience about something, you still must persuade them to pay attention. Why should they listen? What's in it for them? Finding the persuasive heart of a presentation is particularly important because it reformats information from the way we understand it to the way that an audience finds important—often a completely different perspective. This becomes crucial when you aim to present your data in a way that persuades your boss to approve your proposal. When you look at your information like your boss, who wants to make an informed decision as efficiently as possible, your focus shifts to getting to the relevant points as quickly as possible.

When we tackle a new area of information, we usually start by gathering data, analyzing it, and finally distilling the story of the essence of what it means. Problems arise when we want to take our audiences through the same process we did when we learned the information (show the detail first, follow with the analysis, and finally, the story at the end). As described in Chapter 1, if we present too much information at the start, we quickly overwhelm the working memory of our audiences.

TAPPING INTO THE POWER OF PERSUASION Act

I of your story template will make sure that you persuade your audience to focus on your message, and Act II will make sure that you provide the logical reasoning they need to make a decision. You will infuse the entire presentation with personal credibility stemming from verbal clarity and conciseness and add visual credibility by matching your graphics and aesthetics with your audience.

A persuasive story structure solves the problem by focusing information on a real-world decision the audience needs to make, which you'll do in the next chapter. This focus on a "yes-no" decision from the audience will help you dramatically reduce what you *could* say to only what you *must* say to help your audiences decide something.

PRINCIPLE 3: START WITH NO TO GET TO YES

Once you're crafting your message to lead to a yes-no decision, you'll dramatically increase your persuasiveness by starting your planning process by imagining your audience saying the dreaded word—no—to your request or proposal. When you imagine them saying that, and why they would say it, you truly get into their shoes, and with that perspective, you build your presentation to effectively counter their objections and your clear a persuasive pathway to your audience saying yes.

As you go through this process in the next chapter, you'll make your presentation very relevant and personal to your audience. You'll take into account what they already know so you don't waste their time, and you'll realistically address where they are in the decision-making process, so you lower the bar to getting to a yes decision.

PRINCIPLE 4: ALWAYS KEEP THE END IN MIND

Many screenwriting coaches will tell you that the best way to begin writing a story is to start with the final scene and work your way back to how you got there. In a non-fiction presentation, your final scene is the moment when your audience finishes engaging your presentation, and they decide whether to support your ideas. Keeping the end slide in mind will focus you on this crucial moment, so you don't lose sight of it as you're planning your story structure. By always keeping Act III in mind—the last part of your story— you'll be sure to keep the ending in mind as you craft your story from start to finish.

PRINCIPLE 5: THINK LIKE A STORYBOARD

Open a new, blank presentation, add a few blanks slides, and take a look at it in Slide Sorter view, as shown in Figure 3-4.

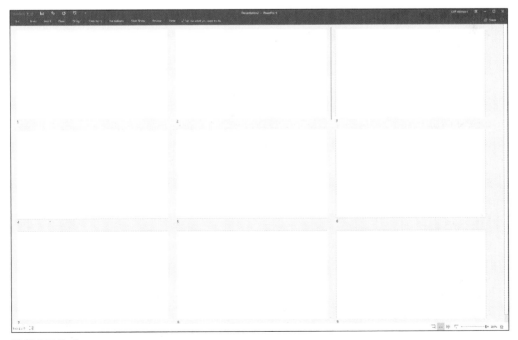

FIGURE 3-4

Slide Sorter view, displaying all of your slides as small thumbnails.

This is how you can always be sure to keep the big picture in view, and as you keep returning to this view, you can look for the ways that your story is flowing from the beginning, through the middle, and all the way to the end.

THE 5 PRINCIPLES OF VISUAL STORYTELLING

1. Nail down the story before the slides.

2. Reformat your information for a yes-no decision.

3. Start with no to get to yes.

4. Keep the end slide in mind.

5. Think like a storyboard.

Everything you do in the story template will shape the visuals and narration to come. The process sets up your ideas in a way that preconfigures and aligns information to best prepare it for its passage through the working memory of your audience. The story template ensures that every presentation accomplishes what you intend—by understanding your audience members, tailoring your material to them, getting to the point, and establishing a priority and sequence for your ideas.

You don't have to be an expert storyteller or an expert in cognitive theory; the template makes structuring your story as easy as filling in the blanks. In the cells of the story template, you'll write out a complete sentence that describes what is happening at each point in your story, similar to writing a newspaper headline. As you fill in the blanks, you'll write the actual story that you'll present. When you've finished, you'll have a completed a script.

ALTERNATIVE STORY TEMPLATE TOOLS This book

shows you how to use a Word document as your BBP Story Template, but it's not the only tool you could use. Readers have found innovative alternatives by re-creating the story template structure with Microsoft Excel, Post-It Notes, a flipchart, and a whiteboard. Figure 3-5 shows a BBP Story Template created using mind-mapping software called MindJet MindManager—an especially flexible and scalable tool for creating presentation outlines. For more resources related to these alternative tools, visit www.beyondbulletpoints.com.

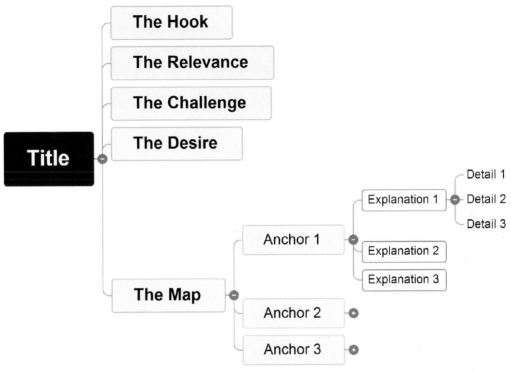

FIGURE 3-5

An alternative version of the story template created with a mind-mapping tool gives you the ability to create presentations using a different tool.

After you complete the template in Word, you'll import the headlines into PowerPoint, where each complete sentence you wrote will become the headline of a slide, as shown in Figure 3-6. This ensures that before you start working in PowerPoint, you already know the main point you intend to make on each slide.

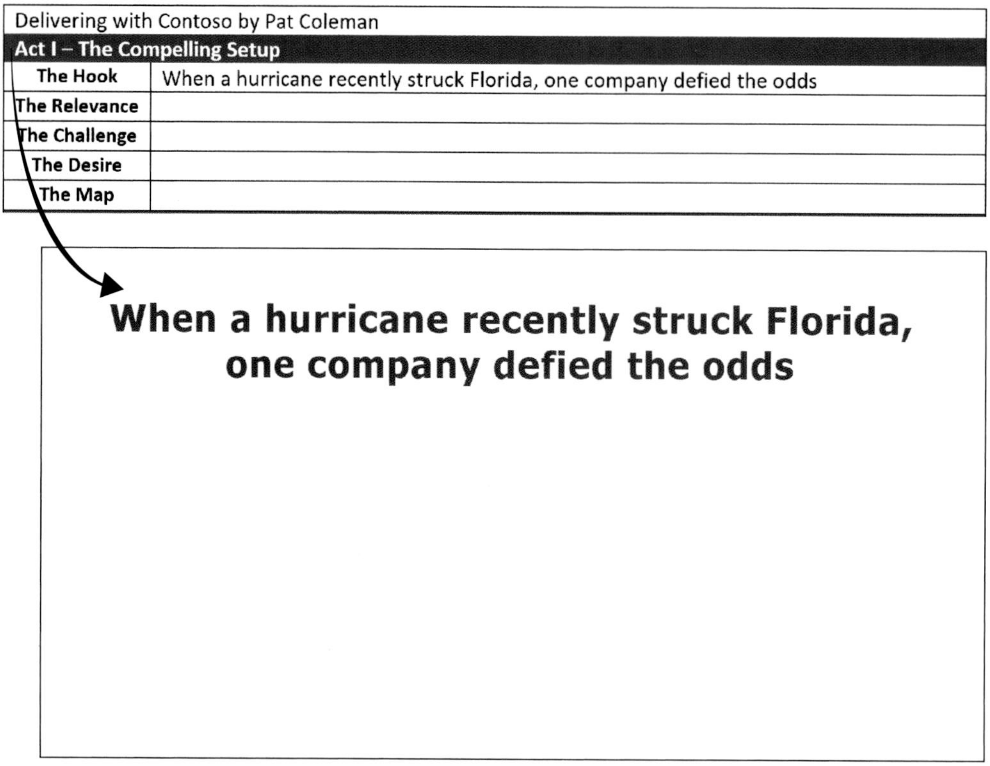

Delivering with Contoso by Pat Coleman	
Act I – The Compelling Setup	
The Hook	When a hurricane recently struck Florida, one company defied the odds
The Relevance	
The Challenge	
The Desire	
The Map	

When a hurricane recently struck Florida, one company defied the odds

FIGURE 3-6

Each headline you write in the story template becomes a headline on a slide.

TAPPING INTO THE POWER OF A TEAM

Get as many people involved in the storyboarding process as possible, especially team leaders, marketers, graphic designers, and even some of your potential audience members. When you bring together these separate groups, the efficient process of producing presentations increases the speed of decision making, reduces revisions, and improves the quality and impact of slides for both presenters and audiences.

The process will also reveal that people on your team have unexpected talents that will surprise you—perhaps computer engineers will turn out to be good at graphic design, and graphic designers will be good at wordsmithing a logical argument.

This pivotal technique of turning your story template into a set of slides will directly transform your written words into the foundation of a visual storyboard. This will make your job of finding visuals easier by establishing what you need to illustrate on every slide and will help your audience understand your new information much faster by indicating clearly in the title area the meaning of every slide.

THE 10 BUILDING BLOCKS OF A PERSUASIVE STORYBOARD

As you begin working your storyboard, you'll find that the hard work you did in the story template will pay off by ensuring that you have the 10 building blocks that create the foundation for a compelling storyboard. These elements are formulated from a combination of classic story structure, psychology, cognitive science, and techniques practiced in filmmaking and advertising—and they automatically will fall into place after you export your story template to your new storyboard.

BUILDING BLOCKS 1-4: THE HOOK, THE RELEVANCE, THE CHALLENGE, AND THE DESIRE

You must quickly make an emotional connection with an audience to motivate them, and you see the specific words that do that in Act I, where you write out the building blocks of a strong story beginning. These include the Hook—the first thing you say to establish the setting and grab your audience's attention. The Relevance is what you say to ensure your audience cares about what you're saying. The Challenge is a burning issue your audience faces, and the Desire is where they would like to be, in the face of that challenge.

The first headlines you write in Act I of the story template form the story thread that will carry attention through the entire presentation.

THE 10 BUILDING BLOCKS OF A PERSUASIVE STORYBOARD

1. Hook
2. Relevance
3. Challenge
4. Desire
5. Map

6. Anchors
7. Explanation
8. Headlines
9. Visuals
10. Flow

After you complete Act I and the rest of the story template, you'll import these headlines into PowerPoint, where each statement becomes the headline of a slide, as shown in Figure 3-7.

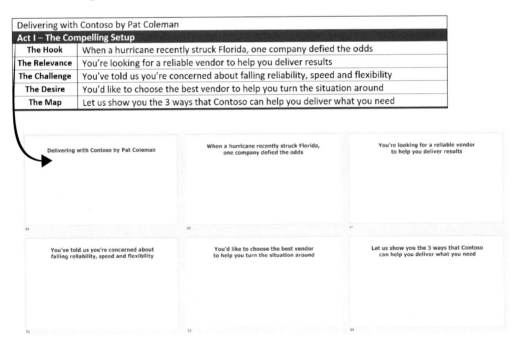

Delivering with Contoso by Pat Coleman	
Act I – The Compelling Setup	
The Hook	When a hurricane recently struck Florida, one company defied the odds
The Relevance	You're looking for a reliable vendor to help you deliver results
The Challenge	You've told us you're concerned about falling reliability, speed and flexibility
The Desire	You'd like to choose the best vendor to help you turn the situation around
The Map	Let us show you the 3 ways that Contoso can help you deliver what you need

FIGURE 3-7

The five sentences you write in the story template become the headlines of your first few slides.

When you view the first five slides in Slide Sorter view, the slide headlines show the story thread that will carry your specific sequence of ideas through the eye of the needle of your audience's working memory, as shown in Figure 3-8; this sequence will also provide the framework for your visuals and narration.

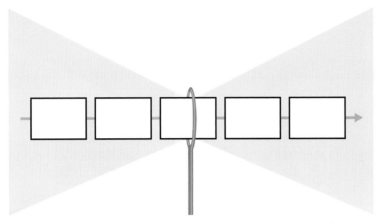

FIGURE 3-8

Act I defines what you'll show to working memory in the first five slides.

BUILDING BLOCKS 5-7: THE MAP, THE ANCHORS, AND THE EXPLANATION

You set in motion some powerful processes in Act I of the story template that continue to play out as you create the rest of the slides in your presentation. Just as in Act I, you'll break up your ideas in Act II into digestible pieces by writing out complete-sentence headlines in the story template. Later, just as in Act I, each sentence will become the headline of a slide, as shown in Figure 3-9.

The challenge of any presentation is not to show all the information you have, but instead to select the most important information to present. The story template guides you through the important process of selecting only the ideas your audience needs to know and breaking them down into digestible chunks that are easier for your audience to understand. As you structure Act II, you lay out the Map for your audience, indicating where they're headed so they don't become confused or disoriented.

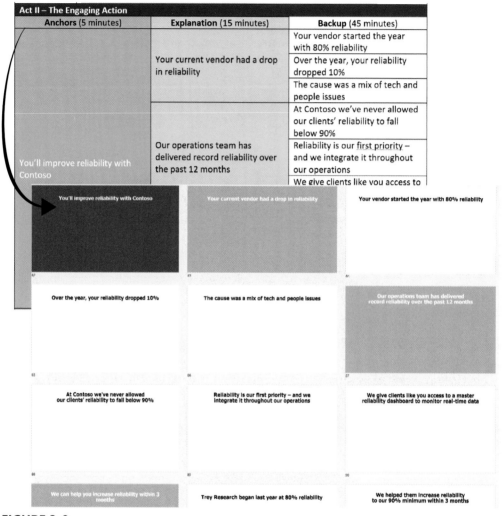

Act II – The Engaging Action		
Anchors (5 minutes)	**Explanation** (15 minutes)	**Backup** (45 minutes)
		Your vendor started the year with 80% reliability
	Your current vendor had a drop in reliability	Over the year, your reliability dropped 10%
		The cause was a mix of tech and people issues
		At Contoso we've never allowed our clients' reliability to fall below 90%
You'll improve reliability with Contoso	Our operations team has delivered record reliability over the past 12 months	Reliability is our first priority – and we integrate it throughout our operations
		We give clients like you access to

(slide thumbnails)

You'll improve reliability with Contoso

Your current vendor had a drop in reliability

Your vendor started the year with 80% reliability

Over the year, your reliability dropped 10%

The cause was a mix of tech and people issues

Our operations team has delivered record reliability over the past 12 months

At Contoso we've never allowed our clients' reliability to fall below 90%

Reliability is our first priority – and we integrate it throughout our operations

We give clients like you access to a master reliability dashboard to monitor real-time data

We can help you increase reliability within 3 months

Trey Research began last year at 80% reliability

We helped them increase reliability to our 90% minimum within 3 months

FIGURE 3-9

The headlines you write in Act II of the story template become the headlines of the rest of your Act II slides.

A logic-tree structure is built into Act II of the story template, as shown in Figure 3-10; this structure helps you put the most important information at the top level of attention, to increase memorability and application. Following the classic Rule of Three that calls for making only three key points in a presentation, you define your most important points, and these become the three Anchors of the presentation. You literally can see them in Act II, where you clarify and identify these top-level points, create a logical and clear structure, and perhaps most importantly, leave out nonessential information. Together, your Act II is the set of slides that provide the Explanation for your story—a mix of anecdotes, examples, and data to back up your case.

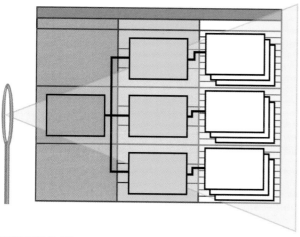

FIGURE 3-10

A built-in logic-tree structure prioritizes your ideas from most important to least, from left to right.

Completing Act II of the story template will sharpen your critical-thinking skills and ensure that the new information in your presentation appears in the order and sequence needed to prevent overloading the working memory of your audience, as shown in Figure 3-11.

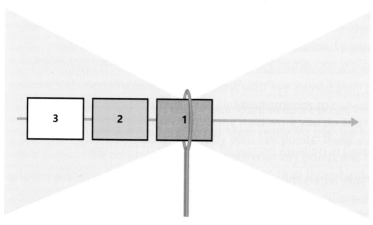

FIGURE 3-11

Act II makes sure that you present the correct priority and sequence of slides to working memory.

BUILDING BLOCKS 8-10: THE HEADLINES, THE VISUALS, AND THE FLOW

After you transform your Word story template into a PowerPoint storyboard, you'll read the next building block of a storyboard—the headlines—across the story frames. From this point forward, you'll work with your storyboard in Slide Sorter view to review your story structure and sequence, check your pacing and flow, and add the visuals to tie together the various parts of your story. This planning ensures that you continually build on and improve your strong story foundation with a single unified set of visuals and words.

Next, you'll quickly apply layouts with slide backgrounds that indicate the three hierarchical levels of Act II slides, as shown in Figure 3-12, to set up preliminary visual cues that designate which slides are more important than others and how those slides fit into a sequence. After you do this, you'll be able to easily see the three most important slides in your presentation—shown in dark blue. You'll also be able to see your second-most important slides—shown in light blue—and your third-most important slides—shown in white—to easily locate and hide them if you need to quickly scale down the presentation to a shorter amount of time. These slides are the foundation for the fully designed layouts and backgrounds you use to cue working memory when you add graphics.

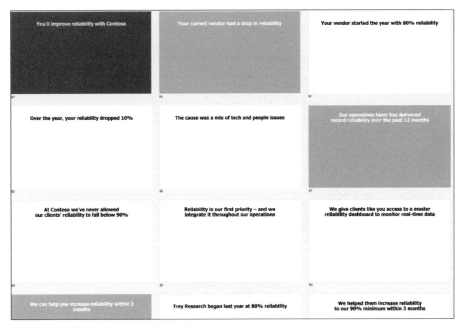

FIGURE 3-12

You'll cue working memory by applying layouts with preliminary slide backgrounds to the three hierarchical levels of Act II slides.

Next, you'll plan the narrated soundtrack of the presentation by writing out the verbal explanation for each headline in the off-screen text box in Notes Page view, as shown in Figure 3-13. If you don't have time to write out your full narration, just take a few notes here. In line with the dual-channels theory described in Chapter 2, this helps you seamlessly integrate each visual with its verbal explanation. After capturing a record of the rich verbal explanation that will accompany the slide and placing it in the notes area, you then choose the simplest possible visual to illustrate the headline of each slide. After you add the visuals as described next, you'll create the flow in your presentation by visually and verbally connecting points from one to the next as you engage your audience.

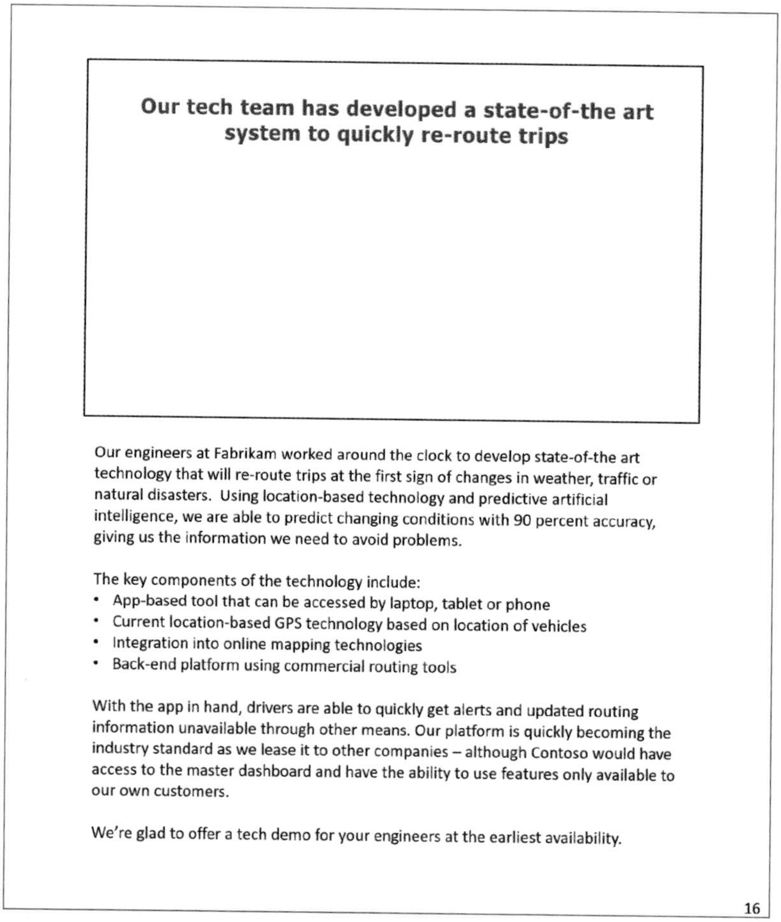

Our tech team has developed a state-of-the art system to quickly re-route trips

Our engineers at Fabrikam worked around the clock to develop state-of-the art technology that will re-route trips at the first sign of changes in weather, traffic or natural disasters. Using location-based technology and predictive artificial intelligence, we are able to predict changing conditions with 90 percent accuracy, giving us the information we need to avoid problems.

The key components of the technology include:
- App-based tool that can be accessed by laptop, tablet or phone
- Current location-based GPS technology based on location of vehicles
- Integration into online mapping technologies
- Back-end platform using commercial routing tools

With the app in hand, drivers are able to quickly get alerts and updated routing information unavailable through other means. Our platform is quickly becoming the industry standard as we lease it to other companies – although Contoso would have access to the master dashboard and have the ability to use features only available to our own customers.

We're glad to offer a tech demo for your engineers at the earliest availability.

16

FIGURE 3-13

First, you write out what you'll say for each headline in the off-screen notes area (bottom). After you have recorded the information that you'll convey with your voice, you next add a simple graphic to the on-screen slide area (top).

SKETCHING THE FIRST FIVE SLIDES

With your clear and concise storyline in place in your slide headlines, and with your narration written out in the off-screen notes area, your next step is to brainstorm an illustration for each headline of each of the Act I slides of your storyboard. In Chapter 7, you'll do that by sketching a visual idea on each of the five slides, as shown in Figure 3-14, using either printouts of the slides or a touchscreen computer.

When you do this, your focus is on making full use of the powerful visual channel of your audience members by sketching out a crisp and compelling visual story that complements your clear and concise headlines. Just as your headlines tell a story with only words, your sketches now should complement, enhance, and intensify that story on individual slides, as well as across slides. Here you'll also plan for both on-screen and off-screen media such as physical props, demonstrations, video, dialogue, or other types of media or interactive techniques.

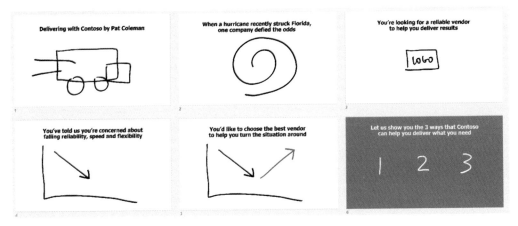

FIGURE 3-14

Once you have a storyboard, sketch a graphic on each of the five slides.

SKETCHING THE REMAINING SLIDES

As with Act I, completing the story template for Act II creates a solid foundation that will help you choose exactly what you'll show and say as you present the working memory of your audience with new information. With this infrastructure in place, you'll have endless creative options to make the crisp and clear underlying story even more powerful. Here on the Act II slides, as shown in Figure 3-15, you'll visually carry through the motif you establish in Act I to help working memory better select and organize the large amount of new information.

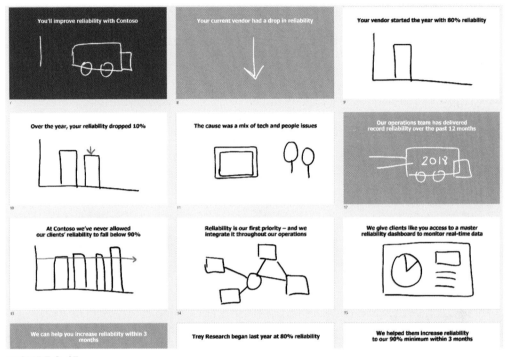

FIGURE 3-15

You'll continue sketching graphics for each of the remaining slides.

APPLYING CUSTOM LAYOUTS

After your team has agreed to and signed off on the sketches, the last step is to find and add a specific photograph, chart, or other graphic to each of the slides. But before you do that, you'll apply custom layouts to each of the different sections of your storyboard, according to the way you sketched the layout of each slide. As shown in Figure 3-16, this creates a visual foundation for the slides based on the hierarchy from the story template.

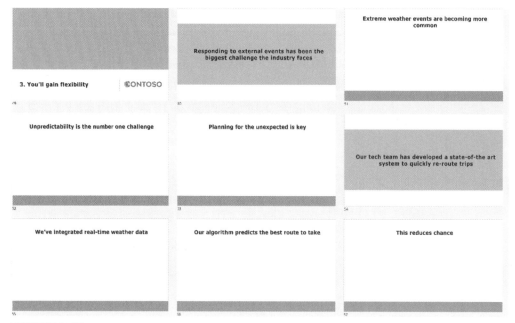

FIGURE 3-16

Storyboard with custom layouts applied.

By applying layouts and backgrounds, you use graphical indicators that cue working memory to the relative importance of each slide, as shown in Figure 3-17. In this example, the slides with the solid sage background are the most important slides; the slides, with the horizontal gold background are the second-most important, and the slides with the white background are the third-most important.

ADDING GRAPHICS TO THE FIRST FIVE SLIDES

The last step is to find and add graphics to each of the slides using your sketches as a guide. Here is where you savor the fruits of the labor of writing Act I in the story template because you know you've got the specific slides that will ensure that you start strong in your presentation, as shown in Figure 3-18. The visual and verbal clarity you achieve is possible through using the story template, which has established the foundation for everything you have done.

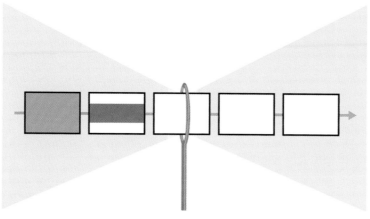

FIGURE 3-17

The slide layouts and backgrounds cue working memory to each slide's relative importance within the big picture.

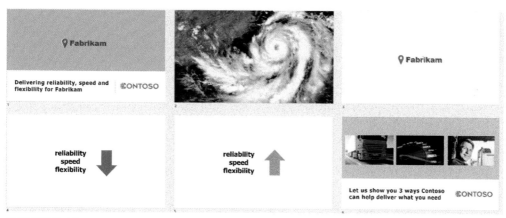

FIGURE 3-18

Adding graphics to the first five slides of Act I.

ADDING GRAPHICS TO THE REMAINING SLIDES

After you add graphics to the Act I slides, you continue by adding graphics to the rest of your slides, as shown in Figure 3-19. Here, you might use photographs, screen captures, logos, charts, and other illustrations.

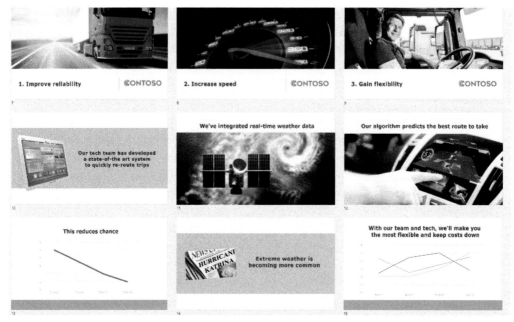

FIGURE 3-19

Adding graphics to the remaining slides.

STEPPING INTO THE SCREEN

Using the approach described in this book, you'll be well-equipped to produce a media experience that will get you the results you want anytime you give a presentation. Focusing and distilling your ideas using a story template and clarifying them using a storyboard blends your message with your media and significantly expands your ability to enhance your presentation with sophisticated media tools and techniques.

Now, the large screen directly behind you, as shown in Figure 3-20, completely integrates your voice and body into a media experience greater than the sum of its parts. This approach brings together a range of media techniques—including those from stage, screen, theater, and television—and blends them with your body and your clear message into a seamless presentation experience.

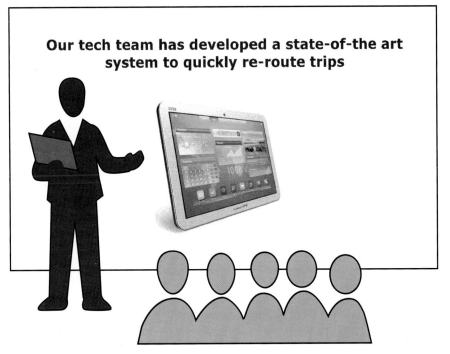

FIGURE 3-20

Your visual story immerses the audience in the experience and ensures that the attention of the audience is not split between screen and speaker.

When you project your slides on a large screen, they work as visual prompts that increase your confidence as a speaker. You're no longer tied to the uncomfortable task of reading text off the screen and unintentionally ignoring your audience. Instead, the clear headline and graphic quickly prompt you to use your natural voice and authority as you explain them.

DOCUMENTING THE EXPERIENCE

As described in Chapter 2, aligning your approach with the dual-channels theory allows you to use PowerPoint in a way that produces both an effective presentation and an effective printed handout, as shown in Figure 3-21. Looking at Notes Page view on the left, the on-screen slide area contains a headline and a simple graphic, while the off-screen notes area captures what is spoken aloud by the presenter. Keeping the narration off the screen creates effective slides (upper right), along with effective handouts (lower right).

When you distribute the PowerPoint file to people who were not present for the live presentation of visuals and narration, you send the notes pages, not the slides. Print out the notes pages to create a physical copy, or create a PDF version that you distribute electronically.

Using Notes Page view taps into the unique value PowerPoint offers you as a communications tool because no other tool can produce a single file that works effectively like this on a screen, on a piece of paper, and even online.

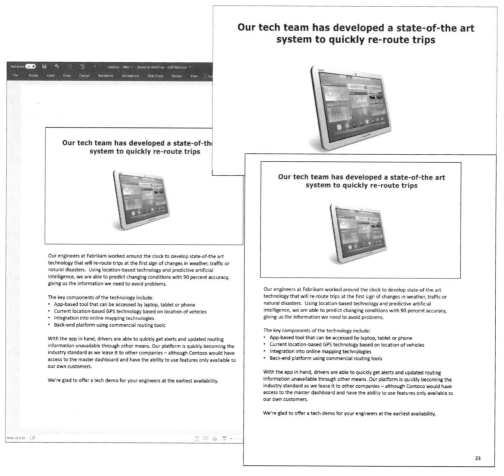

FIGURE 3-21

Notes Page view, showing a well-designed slide and a well-designed handout with the complete verbal explanation of the slide.

GETTING STARTED WITH THE BBP STORY TEMPLATE

To get started, download a copy of the BBP Story Template from www.beyondbulletpoints.com, and save it on your local computer.

WRITING HEADLINES USING THREE GROUND RULES

Everything you do in your presentation from this point forward will build on the headlines you write in your story template. To make your headlines as effective as possible, review the three important ground rules that apply to every statement you write.

GUIDELINE 1: WRITE CONCISE, COMPLETE SENTENCES WITH A SUBJECT AND A VERB IN ACTIVE VOICE

To effectively communicate your message consistently and clearly through your entire story, your headlines must be complete sentences with a subject and a verb. Write the sentences in active voice—for example, "Our top competitors launched five new products last quarter" rather than in the passive voice, "Five new products were launched by our top competitors last quarter." Keep your language dynamic and direct; the same principles, techniques, and rules that define good writing also define good headlines in your template.

MORE ON WRITING CLEARLY For an excellent reference guide to writing the headlines of your story template clearly and concisely, see William Strunk Jr. and E. B. White's *The Elements of Style* (Longman, 2000).

Writing headlines in the form of complete sentences imposes discipline on your ideas by forcing you to turn them into coherent thoughts and removes any ambiguity. Later, when you import your headlines into the title area of your slides, your audience will not doubt what you want to communicate because they can read it for themselves at the top of each slide. Write your headlines using sentence case, with the initial word capitalized and the rest in lowercase.

When you write your headlines for Act I, constrain them to only one line that fills the width of the cell without extending to a second line. The columns in your template for Act II are narrower, so you can extend those headlines to a maximum of about two and a half lines. Constraining your headlines to these limits keeps you from being wordy and ensures that your headlines will fill a maximum of two lines when you send them to the title area of your PowerPoint slides.

GETTING CLEAR ON YOUR HEADLINES If you're looking for practical examples of how to write concisely, look no further than the headlines used in social media or online publications. When writing a headline, a writer has limited time and space to communicate an idea clearly, so the language needs to be clear, direct, and engaging.

It might be a challenge to keep your headlines brief, but that's part of the process of boiling down your complicated ideas to their essence. This distillation will help you get right to the point in your presentations.

GUIDELINE 2: BE CLEAR, DIRECT, SPECIFIC, AND CONVERSATIONAL

Each statement in your story template will speak directly to your audience when it fills the title area of a slide, so use a conversational tone that is simple, clear, and direct. Say what you mean in plain language. When you make your point, include the details that give it specificity, color, and impact. Tailor your words to the level of understanding of everyone in the audience and place nothing in the headline that is not in the audience's vocabulary.

The point of the headline is to help your audience understand your point as efficiently as possible—if you use words unfamiliar to them, you create obstacles to understanding, and they will wonder what the individual words mean instead of attending to the overall message. If everyone in your audience has a clear prior understanding of the technical language you are using, you can use more complex language.

When you write your headlines, imagine that you are addressing a few members of your audience sitting in chairs next to your desk. Because you're simply having a conversation, your voice should be relaxed and casual—not tense and formal. This conversational tone will help you keep your headlines from getting wordy. Later, when your audience reads your headlines in the title area of your slides, the conversational tone will help them feel more relaxed and open to your ideas. Although presenters might assume formal language gives them more authority, research shows people learn better when information is presented in a conversational style rather than a formal style.

THREE GUIDELINES FOR WRITING HEADLINES

Your story template depends on a special writing style that boils down your story to its essence. Follow these three guidelines to keep your writing on point:

1. Write concise, complete sentences with a subject and a verb in active voice.

2. Be clear, direct, specific, and conversational.

3. Guideline 3: Link your ideas across cells.

GUIDELINE 3: LINK YOUR IDEAS ACROSS CELLS

As you'll see later, you'll be breaking up complicated ideas into smaller pieces as you write your thoughts in the cells of the story template. As you do that, make sure that you link your ideas so that they flow to one another as you read them across the cells. By choosing a consistent tense across all headlines, you'll create a more dynamic, in-the-moment feeling to your story. Also, link your ideas by using a parallel sentence structure across cells, which keeps everything sounding clear and coherent.

THE WRITING ON THE WALL   When your story template is projected onto a wall as you work with your team, it becomes a tool for a group of people to see, create, discuss, debate, and agree on the structure of any presentation. Organizations have found the story template tool to be a breakthrough innovation because it guides a collaborative process, gives people ownership, taps into collective brainpower, and gets everyone on the same page.

Now that you've prepared your story template and reviewed the ground rules, it's time to get specific and start with the beginning—the first and most important slides of your presentation.

CRAFTING YOUR STORY STRUCTURE

In this chapter, you will:

- Use a story structure to set up the start of your presentation.
- Write the headlines for your crucial first few slides.
- Explore ways to make your ideas sticky and persuasive.

Story is all the rage today in business communication, and for good reason. Humans are story-making creatures, always looking for ways to make sense out of complicated situations, and continually trying to find a clear narrative that explains what's happening around us. The need for clarity grows greater every day, as ever-increasing amounts of information overwhelm us, and the pace of change quickens.

Though the need for story is quickly growing in importance, it's hard to know how to craft a story if you don't have the fundamentals in place and a tool to help you get started. That's where the Beyond Bullet Points Story Template comes in—it's a tool that guides you along the way of crafting a story, ensuring you include all the classic elements that drive the underlying flow of ideas through classic novels, films, TV shows, and advertising. As you'll soon see in more detail, these elements include capturing attention, making the information relevant, presenting a challenge, naming the desire to overcome the challenge, and laying out a roadmap.

THE STRATEGIC STORY STRUCTURE
There are many types of stories you could tell—including anecdotes that relate a brief incident, a case study that illustrates how you helped someone solve a problem, or a fable that relates a fictional character in a situation. The distinction of the BBP Story Template is that it applies the core fundamentals of a story structure to the entire presentation. Within this overall strategic story structure, any number of other types of stories will back up and further illustrate any points you need to make.

Later, after you set these bedrock story elements in place in Act I, you'll tackle Act II, where you'll do the critical thinking work to distill your ideas to their essence and ensure the story is backed up by solid reasoning and good examples.

WHAT WILL YOU SHOW, SAY, AND DO IN THE FIRST FEW SLIDES?

The beginning of a story is the most crucial part because it is the doorway within which you capture the attention of your audience and keep it. When done well, the beginning also makes efficient use of your audience's limited capacity for new information and your limited time to make a first impression.

The Beyond Bullet Points Story Template gives you a place to begin. With your story template document open, locate the Zoom toolbar on the lower right of the screen, and click and drag it so that Act I fills the screen, as shown in Figure 4-1. Here you see the cells where you'll write the five headlines of Act I following the "Writing Headlines Using Three Ground Rules" section in Chapter 3.

Title and Byline	
Act I – The Compelling Setup	
The Hook	
The Relevance	
The Challenge	
The Desire	
The Map	

FIGURE 4-1

The five cells where you'll write the five headlines in Act I of the story template.

The specific words you write here will become the headlines of the first five slides of your presentation, as shown in Figure 4-2.

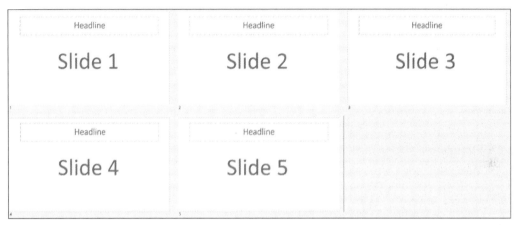

FIGURE 4-2

The five headlines you write in Act I of the story template will become the headlines of the first five slides of your presentation that determine what you'll show, say, and do during the critical first few minutes.

These five slides are the sequence of what you say, show, and do in the critical first few minutes of your presentation. They also represent your opportunity to start strong and to guide working memory through the entire presentation.

Embedded into Act I of the story template are the specific elements that make up the beginning of a well-crafted story, ensuring that you always have the essential pieces to begin your presentation properly. Later, you'll look at a range of ideas for creating the words and images for these first few slides.

But first, you'll see how to write a specific example to see exactly how all the pieces of Act I fit together in a tight and smooth sequence.

STARTING WITH THE "TITLE AND BYLINE"

In the top cell above Act I, replace the text Title and Byline with the title of your presentation—in this example, *Delivering with Contoso*. Type a byline for the script following the title—in this example, *by Pat Coleman*, as shown in Figure 4-3.

Delivering with Contoso by Pat Coleman	
Act I – The Compelling Setup	
The Hook	
The Relevance	
The Challenge	
The Desire	
The Map	

FIGURE 4-3

Type the title and byline in the top cell of the story template.

Now that you've added a title and byline, the story template is ready for you to start writing Act I.

WHY A BYLINE IS IMPORTANT

The byline of the story template is important because it names the person who is responsible for the story's successful delivery: the presenter. In many organizations, slides will pass through many hands as they're being developed, and ownership can easily become lost or unclear. The impact of these presentations diminishes because they are disconnected from the real names and faces of the people who will stand at the podium. Many people can contribute to a presentation, but in most cases, one person will ultimately deliver it. The byline at the top of the story template makes it clear at all times who is behind the slides and whose reputation and credibility are on the line.

CHOOSING A STORY THREAD

Act I of the story template lays down the sequence of headlines of the first few slides that will engage the audience, make the topic relevant to them, engage them, motivate them, and then focus them on a path forward.

In Act I, you structure your ideas in a creative way that awakens the imagination of your audience, connects with their emotions, and persuades them that they want to participate in your story.

CAPTURING ATTENTION WITH "THE HOOK" HEADLINE

When you stand and prepare to deliver your presentation, your audience has many other things on their minds that compete with their attention other than you and your information. You must break through the clutter quickly, or you lose your chance to focus their attention on the new information you'll present.

The Hook headline intends to grab the attention of your audience quickly and keep it. Many television shows are very effective at using a hook when a show begins when they plunge you immediately into some dramatic experience that pulls you into the story immediately.

In addition to quickly capturing attention, the headline of your first slide also establishes the context for your entire presentation. In a film or television show, if a scene takes place in the living room of a house in the daytime, you might first see a shot of the exterior of the house in daylight that then fades into a shot of the living room where the action will take place. This film technique is called an *establishing shot* and quickly shows the audience the where and when of a story.

To begin writing the first headline of Act I, type a headline in the row in the template labeled "The Hook," that describes something your audience will find engaging and compelling about your topic.

This chapter uses one example of a presentation that was described in Chapter 3—the chief operating officer of a transportation company named Contoso is speaking to a group of decision-makers from a company called Fabrikam. The presentation intends to persuade the Fabrikam decision-makers to hire Contoso to handle their transportation needs.

For the Hook headline in Act I of this example, you would enter "When a hurricane recently struck Florida, one company defied the odds," as shown in Figure 4-4. This headline relates an anecdote that when a hurricane struck Florida, Contoso continued to safely complete their work successfully because of their planning, creativity, and ingenuity.

Act I – The Compelling Setup	
The Hook	When a hurricane recently struck Florida, one company defied the odds

FIGURE 4-4

Write your first headline of Act I to hook your audience's attention.

At this early stage in the presentation, the headline should be interesting, intriguing, and something that the audience can accept without raising their defenses.

Starting your presentation with a brief anecdote like in this example is a powerful way to hook your audience's attention. The key is to make it brief and directly relevant to the topic you're about to cover. In some situations, an anecdote from your personal life might help you make your point and to establish a personal connection with your audience. In many business contexts, anecdotes that are pulled from your everyday work experience will make your point quickly and efficiently.

TIPS FOR WRITING THE HOOK HEADLINE

- Start with a brief anecdote that's directly relevant to the topic, as in the example in this chapter.

- Describe a surprising statistic or data point. For example, "We've met our numbers 16 quarters in a row" or, "We thought we were on track, but it turns out that we're behind in our numbers this quarter."

- Ask an intriguing question relevant to the topic; for example, "How many of you predict interest rates will go up this year?" or "How many of you agree that the political climate is affecting our bottom line?"

- Share a relevant item from the news or industry; for example, "Though the economy is sluggish, our industry is growing faster than ever" or "The trends continue to show our industry must face a reckoning."

The Hook headline intrigues your audience, invites them to join you at the same location, establishes a common ground, and leaves no doubt about the context for what you are about to say.

SLIDE 1: THE HOOK   The Hook headline captures your audience's attention with something interesting, intriguing, and engaging.

When you've written the Hook headline, you've grabbed your audience's attention in the first slide of your presentation, as shown in Figure 4-5.

After you write a headline for the hook, it's time to make your topic relevant.

Capture your audience's attention in the first slide.

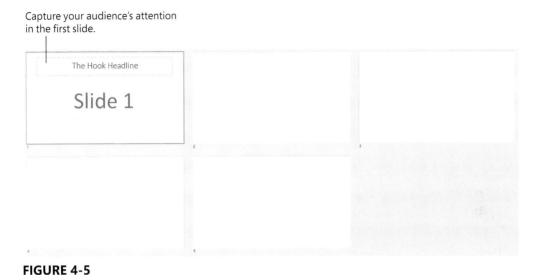

FIGURE 4-5

The headline of the Hook slide grabs your audience's attention.

CONNECTING EMOTIONALLY WITH "THE RELEVANCE" HEADLINE

The headline of your second slide names the main character(s) of your story—your audience. In both fiction and non-fiction stories, the main character is a person—real or imagined—who encounters a series of events. However, in this non-fiction story you are crafting, you dramatically increase the power of a story structure by making your audience the main character and putting them front and center in the series of events that are about to unfold. Establishing your audience as the main characters in your second slide establishes the relevance of your presentation by making it personal to them. Because the audience members have a direct involvement and stake in the outcome, they will pay attention.

Making your audience the main character also helps you to stay focused on them and makes sure that you tailor your presentation to their needs. Many slide presentations tend to be "all about me," with little if any consideration of the audience. With this single slide, you remind your audience that this is "all about you."

REMEMBER The main character of every presentation is your audience, and you are a supporting character. This is the crucial spin on crafting stories for live presentations.

The main character(s) of a presentation could be a single person, such as a customer or client, or it could be a group, such as a committee, a team, a jury, a board, or an organization. In this example, the Fabrikam executives are the main characters because they will decide on which vendor to choose.

Now that you've selected a star for the leading role in your presentation, write a headline in the row labeled "The Relevance" that acknowledges your audience's relevant role following the Hook headline you just wrote. In this example, you might enter a statement such as "You're looking for a reliable vendor to help you deliver results," as shown in Figure 4-6. This headline establishes that the audience ("you") has a personal interest in this topic in the form of "looking for a reliable vendor."

Act I – The Compelling Setup	
The Hook	When a hurricane recently struck Florida, one company defied the odds
The Relevance	You're looking for a reliable vendor to help you deliver results

FIGURE 4-6

Write your second headline of Act I to make your audience the main character and describe the relevance of your presentation to your audience.

TIPS FOR WRITING THE RELEVANCE HEADLINE

■ Consider why your audience cares about the topic and address that reason; for example, "This is at the top of your agenda" or "You've said this is something near and dear to your heart."

■ Ask a question on their minds, such as "What can I do about this?" or "How do we engage this situation?"

■ Use the words "you," "yours," "we," or "ours" to speak directly to your audience and establish a topic of their concern; for example, "You're concerned about this topic" or "We have to do something about this."

An effective way to establish connection and relevance with your audience is to use the words "you," "yours," "we," or "ours" to speak directly to the audience and make them feel central to this story. Now that the "who" of the story is clear, the rest of the headline can simply affirm something relevant about the audience's situation on which everyone in the room can agree.

SLIDE 2: THE RELEVANCE The Relevance headline establishes your audience as the main character of the story and makes the topic relevant to them.

When you've written the Relevance headline, you've made sure that you'll interest the audience by acknowledging their relevant role in the second slide of your presentation, as shown in Figure 4-7.

In the next slide headline, it's time to stir things up for the main character.

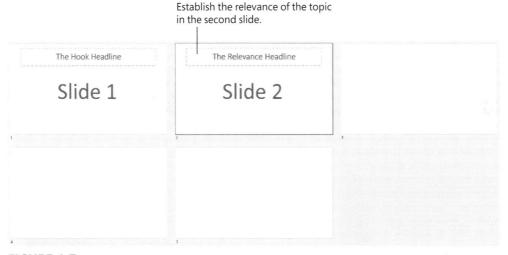

FIGURE 4-7

The headline of the Relevance slide makes your audience the main character(s) of the story with a relevant role to play.

RAISING THE STAKES WITH "THE CHALLENGE" HEADLINE

The headline of your third slide begins the action and presents your most important opportunity to engage your audience quickly. Because you must make an emotional connection within the first few minutes of a presentation, this is the specific slide where you make that concept a reality.

Stories are about characters who encounter a change, how the characters respond to that change, and what their choices reveal about them. When a main character experiences a change, an imbalance is created because things are no longer as they used to be. This imbalance creates a challenge that sets the story in motion—it's where the action begins.

In your story template, you'll specifically define this challenge with the Challenge headline. Later, you'll define the specific point where your audience wants to be in light of this challenge—"The Desire."

The challenge that has brought everyone to the presentation today could be a crisis brought on by an external force that has changed your organization's environment, such as a sudden economic shift or the action of a competitor. It could be the result of an internal change, such as a revised opinion or mindset, a new piece of information, a new research report, or a report from the field.

REMEMBER   The Challenge headline sets your story in motion by defining a specific challenge your audience faces.

A DOZEN STORY TYPES   Although the classical story structure of Act I is the foundation for limitless story variations, there is a more limited set of story types that can help you to frame your own stories. In his book *Moving Mountains* (Crowell-Collier Press, 1989), Henry M. Boettinger describes a dozen story types—summarized in the following list—that reflect various situations that people in organizations might face. Many of these story types can help you to refine the way you set up Act I:

1. **Historical narrative:** "We have a history that makes us proud, and we want to apply our high standards to the current situation."

2. **Crisis:** "We have to respond to the danger facing us."

3. **Disappointment:** "We made a decision based on the best information we had available, but now we know it wasn't the right decision, so we have to try something else."

4. **Opportunity:** "We know something now that we didn't know before, which presents us with a new possibility if we act."

5. **Crossroads:** "We've been doing fine on the path that we're on, but now we have a new choice, and we have to decide which path to take."

6. **Challenge:** "Someone else has achieved something amazing. Do we have it in us to do the same?"

7. **Blowing the whistle:** "Although it appears everything is going fine, we have a serious problem we need to fix."

8. **Adventure:** "We know that trying something new is a risk, but it's better to take a risk than to stay in a rut."

9. **Response to an order:** "We've been told we have to do this, so we're here to figure out how to make it happen."

10. **Revolution:** "We're on a path to disaster if we don't radically change what we're doing today."

11. **Evolution:** "If we don't keep up with the latest, we'll fall behind."

12. **The Great Dream:** "If we can only see our possibility, we can make it our reality."

No matter what type of story you have, read through these story types when you start writing your Act I headlines to determine whether one of them can help you to find the words you're seeking.

On the upside, a change could be brought on by an inspiration, a new idea, a discovery, or the appearance of a new opportunity that the main character hadn't seen before. On the downside, the challenge could be the realization that a mistake was made, there was a fall from grace, there was a loss of market share, profits declined, or there was a sudden drop in status. Whether positive or negative, all these challenges are core reasons why people gather for presentations.

The Challenge headline should establish the challenge that the specific audience faces in this story. In this example, enter the headline "You've told us you're concerned about falling reliability, speed, and flexibility" as shown in Figure 4-8.

Delivering Results for Fabrikam by Pat Coleman	
Act I – The Compelling Setup	
The Hook	When a hurricane recently struck Florida, one company defied the odds
The Relevance	You're looking for a reliable vendor to help you deliver results
The Challenge	You've told us you're concerned about falling reliability, speed and flexibility

FIGURE 4-8

Write your third headline of Act I to describe the challenge—a specific challenge that your audience faces.

TIPS FOR WRITING THE CHALLENGE HEADLINE

- In advance, interview your audience members and industry experts and ask them to identify in a single sentence the top challenges your audience faces; for example, "Artificial intelligence threatens to permanently change our business" or "Millennials are becoming less attached to brands."

- Arrange a brainstorming session with your team to identify the top challenges you think your audience faces, then narrow down the list to the top 10. From that list, choose the top three, such as "The three biggest obstacles to change are corporate culture, lack of resources, and minimal buy-in."

- Be clear in your language and get right to the point. The better you define the heart of the challenge, the more credibility you have. For example, rather than say, "The shifting competitive landscape is impacting our revenue stream," say "Three new competitors are targeting the top 10 percent of our customers."

Refer to Appendix B for more examples.

The point of the Challenge headline is to arrive at an emotional touchstone that clarifies why your audience would want to engage with your presentation. As you're thinking of what to write, answer this question from the audience's viewpoint: "What is it that I would stand to lose if I missed your presentation today?" Their answer might be related to sales, a dilemma, or the opportunity to find clarity or direction. By focusing on what the audience might believe they would lose or gain, you'll find the emotional challenge they really care about that you should address in your Challenge headline.

NOTE It might appear that writing headlines is a straightforward process in which you write what you need in the first pass. However, in reality, headline writing is an iterative process in which you'll write the first draft and then make multiple rounds of changes. As mentioned earlier, you'll get the best results if you develop your headlines with a team so that you get multiple perspectives and distill the best of your collective effort.

As shown in Figure 4-9, the Challenge headline defines your story and helps you focus your topic on something your audience really cares about. Focusing on a specific challenge helps you to narrow your scope to a single story presented to a specific group of people at a particular moment in time.

You might have to go through a difficult decision-making process to choose the one story thread that is the best fit. To write the best Challenge headline, you must know your audience as well as possible and make your decision based on your experience as well as your team's experience, research, competitive intelligence, analysis, and intuition.

SLIDE 3: THE CHALLENGE The Challenge headline names the most important challenge your audience faces.

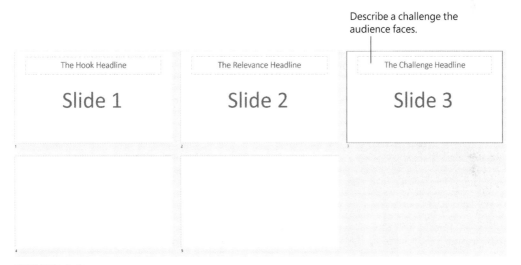

The headline for the Challenge slide engages your audience by describing a challenge they face.

FIGURE 4-9

Although your audience has a formidable challenge in the Challenge headline, you'll provide them with what they want when faced with the challenge in the next headline.

RAMPING UP EMOTION WITH "THE DESIRE" HEADLINE

Generally, when people are challenged, they feel unsettled and emotionally uncomfortable until they bring the situation back into equilibrium. The same holds true for your audience when you present them with the Challenge headline, so your next headline should point to a new state where they will find that equilibrium.

In the Desire headline, you spell out what your audience wants as they face the challenge—whatever it is that would bring them back into the balance they want. The Desire you write in your headline could describe how they could solve a problem, reach their goal, or find a new opportunity.

In the cell labeled "The Desire," type an answer to the question: "What do I want as I face this challenge?" In this example, enter "You'd like to choose the best vendor to help you turn the situation around," as shown in Figure 4-10.

Act I – The Compelling Setup	
The Hook	When a hurricane recently struck Florida, one company defied the odds
The Relevance	You're looking for a reliable vendor to help you deliver results
The Challenge	You've told us you're concerned about falling reliability, speed and flexibility
The Desire	You'd like to choose the best vendor to help you turn the situation around

FIGURE 4-10

Write your fourth headline of Act I to describe where your audience wants to be when facing the challenge you defined earlier.

This headline concisely affirms what the audience wants—namely, to find a better way to do things. Again, this headline establishes the desired outcome that will bring the main character's situation back into balance.

TIPS FOR WRITING THE DESIRE HEADLINE

- Read what you wrote for the Challenge headline and consider where your audience wants to be when they face it. For example, if the challenge they face is "We're losing market share to new competitors," the desire is, "You'd like to do something about it to regain that share."

- Consider the challenge as Point A—where your audience is now—and the desire as Point B—where they want to be. For example, your audience might be at Point A where "You're facing a crossroads, and you're not sure which direction to take," and their Point B would be "You'd like to make the best possible decision to get you where you want to go."

- Paint a clear and concrete picture of the desire to make a strong emotional connection. For example, if the Challenge headline reads, "The team is struggling to maintain focus," your Desire headline might read, "Picture yourself in December with a big bonus check in hand."

Refer to Appendix B for more examples.

When you've written effective Challenge and Desire headlines, the audience sees their challenge and where they want to go, and they'll be fueled by their desire to get there with your help.

SLIDE 4: THE DESIRE
The Desire headline describes where your audience wants to be when they are faced with the challenge you describe.

When writing the Desire headline, make sure that you motivate the audience by affirming what they want, as shown in Figure 4-11.

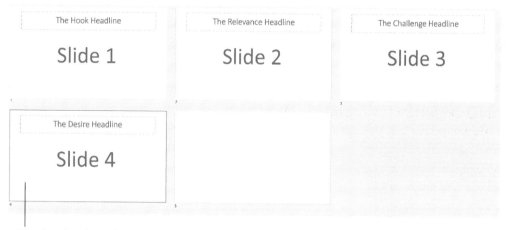

Describe what the audience wants in the face of the challenge.

FIGURE 4-11

The Desire headline motivates your audience by defining where they want to be as they face a challenge.

THE CHALLENGE AND DESIRE HEADLINE STARTERS

Here are a few examples of phrases to start your Challenge and Desire headlines:

CHALLENGE (WHAT CHALLENGE DO I FACE?)	DESIRE (WHERE DO I WANT TO BE?)
You're overwhelmed about x.	You'd like to gain control.
You're unclear about x.	You'd like to be clear.
You're uncertain about x.	You'd like to be certain.
You don't know what to do about x.	You'd like to know what to do.
People don't appreciate your value.	You'd like people to appreciate what you do.

For a longer list, refer to Appendix B.

CREATING DRAMATIC TENSION BETWEEN THE CHALLENGE AND DESIRE HEADLINES

In the story template, the two cells that hold the Challenge and Desire headlines are next to one another physically, yet there is an emotional gap between the two that emotionally charges your presentation.

Remember, the Challenge headline puts your audience in an emotionally uncomfortable state of imbalance, and the Desire headline describes what they want to achieve a state of balance. The gap between Challenge and Desire headlines creates an unresolved tension that drives the plot of every story—a character faces a challenge and has a desire to overcome it. This timeless storytelling technique of creating dramatic tension helps you quickly engage and motivate your audience and to further an emotional connection.

The gap between the Challenge and Desire headlines can also be defined as the core problem your audience faces—they are at Point A and want to get to Point B. Defining this problem helps your audience engage with your presentation, and helps you select and prioritize information. Of all the information available to you, how do you know which information to include? The answer is to select only information that specifically helps your audience close the gap between the Challenge and Desire headlines. Any other information is unnecessary for this presentation and can be set aside for another story on another day.

The problem created by the gap between the Challenge and Desire headlines also forms the purpose of your presentation, so when you make the problem clear, you make your purpose clear. This problem is central to your entire presentation and forms the singular question that your presentation will try to answer. This problem creates a center of gravity that grounds your story and makes it cohere across all of its separate parts.

You and your team might go through several rounds of drafts and revisions to get the Challenge and Desire headlines right, and when you do, the rest of your presentation will fall into place.

TIP   See Appendix B for a list of some of the possibilities for writing your Challenge and Desire headlines.

When you have a clear problem established with the Challenge and Desire headlines, it's time to let your audience know how you propose to solve it.

LAUNCHING THE JOURNEY WITH "THE MAP" HEADLINE

The Map headline defines the reason you're the presenter—you've taken the time to figure out how the main character can solve the problem at hand—getting from the Challenge to the Desire.

To complete the fifth slide, in the cell labeled, "The Map," type an answer to the question: "How do I get from the Challenge to the Desire?" In this case, enter "Let us show you the 3 ways that Contoso can help you deliver what you need," as shown in Figure 4-12.

Act I – The Compelling Setup	
The Hook	When a hurricane recently struck Florida, one company defied the odds
The Relevance	You're looking for a reliable vendor to help you deliver results
The Challenge	You've told us you're concerned about falling reliability, speed and flexibility
The Desire	You'd like to choose the best vendor to help you turn the situation around
The Map	Let us show you the 3 ways that Contoso can help you deliver what you need

FIGURE 4-12

Write your fifth headline of Act I to lay out a map for how the audience can engage the challenge and reach their desire.

This headline closes the gap formed by the Challenge and Desire headlines. The challenge is that the audience is concerned about three key issues. The desire is that they'd like the right vendor to help them turn things around, and the map is that they can get there by understanding how Contoso can help them deliver what they need.

THE MAP HEADLINE STARTERS Try using these phrases to start your Map headline:

Partner with us and you will...

Approve our plan...

Grow better relationships...

Follow three steps to...

Remove the barriers...

Tap into new opportunities...

Refer to Appendix C for more examples of headline starters.

SLIDE 5: THE MAP The Map headline lays out the pathway for your audience to overcome the challenge and achieve their desire.

The Map headline should describe what your audience should do or believe to solve the problem created by the gap between the Challenge and Desire headlines. The Map is the central point of the presentation. Your final wording is important because the Map headline clearly defines what you and your audience want to accomplish, and it offers a clear roadmap that they will be able to follow through the rest of the presentation.

As you go through the process of writing Act II in Chapter 5, you will thoroughly develop and test the Map headline, and you will likely revise its wording as you go along.

TIPS FOR WRITING THE MAP HEADLINE

- Consider using a three-part structure for the Map, such as "Here are three directions we can take" or "These are three reasons why (or how) we should do this."

- Think of the map as a call to action statement, describing what you want your audience to do or think differently. For example, write "Adopt my new plan to get the results you want," "Approve the budget to accomplish our goals," or "Follow three steps to turn around the situation."

- The map should distill your ideas to their essence and get to the point of the entire presentation.

Refer to Appendix C for more examples.

The Map headline also puts your ideas in a decision-making format that's important to people who want to accomplish something. In a single sentence, the wording of the Map headline defines how you know if you were successful in your presentation and whether that success is a next meeting, a sale, an agreement, or a good grade. If your audience accepts the Map headline by the end of your story, you'll know you succeeded.

I'M STUCK! What do you do if you get stuck somewhere in the process of writing the headlines for your first five slides? Visit Appendixes B and C for inspiration. Or when you're stuck in Act I, skip ahead to Act II and return to Act I later. Often the process of working through the structure in Act II will help you define and refine Act I.

When you've written the Map headline in Act I of the story template, you've made sure that you will focus the audience by offering them a way to get from the Challenge to the Desire in the fifth slide of your presentation, as shown in Figure 4-13.

The Map slide in this illustration now has an orange background, making it stand out from the others because it is, in fact, the most important slide in a presentation. If you had only one slide to show, it would be the Map slide. By the time you have finished with the Map slide in Chapter 8, that slide will distill your entire presentation into a single visual accompanied by your verbal narration.

FIGURE 4-13

The Map headline focuses Act I and the rest of the story to come.

ADDING A STORY THEME

A theme carries your ideas all the way through your story in a coherent way and adds color and interest to your language. It also makes the job of searching for graphics to add to your slides significantly easier because you only search for visuals related to your theme.

A theme might seem like a "nice-to-have" addition to making the presentation colorful and interesting, but research shows that it can provide much more than just an interesting take on your presentation. Working memory cannot possibly process all the new information it experiences, and without a clear structure to organize the new information, it has to create a structure from scratch—a very inefficient process.

However, with a memorable story theme that works, you help working memory select, organize, and integrate the new information much more effectively. The themes that happen to work best are ones the audience already holds in long-term memory—they might take the form of a familiar metaphor, an organizing system like 1-2-3, or any number of familiar story themes.

For example, most people are familiar with the process of putting together a puzzle, so a puzzle-making structure already exists in their long-term memory. When you apply a puzzle theme to the structure of your story, as shown in Figure 4-14, you increase the efficiency of the working memory of your audience so that they can much more quickly make sense of the new information. Introducing a preexisting structure reduces cognitive load because working memory doesn't need to exert as much energy to create a structure from scratch.

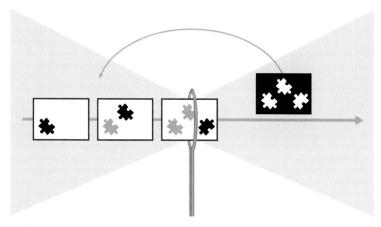

FIGURE 4-14

When you pull a familiar structure from long-term memory and use it to structure a presentation, you make working memory more efficient.

There are many different themes to apply to your presentation, which are incorporated into some of the example phrases in Appendix C. To apply a theme to your presentation, integrate it through your headlines as in the following variations of the Act I example in this chapter. Keep the following general principles in mind when you search for a theme for Act I:

- **The theme should exist already in your audience's long-term memory.** That means you need to get into the minds of your audience to find the right theme because the structure has to exist already in their long-term memories. You need to figure out what they think, and what they know, through your research, interviews, and analysis. In legal trials, lawyers create juror questionnaires designed to find out what potential themes might resonate in a legal presentation. You might need to do similar in-depth research if your presentation is particularly important. If you don't know your audience or can't find enough information about them, choose a general metaphor like the checklist theme shown in Figure 4-15.

The Map	Check off the 3 most important items on your list to get results

FIGURE 4-15

The checklist theme is familiar to most audiences.

■ **The theme should resonate with your audience.** Your theme needs to be a good match with your audience, and they should be able to easily relate to it. A theme can work against you if the structure is a mismatch because it distracts your audience or misleads them into thinking you're not serious. The theme should also resonate with you as the presenter—choose one that you personally can relate to so that it draws out your personality and warmth and brings your ideas to life with your natural enthusiasm. Only use a complex or special theme if everyone in your audience shares knowledge of it, as in the formula example shown in Figure 4-16.

The Map	Reliability + speed + flexibility = results

FIGURE 4-16

The formula theme can resonate with those who deal with numbers.

■ **A theme is more memorable if it is unexpected.** Introducing a surprising theme in Act I will also increase memorability. Choose a surprising insight, a different way of looking at things, or another unexpected way to introduce your idea, as shown in Figure 4-17. Creatively applying a theme by putting it in a surprising context can heighten interest and stimulate creative thinking and mental participation. The more surprising and interesting and engaging the theme is, the more memorable it will be. However, as mentioned earlier, make sure that in every case the theme is a good match for your audience.

The Map	Return to our past principles to get the results we need now

FIGURE 4-17

Telling someone to go backward instead of forward gives a twist to a journey theme.

SEE ALSO Some of the most powerful presentation themes are drawn from popular culture, such as the opening statement of a jury trial in Chapter 1 that used a CSI theme inspired by the popular television show. Finding a blockbuster theme that works well for your audience is a blend of science and art—the science of doing thorough research to know your audience and the art of applying an interesting theme in an innovative way to your information.

■ **The best themes are extendable.** The more elegantly a single theme can extend through the presentation, the more impact it will have. Sometimes a theme is straightforward, and other times it will be clever, humorous, or surprising. The deeper and more broadly your simple theme extends through the presentation, the more cohesive and elegant the communication.

You should invest a good amount of time considering your theme and trying on different ones for size because if you find a good one, it transforms the fiber of your story thread into fiber optics as your new information travels through working memory.

CLOSING THE CURTAIN ON ACT I

Now that you have five headlines, you've completed the first draft of Act I. Review your headlines. They might seem simple, but they've helped you to accomplish many important tasks, such as tailoring your presentation to your audience and establishing criteria to narrow down the information you want to communicate. Consider these headlines a working draft as you complete the rest of the story template; you might need to return to them and revise them as you develop the rest of your presentation.

NOTE When a journalist puts the most important information somewhere else in the article rather than up front, it's called burying the lede. The structure of Act I ensures you don't bury your lede by making sure that you always bring the most important information to the top level of attention at the start of every presentation.

If you haven't already done so, take the time now to review your five headlines with your team and anyone else who needs to approve your presentation. These headlines determine everything that will unfold next in your story, so it's important to get other people involved early in this writing process to make sure that you're on the right track.

Never rush through the process of writing your Act I headlines. The words you write in Act I will make the difference between a strong start and a weak one. It's not uncommon for an individual or a team to completely revise Act I several times until the story is exactly right for the audience. An executive team might spend a great deal of time fine-tuning Act I because, in a bigger sense, these five headlines can define the way the organization understands and relates to its customers. These five simple headlines are in fact a communications strategy and are worthy of whatever resources you normally invest in developing strategic issues.

Review the tips at the end of this chapter to develop and refine your Act I headlines. Here are a couple of ways to test and review the headlines now.

APPEALING TO YOUR AUDIENCE'S EMOTIONS

Your audience—including business executives—is made up of both rational and emotional beings. You avoid a strictly rational approach by using your Act I headlines to make an emotional connection with your audience and persuade them that the information is important to them. You achieve this connection by including the most important elements of a strong story beginning, in the form of headlines for the Hook, Relevance, Challenge, Desire, and Map slides. By tailoring each of these elements to your audience and presenting them in Act I, you make your story personal to your audience and ensure that you are off to a strong start.

REMEMBER   Your Act I headlines make an emotional connection with your audience.

FOCUSING YOUR IDEAS

As you saw in Chapter 2, if the volume of information overwhelms your audience, especially at the start of a presentation, their minds will shut down, and you won't achieve the results you want. Act I of the story template helps you to establish criteria to narrow down all the things you could say to only the most important things you should say to this audience during this presentation. When you begin writing the Act II headlines in Chapter 5, you'll find that these Act I headlines have set up your story in a way that will limit the quantity of information to only what is necessary and the quality of information to the high standards you expect.

BBP CHECKLIST: PLANNING YOUR FIRST FIVE SLIDES

Do the first five slides of your presentation accomplish the following:

- Grab attention and orient your audience to the setting of the presentation with the Hook headline

- Interest them by acknowledging their role in the setting with the Relevance headline

- Engage them emotionally by describing a challenge they face with the Challenge headline

- Motivate them by affirming what they want with the Desire headline

- Focus them by offering a way to get from the Challenge to the Desire with the Map headline

The process of writing the five slide headlines described in this chapter covers the fundamentals that apply to any presentation story and helps you appeal to emotion and focus your ideas. Once you learn the basics, you'll apply a broad range of creative resources, tools, and techniques to help you adapt this structure to your own style and circumstances.

When you're satisfied with your Act I headlines, it's time to flesh out your story in Act II. But before you move on to Chapter 5, scan through the 10 tips in the following sections to find ideas that might inspire you to improve on Act I after you're comfortable with the fundamentals.

10 TIPS FOR ENHANCING ACT I

The Act I structure in the story template is a basic platform with the potential for endless innovation and improvisation based on the specifics of your situation. Just as writers can create endless story variations using this pattern, you likewise have the potential to create endless presentation variations with this tool. After you learn the fundamentals, there's plenty of room to adapt and improvise to suit your personality, audience, and situation.

If you're ready to take your presentations to the next level, here are 10 advanced tips for building on the basic structure of Act I.

TIP 1: INSPIRATION FROM THE SCREENWRITERS

Spark your creative energy by going back to the past to see the future of presentation stories. All you need to do is consult with the original expert on story structure. Start by picking up copies of Aristotle's classic works *Poetics* and *Rhetoric*. For a more recent adaptation of Aristotle's ideas, these excellent books on screenwriting can help you with writing your Act I headlines, including:

- *Substance, Structure, Style, and the Principles of Screenwriting*, by Robert McKee (Regan Books, 1997)

- *Screenplay: The Foundations of Screenwriting*, by Syd Field (Dell, 1984)

- *Stealing Fire from the Gods: The Complete Guide to Story for Writers and Filmmakers,* by James Bonnet (Michael Wiese Productions, 2006)

Any of these titles will help you learn more about the key elements of the first act of every story, including settings, character development, inciting incidents, and plot points. As you read these books for inspiration, keep in mind that your presentation is a specific type of story in which your audience is the main character, and you are in a supporting role. Maintaining this focus will ensure that all of your stories align with the specific needs of your presentations.

TIP 2: VARYING YOUR STORY

After you've mastered the basics of the five Act I headlines, try improvising in your stories. For example, your story structure might involve changing the order of headlines in Act I. You could place the Challenge and Desire headlines first and define the Hook, Relevance, and Map headlines later. You could begin with the Map headline to grab people's attention and then continue with the other headlines. At times, you might be able to delete a slide if the audience is absolutely in agreement about a situation, although it rarely hurts to clearly restate information to bring everyone to the same starting point.

TIP 3: YOUR ACT I SCREEN TEST

In filmmaking, a screen test puts actors in front of a camera to test how they will do on-screen. In a presentation, your first screen test is for your Act I headlines, and your first audience is the members of your team. It's important to include other people at this stage of your presentation to get early feedback and fresh perspectives. If you're working on a small or informal presentation, ask a colleague or your boss to look over your Act I headlines.

Once you get the hang of writing an Act I with your group, try applying these techniques to other communications scenarios beyond your presentations. Crafting Act I of a presentation is a problem-solving framework that also helps a group to clarify strategy, develop marketing messages, create project plans, and resolve other challenges. Sharing your Act I headlines with a team is also a great way to kick off a project or orient someone new to a team. By reviewing the five headlines of Act I and the clarifying questions, team members learn the situation quickly and efficiently.

TIP 4: MULTIPLE STORIES AND MULTIPLE TEMPLATES

When it comes to presentations, one size might not fit all.

The beauty of your Act I headlines is that they are finely tailored and tuned to solve the specific problem of a specific audience. But what if your audience has more than one problem? What if you give the same presentation to different audiences that have different problems to solve? For example, you might need to present a marketing plan to different audiences, including the board, your advertising agency, and your sales team. In each instance, the presentation will have a different focus and will need a different version of Act I. If you don't tailor your presentations to your audiences, you won't connect with them.

One way to plan for these different situations is to create several versions of Act I, each of which is tailored to a specific audience. Create a copy of the document that contains the five Act I headlines from your current story template. In the new document, revise the Challenge and Desire headlines, which describe the central problem that your new audience faces. When you change these headlines to reflect a new problem, you might find that you need to revise the Hook and Relevance headlines if a different set of circumstances led to this problem. And you most likely will also need to revise the Map headline because the solution for the new problem will probably be different from the solution to the previous problem. After creating separate versions of Act I, you choose the most appropriate version for your next audience.

This multiple-version approach also works if you find that you have more stories to tell in addition to the one you're working on. If you sense another story emerging, open up a new story template, and keep it open while you're working on your current presentation, adding headlines to your second story as you go. As you develop your second presentation in parallel to the first, you might find that you're able to refine both versions at the same time.

TIP 5: VISUALIZE YOUR AUDIENCE

The more clearly you know your audience, the clearer your communications will become.

When you start writing your Act I headlines, take some time with your team to visualize everything that you know about your specific audience. To do this, create a blank slide and insert a picture of a specific audience member or just type a specific name on the screen. If you're speaking to a large audience, consider creating a composite of the average audience member on the slide.

Ask your group questions like these:

- What do we know about this person?
- What have we heard about his personality type?
- How does she make decisions?
- What can we learn from a Web search about his thinking process?
- What can we learn from our social network about how she works with other people?
- How do we effectively fashion an experience that aligns with his interests and personality type?

Type the information on the slide as your group gives feedback so that everyone has all the information captured on the slide. When you do this, you tap into the collective thinking of your group to better understand your audience. And you think more deeply about your audience and your purpose, which will significantly improve the quality of your headlines.

TIP 6: WHAT PROBLEM IS YOUR AUDIENCE FACING?

To accurately define the problem your audience is facing, try putting yourself in the place of the audience.

Your Act I headlines identify a problem that your audience faces and a solution that you propose. But it's not always easy to figure out the problem to be sure you have the right solution. The visualization exercise described in Tip 5 helps you to see into the mindset of your audience so that you'll be in a better position to write the appropriate headlines for them.

Another technique is role-playing. When you review the rough draft of your Act I headlines, ask a member of the group to play the role of a decision maker or representative member of your audience. She will review the material you gathered from the preceding profiling exercise to help her get into character.

Request that this person be a devil's advocate during your review session, continually asking questions such as these:

- What's in it for me?
- Why do you think this is important to me?
- Why should I care?

When you hear this critical voice during your review, you'll be able to test your headlines to make sure that you're hitting the mark. It's better to hear the questions from a fictional audience than to have them pop up unexpectedly during your actual presentation.

Once you've identified your audience's problem, don't be surprised if your presentation holds tightly together and your ideas start to emerge into clear meaning.

TIP 7: STRATEGIC COLLAGE

If you have a high-stakes presentation to make, you might need to invest extra effort to get to know your audience in advance. One way to get to know them is to spend a day in their shoes—at least symbolically. Create six blank slides, and on each of these slides, type one clarifying question: Where? When? Who? What? Why? and How?

Take pictures of the objects your audience uses every day or of the environments where they live and work and the people they might see. Your visuals should represent whatever data you have about your audience, whether it's market research, demographics, or focus group information. Go through your organization's photo libraries to find licensed photographs and clip art to show the buildings in which these people work, the products they use, and the places they visit. Use a digital scanner to insert pictures of documents, a pen tablet to make sketches, a video camera to insert video clips, and a microphone to collect sound.

When you've collected these multimedia elements, arrange them on each of the six slides to create six collages. Size the different elements according to how important you think each is to your audience—for example, if mobility is most important, make the picture of a car larger than less important elements.

Present the file to your team as you discuss what it's like to spend a day in your audience's shoes in the context of these six slides. Then open your story template and start working on Act I. Discuss with your team how well the headlines match the collages and then edit the headlines to provide a good fit. The better your Act I story matches the reality of your audience's lives, the better your presentation.

TIP 8: THE STORY OF ADVERTISING

Some of the most powerful examples of Act I story structure pass right before your eyes every day. If you look for them, you'll find an endless stream of ideas for your presentations. These stories are all around us—in the form of advertising.

Advertisers are well aware of Aristotle's ideas and techniques of storytelling and persuasion because at its core, every advertisement is a persuasive story. Whether you look up at a billboard, open a magazine, or watch television, you see a mini-story built on the fundamentals of persuasion. Each advertisement has a singular goal in mind: to persuade you to do something—usually, to buy a product.

To persuade you, an advertiser will use the most current and sophisticated blend of multimedia possible. But beneath the media mix are the same classical story elements you've been working on in Act I of the story template. As in a presentation, the main character of an advertisement is usually the audience—in this case, you—because the advertiser's goal is to persuade you to buy or think something new.

If you're watching a commercial for laundry detergent, compare the core elements of your five Act I headlines with what you see on TV. It goes something like this:

- What's happening? I'm at home, and it's the afternoon.
- How is this relevant? I'm getting ready to go out for the evening.
- What challenges do I face? I dropped spaghetti on my favorite shirt.
- Where do I want to be? I want to impress my date tonight by looking my best.
- How do I get from here to there? If I buy Product X laundry detergent, my shirt will be clean in time for my date.

There's usually a one-to-one correspondence between your Act I story elements and most advertisements because both have the same intent: to make an emotional connection and to persuade. And both creatively interpret the fundamentals of story structure to get the job done. The next time you notice an advertisement, observe the structure that gives it form. Sometimes the story elements might be implied or communicated using a photo, sound, or movement instead of words, but they will usually all be there.

As you begin to see this common persuasive story structure in advertising, you'll be more aware of the range of storytelling approaches, and you'll be able to apply these techniques to your own Act I headlines.

TIP 9: PERSUASIVE EDUCATION

Educators and trainers are in the same boat as the rest of us when it comes to the challenges of communicating today. They also are affected by the expectations of audiences who now are fluent in the visual language around them and expect the same level of media sophistication in the classroom.

For example, a university professor who's struggling to find a way to make his architecture course more interesting and engaging is struck by the fact that every one of the architects he'll discuss also struggled with change—economic change, social change, demographic change, and technological change. Consequently, he decides to adopt a classical persuasive technique and chooses the singular topic of change as the key theme of his course. The persuasive story in Act I goes like this:

- ■ What's happening? Architects stand at the epicenter of economic change, social change, and technological change.

- ■ Why is this relevant? As a new graduate, you will be facing the reality of the situation soon.

- ■ What challenges do I face? As a new hire, you are most in danger of instability because of the forces of change.

- ■ What do I want? You'd like to learn the skills to handle the situation no matter what changes occur.

- ■ How do I get from here to there? Learn three crucial techniques to ensure that you keep a firm footing.

This persuasive Act I structure provides an elegant framework for the entire course. It gives students a way to understand the single theme and follow it through the various events in the complicated history of architecture. And the dramatic and persuasive elements give students a way to relate personally to the material.

Finding a defining structure like this is not always easy, but it can make the difference between a boring lecture and an engaging presentation. Try applying the persuasive model the next time you teach or inform, and see whether you make things more interesting for both yourself and your audience.

TIP 10: GET THE WRITING RIGHT

Beyond the nuts and bolts of writing down the words, consider ways to apply literary techniques to convey clear meaning across your headlines. Act I is so brief and elegant that you are actually telling a rich but concise story in only five sentences. Using a theme is one powerful technique; look for other techniques from professional writers whose work you admire.

Writers such as poets are extremely good at communicating a great deal of information in a limited number of words. Pick up a book of good poetry, and pay attention to how the author uses words, metaphor, and pacing. Scan through the text in a range of newspapers, and consider how the writers manage to tell a complicated story in only a brief article. Listen to people speak, and try adapting the direct and clear phrases you hear to the words in your Act I headlines. If you have good writers on your team, ask them to help write your Act I headlines, and if you have the resources, hire a professional writer to help. The success of your entire presentation rests on the language you use for Act I, so invest the resources necessary to get it right.

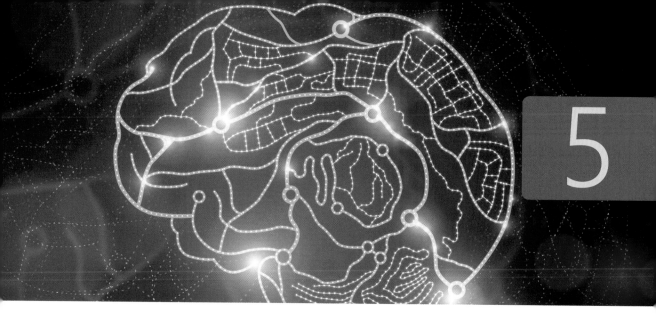

ANCHORING YOUR STORY IN YOUR AUDIENCE'S MINDS

In this chapter, you will:

- Write the headlines for the rest of the slides of the body of your presentation.
- Distill your ideas to their essence.
- Prioritize your ideas, and put them in a meaningful sequence.

The headlines you wrote for Act I will prepare the working memory of your audience for the crucial first few minutes of a presentation by orienting, interesting, engaging, motivating, and focusing them. Now it's time to move on to the rest of the slides in the body of your presentation.

AND NOW PRESENTING...ACT II

As in Act I, completing the story template for Act II creates a solid foundation that will help you choose exactly what you will show and say as you present the working memory of your audience with new information. With this foundation in place, you'll have endless creative options to make the crisp and clear underlying story even more powerful.

To begin, go to the BBP Story Template and zoom out so that Act II fills the screen, as shown in Figure 5-1. Here you see the empty cells where you will write the rest of the headlines of Act II following the three ground rules described in the section "Writing Headlines Using Three Ground Rules" in Chapter 3.

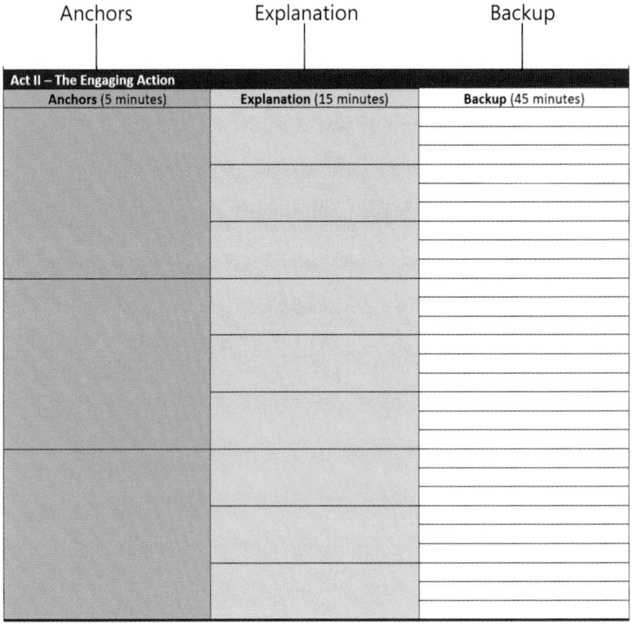

FIGURE 5-1

The cells where you will write the remaining headlines in Act II
of the story template.

The specific words you write in these cells in Act II of the story template become the headlines of the rest of the slides of your presentation. However, whereas the Act I headlines help you plan only five slides, your Act II headlines will help you plan most of the rest of the slides in the body of your presentation.

A SPECIAL TYPE OF OUTLINE

Act II in the story template contains three columns, labeled "Anchors," "Explanation," and "Backup," as shown in Figure 5-2. In the Anchors column, you give the top three reasons your audience should accept and follow your Map headline. The Explanation column contains an additional level of information about the Anchors column headlines, and the Backup column contains the next level of information about the Explanation column headlines.

Act II – The Engaging Action		
Anchors (5 minutes)	**Explanation** (15 minutes)	**Backup** (45 minutes)

FIGURE 5-2

The three column headings: Anchors, Explanation, and Backup.

One way to understand how Act II works is to see it as a sentence outline where you begin with a single thesis statement, then write out your topic sentences, explanation, and backup and organize them by using numbers and letters along with indentation. For example, you write out your first topic sentence and then number it as 1. You then indent and number the next sentence as 1.a. because it is the first explanation that follows the topic sentence. Then you indent and number the next sentences as 1.a.i., 1.a.ii., and so on, because they are the backups that follow the explanation, as shown here:

1. Topic sentence (Anchor)

    a. Explanation

        i. Backup

        ii. Backup

        iii. Backup

    b. Explanation

        i. Backup

        ii. Backup

        iii. Backup

You continue numbering and indenting your sentences in this fashion as you write the rest of the outline.

When you write your outline using your story template, instead of indenting and numbering your headlines, you write them in the corresponding columns of Act II, which are colored according to the levels of hierarchy. For example:

- When you view Act II as a sentence outline, as shown in Figure 5-3, your thesis statement corresponds to the Map headline in Act I (top).

- Your topic sentences in the first numbered level of your outline correspond to the dark blue Anchor column in Act II (left).

- The next level of indentation corresponds to the medium blue Explanation column (middle).

- The next level of indentation corresponds to the white Backup column (right).

OTHER ACT II OPTIONS
Write Act II in a blank Microsoft Word document using a traditional sentence outline if that works better for you. Just be sure to write complete sentences as described in the section "Writing Headlines Using Three Ground Rules," in Chapter 3, and aim to keep your indented headings to only three levels. Some BBP practitioners use tools other than Word to write their story templates, including Microsoft Excel, mind-mapping software, and even sticky notes.

The Map	Thesis statement		
Act II – The Engaging Action			
Anchors (5 minutes)	**Explanation** (15 minutes)	**Backup** (45 minutes)	
Topic sentence 1	**1.a.**		
	1.b.		
	1.c.		
Topic sentence 2	**2.a.**		
	2.b.		
	2.c.		
Topic sentence 3	**3.a.**		
	3.b.		
	3.c.		

FIGURE 5-3

The relationship between the three columns of Act II is like the indented levels of headings in a sentence outline.

BUILT-IN SCALABILITY

You'll notice that the column headings in this story template also include time estimates:

- The Anchors column heading includes the phrase "5 minutes."
- The Explanation column heading includes the phrase "15 minutes."
- The Backup column heading includes the phrase "45 minutes."

These time estimates indicate that for any presentation, you choose to complete the columns that correspond to the level of information and length of presentation you want.

The entire story template, including Act I and all three columns in Act II, contains 44 cells, each of which contains a single headline.

- If you spend an average of one minute per headline, you have enough material for a 45-minute presentation.

- If you skip the Backup column, you end up with a total of 17 headlines in your story template, and if you spend an average of 50 seconds on each headline, you have enough material for a 15-minute presentation.

- If you skip the Explanation and Backup columns, you have eight headlines. If you spend an average of 40 seconds on each headline, you have enough for a 5-minute presentation.

In this chapter, every cell in the example will eventually contain a headline so that you see how the entire process works to create a 45-minute presentation. Many presentations these days are shorter, so if you have a 15-minute presentation, you only need to complete the Anchors and Explanation columns, leaving the Backup column blank.

SEE ALSO   The headings in Act II of the story template describe the most common division of levels of information in a presentation. If you want to adapt the headings to align more closely with your profession, see "Tip 3: Tailor Your Act II Column Headings to Your Profession" later in this chapter.

TAPPING THE POWER OF HIERARCHY

Act II might look bland and unassuming with its various rows and cells in a Word document, and the idea that it is a form of a traditional sentence outline does not make it seem exceptional. But appearances are deceiving—it is, in fact, a powerful critical-thinking tool that has helped many people in a range of professions to break through the intellectual clutter and find a compelling story structure beneath mountains of data, charts, and bullet points. Built into the arrangement of these simple cells is a process that wields tremendous intellectual power to help you get right to the point.

When you use indentations in a sentence outline, as described earlier, you are applying a *hierarchy* to your ideas by consciously specifying some ideas (your topic sentences) as more important than other ideas (your explanation), which are in turn more important than other ideas (your backup). The relationships between levels of ideas in a hierarchy become clear in a *logic tree*, also called a tree diagram, which is a concept that dates back at least 1,700 years. The basic look of the logic tree diagram is recognizable today in the form of an organizational chart. When the logic tree that is built into Act II of the story template is placed on its side, a triangle drawn around the logic tree shows its shape, as in Figure 5-4. This triangle shape is the powerful tool you use to distill your ideas to their essence, prioritize them, and arrange them in the sequence in which you will present them in the form of slides to your audience.

These days, the trend is toward free-flowing, organic, free-association relationships among people and ideas. However, you need an *idea hierarchy* to help you decide which of your ideas are more important than others. You cannot present the working memory of your audience with an unprioritized and unstructured sequence of slides because you will quickly overwhelm it. A hierarchy breaks up a complex body of information into smaller pieces that are easier for working memory to handle and then prioritizes those pieces and places them in a particular sequence.

A hierarchy is a natural way people routinely go through a reasoning process. If you are completely new to a topic, you might start with a large amount of unstructured information (bottom of a hierarchy). You then apply your reasoning process to sort the information into smaller related groups to explain what it means (middle of the hierarchy). Last, you develop the key points or conclusion about what you analyzed (top of the hierarchy).

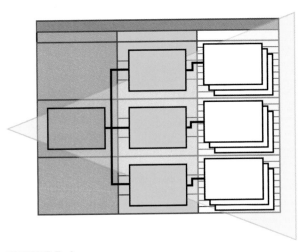

FIGURE 5-4

Act II of the story template is built on the powerful foundation of a hierarchy.

However, when you present new information to an audience, you must front-load what is most important, so you provide a clear cognitive roadmap to where you're going. That means that you flip the way you originally approached the information and begin with the key points you want to make, followed by your explanation and backup.

With the hierarchy concept firmly established as the foundation of Act II, it's time to make things practical and apply the hierarchy to the specific slides in the example presentation.

THE POWER OF A PYRAMID
The design of Act II of the story template is inspired by Barbara Minto's book *The Minto Pyramid Principle: Logic in Writing, Thinking, and Problem Solving* (Minto International, 1996). The book is a sophisticated, thorough, and comprehensive application of a logic tree technique that Minto developed more than 30 years ago to teach management consultants to write business documents more effectively, and she now teaches her approach as an independent consultant to senior executives around the world.

PRIORITIZING YOUR SLIDES

To recap your story so far:

1. Your Act I headlines define the Hook, Relevance, Challenge, Desire, and Map slides.

2. You make your audience's problem clear with the gap between the Challenge headline and where they want to be in the Desire headline.

3. The gap between these headlines forms the dramatic tension for the entire presentation, causing your audience to now pay close attention to find out how they can solve this problem.

4. With this gap wide open, you focus the entire presentation with the Map headline. This makes the headline of the Map slide the top of the triangle, as shown in Figure 5-5, and Act II is the rest of the triangle that will pull your slides through the eye of the needle of your audience's working memory based on a sensible sequence and priority.

The Map headline focuses all the slides in the hierarchy.

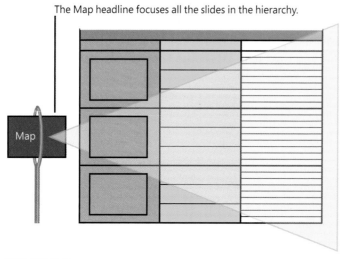

FIGURE 5-5

The tip of the hierarchy is the headline of the Map slide from Act I.

In the example presentation, your proposed Map headline is to *Let us show you the 3 ways that Contoso can help you deliver what you need,* as shown in Figure 5-6.

The Map	Let us show you the 3 ways that Contoso can help you deliver what you need

FIGURE 5-6

The Map cell from Act I with the headline completed.

Now that your audience knows your recommended Map headline, they're eager to hear why and how it is a good idea, which is what you'll justify next. Focusing exclusively on explaining your Map headline in Act II gives you the criteria you need to reduce the amount of information in your presentation. You'll include only information that supports your reasons for recommending the Map headline and exclude everything else.

JUSTIFYING THE MAP HEADLINE WITH THE ANCHOR HEADLINES

As you begin Act II, your first goal is to write the headlines for the most important slides you will present. If your audience will remember only the three Anchors in your presentation, you need to know specifically where those corresponding slides are in your presentation and allow ample time to show them and speak about them. To create these important slides, you will justify your Map headline. You'll do this by boiling down to only three Anchor headlines the reasons why your audience should accept your recommended call to action or the main steps that describe how they should implement it. You will accomplish that by writing three headlines in the first column of Act II.

SEE ALSO It's always a good idea to limit your ideas to groups of three, as described in "Tip 1: The Power of Three," later in this chapter. However, if you need to expand your groupings to four, use the expanded template version that's described in "Tip 2: Make Room for Four." Remember that working memory can hold three to four chunks of new information at any one time, so if you try to present more than that, you'll quickly overwhelm it.

To begin filling in Act II in the story template, position your cursor to the right of the Anchors column heading. If the Map headline recommends your audience do something, they will want to know *why* they should do it. If your Map headline recommends they follow a set of steps, they will want to know *how*. This is a critical decision-making point because whether you choose *why* or *how* will shape every slide to follow in Act II.

- If you choose *why*, you are giving the entire presentation a persuasive orientation.

- If you choose *how*, you are giving the entire presentation an explanatory orientation.

When the singular focus of the presentation is to persuade someone to do or think something, choose *why*. When the audience already has agreed to the idea, and now your singular focus is to explain something, choose *how*. Create a hybrid persuasive-explanatory presentation by choosing *how* for the first column and *why* for the others, or vice versa.

Choose the question that best describes what your audience will want to know next about your Map headline, and enter the question to the right of the Anchors column heading. In this case, the question is How? as shown in Figure 5-7.

Anchors (5 minutes) How?	Explanation (15 minutes)	Backup (45 minutes)

FIGURE 5-7

The Anchors column indicates the question "How?"

THREE CRITICAL DECISION POINTS The three critical decision

points that have the biggest impact on your presentation are:

1. Identifying in Act I the gap between a challenge the audience faces in the Challenge headline and where they want to be in the Desire headline

2. Defining in Act I the Map headline that focuses the entire presentation

3. Choosing in Act II *why* or *how* for your Anchors headlines, which determines whether the rest of your presentation will have a persuasive or an explanatory orientation

Your Anchors column now presents the question, *How will Contoso deliver what we need?* You'll answer this question by explaining the three main ways Contoso will deliver.

Follow the three guidelines described in the section "Writing Headlines Using Three Ground Rules," in Chapter 3 to write out your headlines in each of the three medium blue cells of the Anchors column, prioritizing them in descending order of importance. The more concise your Anchor headlines are, the easier they will be to remember, so limit them to a maximum of about two and a half lines, as shown in Figure 5-8.

> In this example, the first Anchor headline states, *You'll improve reliability with Contoso.*
>
> The second Anchor headline states, *You'll increase speed with Contoso.*
>
> The last Anchor headline states, *You'll gain flexibility with Contoso.*

These three Anchor headlines are clear, concise, and literally to the point(s), giving your audience a sense of coherence and focus as you develop the coming backup. It will be relatively easy for working memory to hold on to these most meaningful visual and verbal pieces and integrate the information into long-term memory.

Your three Anchor headlines might come easily if you've been thinking about these issues for a long time and you simply write them down. Or they might take some work because you're still figuring them out and you need to organize related ideas into a single main idea. If you're at a loss for words, try an interviewing technique by asking someone to read the Anchors column question out loud to you. Speak your answers out loud as you formulate them, and then type them in the Anchors column cells.

Act II – The Engaging Action		
Anchors (5 minutes) How?	Explanation (15 minutes)	Backup (45 minutes)
You'll improve reliability with Contoso		
You'll increase speed with Contoso		
You'll gain flexibility with Contoso		

FIGURE 5-8

Act II of the story template, with the Anchors column cells completed.
Note that the headlines across the cells have parallel construction—
meaning they all are worded similarly.

Tip   It is not always easy to boil down complexity to its essence, but it's critical that you do so to reduce the amount of information you present to the limited capacity of your audience's working memory. You simply cannot show and narrate 100 possibilities; rather, the aim is to distill the information to the three most meaningful concepts. Finding the essence is about simplicity rather than simplification; it's about raising the cream of your critical thinking to the top, not the fluff.

If you're still not sure of your answers, draft a placeholder set of Anchor headlines so that you have a place to start. You will want to spend ample time on writing the Anchor headlines because together with the Map headline, they are the most important information you want your audience to remember and apply.

As you formulate your Anchor headlines, think of how they will read when you present them in their corresponding sequence of slides. After you create a slide from each of these headlines in Chapter 6, as shown in Figure 5-9, you will sketch initial ideas to illustrate each of these headlines. When you imagine your headlines visually as slides like this, you get a better sense of how they will relate to one another as you present them. The goal is to make these three Anchor headlines a neatly coordinated package that flows together from one idea to the next so that it will be easy to illustrate them when you get to your sketches later. These three slides should become the most memorable to your audience.

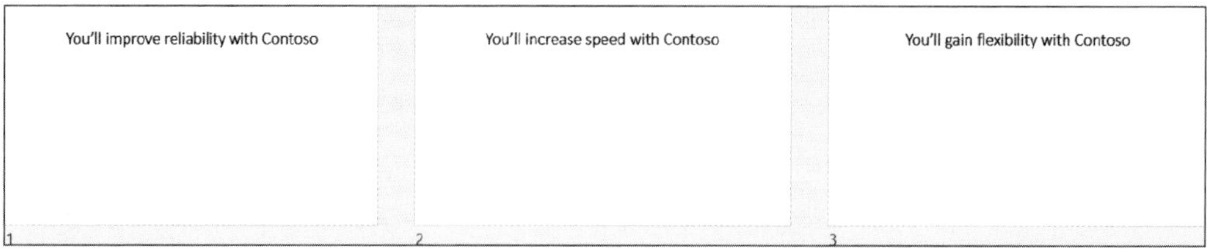

You'll improve reliability with Contoso	You'll increase speed with Contoso	You'll gain flexibility with Contoso
1	2	3

FIGURE 5-9

Keep in mind how your Anchor headlines will become the foundation for a visual story you tell across the corresponding slides in the storyboard.

IMPROVING YOUR ANCHORS

Tighten the relationship among these three Anchor headlines, and increase their memorability by carrying your theme from Act I through their wording. Remember, a theme is about much more than being clever. A theme is about finding a familiar structure from your audience's long-term memory that will ease the introduction of new information into working memory. For example, if you use the puzzle theme in the Map headline, *Put the three pieces of the puzzle together to change your way of thinking,* place in front of each Anchor headline the corresponding phrase: Puzzle Piece 1, Puzzle Piece 2, and Puzzle Piece 3. You could use a puzzle motif in two different ways, with the puzzle pieces of the three points either revealing or concealing the final picture.

There are endless ways to lay out the top-level story thread across your Anchor headlines. Whatever you decide depends on what you carry through from the Map headline in Act I. For example, extend a chronology across your Anchor headlines based on the Map headline, *Follow the story through the three crucial time periods,* or use a simple list format based on the Map headline *Check off the three items* or *Follow the three parts.*

You can heighten engagement and suspense through the three Anchor headlines by withholding what will happen, as in "Uncover the three secrets" or "Follow the three clues," allowing the audience to get involved and fill in the blanks for themselves. A trial attorney might tap into a familiar story structure for an opening statement at a jury trial by following a formula such as *motive + means = death* or one of its variations such as *denial + deception = injury*. For inspiration on motifs, review the sample phrases to begin your Map headlines in Appendix C, and consider how you could carry the same themes through the language of the Anchor headlines.

Whichever way you decide to go with your motif, make sure you integrate it through the wording of the map and the Anchor headlines because later, you will apply a similar visual design related to the motif to the corresponding slides. Although it is sufficient to integrate a motif only through a set of Map and Anchor headlines, you might want to extend it through the Explanation headlines if it works. Don't stretch a motif beyond its sensible limits, though. Remember from Chapter 4 that a motif must resonate with your audience, and if it starts to sound trite or overused, it will hurt your message rather than help it.

When you've entered your three headlines in the Anchors column, test them by filling in the blanks in this sentence:

> *The three main reasons/ways my audienc should* (insert Map headline) *are* (insert Anchor headline 1), (insert Anchor headline 2), *and* (insert Anchor headline 3).

In this presentation example, the completed sentence reads:

> *The three main ways that Contoso can help you deliver what you need are by improving reliability, increasing speed, and gaining flexibility.*

THE ANCHOR HEADLINES TEST   Test the three Anchor headlines by filling in the blanks in this sentence:

The three main reasons/ways my audience should (insert the Map headline) *are* (insert Anchor headline 1), (insert Anchor headline 2), *and* (insert Anchor headline 3).

For this sentence to sound right, each Anchor headline should be written in a similar form and should contain a similar type of information. Just as the Anchor headlines explain the Map headline, the Map headline should also summarize the Anchor headlines.

Your Map and Anchor headlines should neatly distill to the essence what you want to communicate in your presentation and define your measure of success. If your audience can remember and apply these points, you've succeeded in your presentation mission. If your measure for success is not present in the wording of your Map and Anchor headlines, go back and change the wording so that the core of your message is clear and visible without a doubt.

As you test your three Anchor headlines, you might find that the Map headline isn't exactly what you intended and you need to go back and revise it or entirely rework Act I. Or, you might need to revise your three Anchor headlines to make sure that each supports the Map headline in a way that makes your test sentence sound right. You'll probably need to do a couple of rounds of testing and revising before you are satisfied with your results and are ready to move on to the next step.

When you have written your three Anchor headlines, ensure that you justify the map slide with the anchor slides that follow it. Your Map and Anchor headlines form the most important information at the top level of the hierarchy, as shown in Figure 5-10, which defines the most important and meaningful information that you want your audience's working memory to engage and integrate into long-term memory.

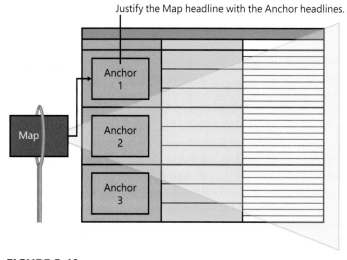

FIGURE 5-10

The top of your slide hierarchy consists of your most important slides—the Map slide and the three Anchor slides. In a sentence outline, the Map slide corresponds to the thesis statement, and the Anchor slides correspond to topic sentences 1, 2, and 3.

CLARIFYING EACH ANCHOR HEADLINE WITH ITS EXPLANATION HEADLINES

Now that you've written the headlines for the Anchor slides, the next step is to write the headlines for the second-most important slides—the Explanation slides. Each Act II *scene* in your story template is represented by a horizontal row of cells that begins with each Anchor cell and extends to the right to include all the adjacent cells in the Explanation and Backup columns, as shown in Figure 5-11.

Act II – The Engaging Action		
Anchors (5 minutes)?	**Explanation** (15 minutes)	**Backup** (45 minutes)
You'll improve reliability with Contoso		

FIGURE 5-11

Act II, scene 1, extends horizontally from left to right in the story template.

As in this example, the headline in the single Anchor cell anchors each Act II scene by maintaining a singular focus horizontally across all three columns. The Explanation and Backup columns will flesh out the main idea in increasing depth as you enter the headlines of your scene from left to right, top to bottom. This keeps all the pieces of information related to the single Anchor headline organized and coherent.

To start writing the rest of Act II, scene 1, position your cursor to the right of the Explanation column heading and type the question (either *why* or *how*) that your audience will want to know next about your three Anchor headlines—in this case, *How?* Reread your Anchor headline, and ask yourself *how* this is true—in this case, "*How* will you help us improve reliability?" As you did in the Anchors column, type your three answers in descending order of importance in the three cells of the Explanation column. When you enter your first reason in the top cell of the Explanation column, your story template should look like Figure 5-12.

Act II – The Engaging Action		
Anchors (5 minutes)	**Explanation** (15 minutes)	**Backup** (45 minutes)
You'll improve reliability with Contoso	Your current vendor had a drop in reliability	

FIGURE 5-12

Act II, scene 1, with the top cell of the Explanation column completed.

Enter your second answer in the cell below, and enter the third answer in the cell below that, as shown in Figure 5-13. Your Explanation column answers should offer more support for your Anchor headline and cite specific evidence, such as findings from research, case studies, financial analysis, or anecdotes.

Act II – The Engaging Action		
Anchors (5 minutes)	**Explanation** (15 minutes)	**Backup** (45 minutes)
You'll improve reliability with Contoso	Your current vendor had a drop in reliability	
	Our operations team has delivered a record reliability over the past 12 months	
	We can help you increase reliability within 3 months	

FIGURE 5-13

Testing the three headlines in the Explanation column to make sure that they support the Anchor to the left.

Test the three answers in the Explanation column by filling in the blanks in this sentence:

The three main reasons/ways (insert Anchor headline) are (insert Explanation column, answer 1), (insert Explanation column, answer 2), and (insert Explanation column, answer 3).

In this example, the test sentence reads as follows:

The three main reasons that we'll help you improve reliability are: Your current vendor had a drop in reliability, our operations team has delivered a record reliability over the past 12 months, and we can help you increase reliability within three months.

As in your earlier test sentence, for this sentence to sound right, each answer should be written similarly and flow from one point to the next. Apply this test visually by reading the test sentence from the left column to the right. You should also test the headlines the other way, from the right column to the left. After you read your three Explanation column headlines, you should find that the Anchor headline summarizes them.

Just as you thought of the three Anchor headlines as a tightly related package of thoughts that you will show over a sequence of slides, think of the Explanation headlines the same way. The headlines from the three Explanation column cells in Figure 5-13 will form the headlines for the corresponding explanation slides in the storyboard, and the slide thumbnails in Figure 5-14 show how the sequence of ideas in this example is the foundation for a three-part visual story.

FIGURE 5-14

Keep in mind how your Explanation headlines will become the foundation for a visual story you tell across the corresponding slides in the storyboard.

Breaking up the explanation of each Anchor headline into smaller pieces that you will show and narrate reduces cognitive load across a sequence of slides. This aligns with the research-based *temporal contiguity principle*, which explains that people learn better when animation and narration are presented simultaneously. For example, if you were to show an entire diagram first and then the narration later, you would split the attention of your audience as their working memory struggles to coordinate what it sees and what it hears. The story template ensures that you break up every explanation into digestible pieces, so you end up tightly coordinating what you say and what you show, one idea at a time.

Organize your ideas within the cells of the Explanation column using a "checklist" structure, a chronology, a list, a 1-2-3 sequence, or any other way you might explain an idea in three parts.

THE EXPLANATION HEADLINES TEST Test the three
Explanation headlines by filling in the blanks in this sentence:

The three main reasons/ways (insert Anchor headline) *are* (insert Explanation column, answer 1), (insert Explanation column, answer 2), *and* (insert Explanation column, answer 3).

When you have written your Explanation headlines, you have made sure that you will clarify each anchor slide with the explanation slides that follow it. The explanation slides form the middle of the slide hierarchy, as shown in Figure 5-15, which presents the second-most important informational pieces to working memory—the sub-parts of your Anchor headlines.

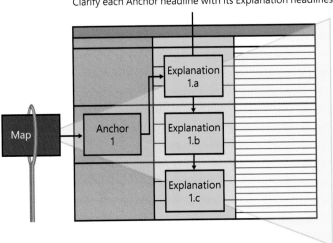

FIGURE 5-15

The middle of your slide hierarchy consists of your second-most important slides— the explanation slides. In an indented sentence outline, these slides correspond to outline items 1.a., 1.b., and 1.c.

BACKING UP EACH EXPLANATION HEADLINE WITH ITS BACKUP HEADLINES

Now that you've written the headlines for your anchor and explanation slides, the last step is to back up each Explanation headline by writing headlines for its backup slides. Fill in the Backup column using the same techniques you used for the Explanation column. Position your cursor to the right of the Backup column heading, and type the question (*why* or *how*) your audience will want to know next about your Explanation headlines. In this case, the question is *How?* The questions you choose for your column headings will vary according to your topic, and sometimes they might be all *why*, all *how*, or combinations of the two. Now, read each headline in the Explanation column, and ask why or how that headline is true. In this example, you'll be asking the question *how*, as in: "*How* did your current vendor have a drop in reliability?"

As you did in the Anchors and Explanation columns, type your three answers in the three cells of the Backup column in descending order of importance. The cells will expand to hold your text. Keep your headlines limited to about two and a half lines, as you did in the other two columns. The answers you enter in the Backup column should offer more support for the Explanation headline and cite specific evidence that backs it up, as shown in Figure 5-16, such as quantitative information, case studies, charts, graphs, anecdotes, analysis, and any other support.

Act II – The Engaging Action		
Anchors (5 minutes)	**Explanation** (15 minutes)	**Backup** (45 minutes)
		Your vendor started the year with 80% reliability
	Your current vendor had a drop in reliability	Over the year, your reliability dropped 10%
		The cause was a mix of tech and people issues
You'll improve reliability with Contoso	Our operations team has delivered record reliability over the past 12 months	
	We can help you increase reliability within 3 months	

FIGURE 5-16

Testing the three Backup headlines to make sure they back up the Explanation headline to the left.

As with the Anchor and Explanation headlines, think of the way you will end up presenting these headlines visually in a sequence of slides, as shown in Figure 5-17. As before, you are breaking up the previous column's headline into smaller pieces that you will present visually and verbally across slides. Whatever specific wording you choose for each Backup headline, you will back it up by the appropriate type of visual evidence, whether it is a screen capture, chart, graph, photograph, diagram, or other illustration. And just as you did in the previous columns, feel free to organize your headlines in a range of formats, including chronological, before-and-after results, 1-2-3 lists, and more.

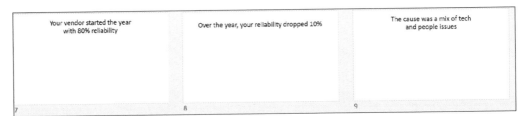

FIGURE 5-17

Keep in mind how your Backup headlines will become the foundation for a visual story you tell across the corresponding slides in the storyboard.

After you've entered three answers in the Backup column, test them by filling in the blanks in this sentence:

> *The three main reasons/ways* (insert Explanation column headline) *are* (insert Backup column, answer 1), (insert Backup column, answer 2), *and* (insert Backup column, answer 3).

In this example, the test headline would read as follows:

> *The three main ways your vendor had a drop in reliability were they started the year with 80 percent reliability; over the year, your reliability dropped 10 percent; and the cause was a mix of tech and people issues.*

After you test your Backup column answers, go to the second Explanation headline and repeat this process for its corresponding Backup headlines. Then go to the third Explanation headline and repeat the process for its Backup headlines. When you've finished, you will have completed Act II, scene 1, of your story template, as shown in Figure 5-18.

Act II – The Engaging Action		
Anchors (5 minutes)	**Explanation** (15 minutes)	**Backup** (45 minutes)
You'll improve reliability with Contoso	Your current vendor had a drop in reliability	Your vendor started the year with 80% reliability
		Over the year, your reliability dropped 10%
		The cause was a mix of tech and people issues
	Our operations team has delivered record reliability over the past 12 months	At Contoso we've never allowed our clients' reliability to fall below 90%
		Reliability is our first priority – and we integrate it throughout our operations
		We give clients like you access to a master reliability dashboard to monitor real-time data
	We can help you increase reliability within 3 months	Trey Research began last year at 80% reliability
		We helped them increase reliability to our 90% minimum within 3 months
		We can do the same for you by assigning a reliability project manager to get you on the road

FIGURE 5-18

Act II, scene 1, of the sample story template, with all cells completed.

THE BACKUP HEADLINES TEST Test the three Backup headlines
by filling in the blanks in this sentence:

The three main reasons/ways (insert Explanation headline) *are* (insert Backup column, answer 1), (insert Backup column, answer 2), *and* (insert Backup column, answer 3).

As always, it is helpful to think of how your headlines will play out across the slides of your storyboard. In Figure 5-19, the Backup headlines tell the story of the second Explanation headline in the form of an anecdote told chronologically across the three slides.

When you have written your Backup headlines, you have made sure that you will back up each explanation slide with the backup slides that follow it. This is the bottom of the hierarchy, as shown in Figure 5-19, which presents the third-most important informational pieces to working memory.

Now that you've finished writing the headlines for Act II, scene 1, it's time to move on to scenes 2 and 3.

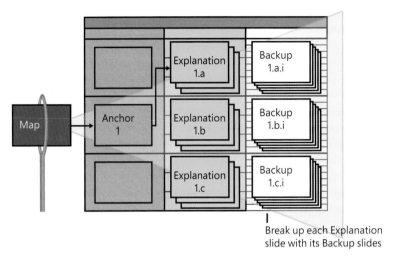

Break up each Explanation
slide with its Backup slides

FIGURE 5-19

The bottom of your hierarchy consists of your third-most important slides—the backup slides. In a classical indented outline, these slides correspond to outline items 1.a.i., 1.b.i., 1.c.i., and so on.

FLESHING OUT THE REST OF ACT II

With Act II, scene 1, complete, your final job is to write the headlines for the rest of the slides in Act II. You'll do this by applying the same process to both scene 2 and scene 3. Continue to check your reasoning with test sentences at each level, and revise your story template headlines as needed to keep the test sentences clear and consistent.

Act II of the story template is structured using groups of three ideas to make your ideas easier for your audience to understand, but you might find that you don't have exactly three supporting headlines to write at any level in the template. If you want to use only two headlines, simply leave the third cell blank. If you need to add a fourth cell to the Explanation or Backup column, position the cursor in a cell, right-click, and select Insert Row. If the extra row creates extra cells in the Anchor and Explanation columns, merge the new cells into adjacent cells within the column.

If you need to create four Anchor headlines, see "Tip 2: Make Room for Four," later in this chapter. If you have more than four Anchor headlines, find a way to reduce that number, either by reworking your ideas or by merging several ideas into one main headline.

If you are having difficulty completing any point of the story template, try tackling it from a different direction. This chapter followed a process of completing Act II working from the top of the hierarchy to the bottom (from left to right in the story template), which you may choose to do if you know your topic well. If you're not completely sure of your message or your Anchor headlines, start first from the Backup column on the right, and work left through the Explanation column and finally the Anchors column.

When you complete the three scenes of Act II, your story template will likely extend across more than one page. In the completed Act II section of this story template, shown in Figure 5-20, the Backup column headlines have been abbreviated to display the three scenes on a single page.

Act II – The Engaging Action		
Anchors (5 minutes)	**Explanation** (15 minutes)	**Backup** (45 minutes)
	Your current vendor had a drop in reliability	Your vendor started the year with 80% reliability
		Over the year, your reliability dropped 10%
		The cause was a mix of tech and people issues
You'll improve reliability with Contoso	Our operations team has delivered record reliability over the past 12 months	At Contoso we've never allowed our clients' reliability to fall below 90%
		Reliability is our first priority – and we integrate it throughout our operations
		We give clients like you access to a master reliability dashboard to monitor real-time data
	We can help you increase reliability within 3 months	Trey Research began last year at 80% reliability
		We helped them increase reliability to our 90% minimum within 3 months
		We can do the same for you by assigning a reliability project manager to get you on the road
	Your speed of delivery has been on a plateau	You began the year at an average speed of 2 hours
		Weather conditions have been better than average
		Speed has not improved
You'll increase speed with Contoso	Our drivers have safely increased the speed of delivery of our customers by 12%	Contoso began the year with a similar average speed of 2 hours
		Conditions were the same
		Speed improved by 26 percent
	We can quickly integrate with your systems to delivery similar results to you	Our technology systems are built on the same foundation as yours
		The data transition is easy
		Integration will take two weeks
You'll gain flexibility with Contoso	Responding to external events has been the biggest challenge the industry faces	Extreme weather events are becoming more common
		Unpredictability is the number one challenge
		Planning for the unexpected is key
	Our tech team has developed a	We've integrated real-time

FIGURE 5-20

Act II of the sample story template, with all three scenes completed.

Each idea you introduce in the presentation might prompt your audience to wonder, "*Why* or *how* is this true?" Because each column in your story template is set up to answer the question *why* or *how*, you provide immediate answers. In story terms, this creates a steady dynamic of action/reaction; one column is an "action," and the next column is a "reaction" to it. This dynamic structure in Act II helps you to examine all the possible directions for your story. It also helps you to align your information with the way people naturally think and reason, making your story more interesting and engaging.

THE POWER OF CUTTING
Just as much as you need to identify what you want to include in a presentation, the hierarchy in Act II is equally important for the *potential* slides it leaves out of a presentation. The built-in hierarchy of Act II guides you through a sometimes difficult but disciplined critical-thinking process that forces you to decide what to include in a presentation and what to leave out. The process of completing Act II acts like an intellectual machete that chops away unneeded data so that clarity shines through.

You will find that there is a great deal of information that did not make it into your presentation. If you're missing something important, go back and include it in your headlines. What does not make it into the hierarchy, such as detailed quantitative analysis, can be captured and documented and can then be handed out before, during, or after the presentation.

When you have written the rest of your Act II headlines, you have made sure that you have fleshed out the rest of the slides of your presentation. Now, every slide in your presentation will be prioritized in your slide hierarchy, as shown in Figure 5-21.

Don't worry about Act III of your story template at this point. You'll quickly take care of that soon when you add graphics to the storyboard in Chapter 8.

BBP CHECKLIST: PLANNING THE REST OF YOUR SLIDES
Do the rest of your headlines in Act II accomplish the following:

- Justify your Map headline with your anchors?
- Clarify your Anchor headlines with further explanation?
- Back up your Explanation headlines with the appropriate backup?
- Put your ideas in a logical sequence and priority?
- Integrate your theme verbally through your headlines where it makes sense?

Flesh out the rest of the headlines in Act II.

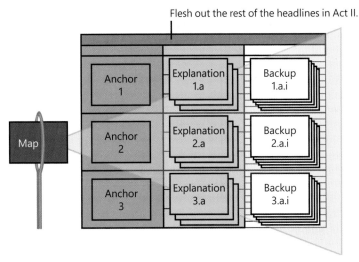

FIGURE 5-21

You determine the rest of your slide hierarchy when you flesh out the rest of your slides in Act II, and in the process, you have prioritized every slide.

PULLING THROUGH WHAT'S MOST IMPORTANT FIRST

Now that you've completed the story template, you have accomplished what you set out to do at the start of the chapter—that is, prioritizing your ideas and finding the right sequence in which to present them. The three columns of Act II established the priority of your idea, from Anchor headlines at the top of the informational hierarchy to Explanation headlines in the middle to Backup headlines at the bottom. The process of creating Act II helps you write out information in complete thoughts, rather than lists and fragments that the audience must sort through. Now there is a clear flow that connects each idea to the next in a logical way.

Next, when you import your headlines into PowerPoint to become your storyboard in Chapter 6, your slides will automatically appear in the same order you wrote them in Act II, as shown in Figure 5-22. In your storyboard, you will cue the audience to the levels of the hierarchy with the slide layouts and backgrounds as you present each idea in the sequence you wrote them. This is an important innovation of the BBP approach that has both prioritized your ideas with a hierarchy and prepared them for a logical sequence in your storyboard.

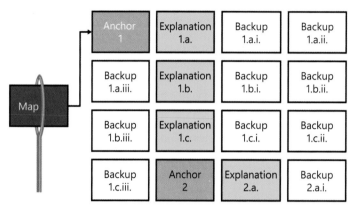

FIGURE 5-22

The hierarchy provides both a priority for your slides and a proper sequence in which to show them.

As described earlier, writing your slide headlines using the Act II columns has now given your presentation an important scalability that will play out when you work in PowerPoint. By creating a presentation with three columns, you are prioritizing your ideas in order of importance, from left to right. If you have a 45-minute presentation, you'll present all your slides in Act II. If your time is unexpectedly cut to 15 minutes, you'll skip the backup slides, and if your time is cut to 5 minutes, you'll also skip the explanation slides. Because you have applied the power of a hierarchy to prioritize your ideas, you scale up or down to the level of information appropriate to the time you have, without sacrificing the integrity or the clarity of your thinking at any level.

However, perhaps most important, what you've done in Act II reduces cognitive load by easing working memory into new information by presenting what is most significant first. Typical presentations show the detailed backup first, then the explanation of the backup, and finally the anchors—the recommendations or conclusions—at the end. Other presentations simply display lists of backup without any explanation or anchors at all to provide context or a framework for understanding the backup. Either way, this approach tries to jam the wide bottom of the hierarchy through the eye of the needle, as shown in Figure 5-23. If you present all the backup first, the working memory of your audience must struggle to retain that information until it knows where your presentation is going.

With BBP, you always pull through the eye of the needle what's most important first, as shown in Figure 5-24. That's because Act II of your story template flips the typical outline around, presenting the most important information first and the supporting information after. By presenting the tip, and the top, of the hierarchy first, you reduce the cognitive load on your audience by focusing first on what's essential and leaving out extraneous information that could overwhelm the eye of the needle.

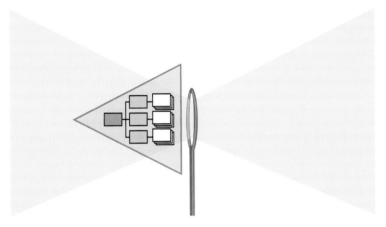

FIGURE 5-23

When you present the backup information first, you quickly overwhelm working memory.

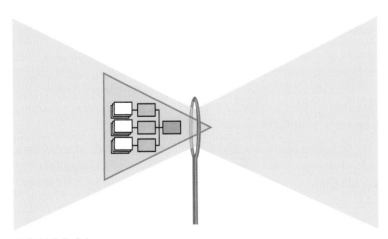

FIGURE 5-24

When you present the most important information first, you properly manage working memory and provide a framework for the rest of the explanation and backups to come.

Now, instead of the backup and detailed data overwhelming your audience, the proper management of the working memory is driving the presentation, which aligns with the three research described in Chapter 2.

LOWERING THE CURTAIN ON YOUR STORY TEMPLATE

One benefit of your BBP Story Template is that you now see all your ideas in one place and quickly grasp how each idea relates to the others. A printout of your story template at this point will guide you through an initial reading of your story to make sure that everything sounds right.

Review your story template before you print it. If it extends over multiple pages, you might need to split Act II into separate scenes that each fit on a page. To do this, position the cursor in any cell in the Anchors column, and on the Table Tools tab, click Layout; and then in the Merge group, click Split Table to split that row from the row above. If you change your mind, click the Undo button on the Quick Access toolbar or press CTRL+Z.

As this book describes, the story template is the hard-working intellectual and structural engine that makes everything in your presentation work, or not. It is the workspace that determines whether your presentation is a success or failure. If you have an elegant infrastructure, the more time you spend on the presentation, the simpler it will get. If you don't have a solid structure, the more time you spend on it, the more confusing it will get.

If you get the headlines right, they will clarify and expand understanding; but if you get them wrong, you will lead your audience in the wrong direction, in a fruitless, frustrating waste of time. That's why it's important to spend as much time as possible reviewing the big picture, editing, tightening, and clarifying your words.

Just as you use your story template to see and manage all your headlines at a glance, other people can use it to review your story, too. If you're working with only a few people, display the story template on your computer screen and make edits together. If you're working with a larger group and want to call a meeting to review your headlines, send a copy of the story template document through email to all the members of the team in advance.

Get agreement on the story template from anyone who has a stake in the presentation. This includes the members of your team, people in other departments of your organization, and anyone who needs to give clearance and approval for what you'll say.

Using your story template as a review document, make quick adjustments to your wording or structure and invite others to contribute their expertise and take owner- ship in the success of your presentation. Getting approval for your story template allows everyone to focus on your ideas instead of on design issues, which would prove distracting right now. When you get final approval of the structure and sequence of your story up front, you'll reduce the likelihood that you'll need to spend unnecessary time and effort later, after you've invested time in the design process.

TIP   When you meet with others in person, either project the story template on the wall or print copies of your story template and bring them to the meeting. Talk through the ideas in the order in which you rehearsed them, and discuss the options you have to scale down the story if your presentation time is reduced from 45 minutes to 15 or 5.

Before you move on to the next major step in the BBP approach—turning your script into a storyboard—read through the following 10 tips to find ideas that might improve your story template.

10 TIPS FOR ENHANCING YOUR STORY TEMPLATE

With your story template in hand, rest assured that you have a focused tale to tell at your next presentation. When you're comfortable with the basics of completing your template, try improvising on the concept using these 10 tips.

TIP 1: THE POWER OF THREE

As much as you might want to load up your slides with data, the quantity of new information that people can understand is always constrained by the limitations of working memory. As mentioned in Chapter 2, you help your audience to understand information better by presenting new information to working memory in groups of three.

Your story template helps you to organize your ideas in groups of three in mul- tiple ways. The essence of your story consists of your Map headline and your three Anchor headlines. Each Anchor headline has three supporting headlines, listed in the Explanation column. Each Explanation headline has three supporting headlines as well, listed in the Backup column. It might be challenging to boil down your headlines to groups of three in this structure, but your hard work will pay off: your audience will more easily absorb, remember, and understand your ideas.

TIP 2: MAKE ROOM FOR FOUR

Although three is a powerful number, you might find while working in Act II of your story template that you have four points to make in a column. As described earlier in this chapter, if you have fewer points to make in any section than you have cells, simply leave the cells blank; if you want to add another cell, you insert one. The disadvantage of using a template with four levels of information is that the number of cells might significantly increase the size and complexity of your presentation. Keep in mind that the more headlines you have, the more time you need and the more information people need to process. To avoid long and complicated presentations, try to stick to three points rather than four.

TIP 3: TAILOR YOUR ACT II COLUMN HEADINGS TO YOUR PROFESSION

The headings of the three columns of Act II are based on the most common categorization of information in a hierarchy. However, there are many other ways to look at these columns. If one of the alternatives shown in the following list works better for you in your profession, simply type over the existing headings in your story template to replace them with new headings.

- The most common categories for the three columns are Anchors, Explanation, and Backup.
- If you're a market researcher, your column headings might be Recommendation, Explanation, and Data.
- If you're a lawyer, your column headings might be Main Point, Explanation, and Evidence.
- If you're an analyst, your column headings might be Conclusion, Analysis, and Fact.
- If you're an executive, your column headings might be Summary, Breakdown, and Backup.
- If you're a salesperson, your column headings might be Benefit, Feature, and Demonstration.

- If you're a writer, your column headings might be Act, Scene, and Action.

- If you're a journalist, your column headings might be Lead, Body, and Backup.

- If you're a teacher or an instructor, your column headings might be Lesson, Explanation, and Backup.

TIP 4: STORY TEMPLATES FOR TEAMS

Act II works well for teams and organizations that have multiple points they have to make to different audiences. For example, most groups have a finite set of Anchor headlines they might want to write about a topic, so someone in the group can create additional Act II scenes to cover those. When you are ready to present, you display only the scenes you choose and hide the rest. This can also be done with Act I variations as you create a range of story templates from frequently used story structures.

TIP 5: THE STORY NUGGET

A *story nugget* is a telling Backup that encapsulates, distills, and frames the entire story. For example, a $6,000 shower curtain represented to many people the excess of company executives found guilty of taking money from a large international corporation, as reported in the news. Place a story nugget in one of the headlines in Act I as an encapsulation of the whole story, or place it as a backup in a strategic place in the Backup column. If the information is truly important and you want to be sure it's remembered and applied, integrate it into the Anchor headlines. If your points are already clear, place the story nuggets somewhere in your presentation for your audience to discover and remember.

TIP 6: BBP BEYOND POWERPOINT

People have reported using the BBP Story Template for a wide range of purposes beyond presentations, including to structure email messages, curriculum design, radio spots, ads, and classroom outlines. When you're at a loss for words or are bogged down or frustrated with writing or communicating, open up a story template. The reliability and simplicity of the structure can break an intellectual or creative logjam by providing clarity and focus. Give it a try, and see what clarity it can help you uncover beyond PowerPoint.

TIP 7: BUILD AN OUTLINE IN A BRAINSTORM

Your Act II headlines must come from somewhere. If they don't flow easily from your imagination, you might need to loosen things up with a little brainstorming. Some excellent books and online resources are available to help you to brainstorm new ideas either on your own or with your team. Whatever technique you decide to use, you need to understand the relationship between the fruit of your brainstorming labor and the story template process you undertake in Act II.

Brainstorming is the art of generating ideas for a purpose; it supports an environment of free-flowing thinking without constraints. *Presentation development* is the art of selecting and prioritizing ideas; it calls on a different set of skills, including critical thinking, selection, prioritization, and reasoning.

When you've finished your brainstorming exercises, the story template helps you select the ideas that best support the focus of your presentation. As you begin to work on Act II, gather all the brainstorming ideas you might have on hand, whether they're in the form of lists, note cards, whiteboard diagrams, or other formats. Then apply the process of writing your Act II headlines described in this chapter.

At times, you might need to switch back into a brainstorming mode when you're stuck on a headline or if your Act II structure isn't working. But when you've generated fresh ideas, it's time to switch back into story template mode to select appropriate ideas that support the focus of your presentation.

Brainstorming and using the story template are different but complementary techniques, and when you alternate the two, you have the best of both worlds—the correct selection of the freshest ideas that support your singular story.

TIP 8: TAP YOUR TEAM'S TALENTS

Consider working with your team to structure your ideas in Act II. By connecting a projector to your computer, you can display some software tools that allow you to work with your team to develop your Act II headlines. Or build your own tables or logic trees using Microsoft OneNote, or the PowerPoint organization chart feature.

If you don't have a projector or you prefer a hands-on approach, use a sheet of paper, a flip chart, or a whiteboard to draw your logic tree. Or write your draft Act II headlines on sticky notes and affix them to a wall to build a logic tree, as described in David Straker's *Rapid Problem Solving with Post-it Notes* (Fisher Books, 1997). Experiment with a range of techniques and tools until you find what works best for you and your team to focus and prioritize your ideas. When you've finished, return to your Word document and enter your headlines in the story template.

Some people think clearly and quickly at the top level, others at the Backup level. If you're caught up in the Backup, step back and ask a top-level thinker/organizer to help.

When it comes to creating the story template, you'll probably find that tapping into the talents of your team will build the best presentation possible.

TIP 9: TAKE THE EXPRESS ELEVATOR

When entrepreneurs begin to approach investors to raise money for a venture, they're expected to have something called an *elevator pitch*. The idea is that they pitch their company within the length of time of an elevator ride. Even if you're not trying to raise money for your company, you might need to give your own version of an elevator pitch if you get a call from your boss before you give your presentation and she says, "I'm sorry, but I can't make it to your presentation. Can you tell me quickly what you're going to say?"

In every case, you'll be clear about what you're going to say after you complete your story template. To respond to your boss, give your own elevator pitch by first summarizing your Act I headlines and then describing each of your Anchor headlines in Act II of your story template. This sets the context for the presentation and covers the high-level points. If your boss is interested in knowing more about any point, elaborate more as needed by providing more supporting information from the Explanation and Backup columns.

This handy technique is not just for elevator pitches and verbal summaries. If you have to write the marketing description for your talk, you've got the outline already written in the story template in the form of your Act I and Act II Anchors column headlines. If you want to let other people know the structure of your talk in advance, summarize it in the same way in an email message. In all these situations, your story template keeps you speeding along with effective communication.

TIP 10: THE HIERARCHY IN YOUR MIND

There are many reasons why the ancient concept of hierarchy still holds such power today. Some researchers believe that the mind uses hierarchical structures to store information in and retrieve information from long-term memory. For example, the idea of chunking is based on the idea that long-term memory applies a higher category to smaller pieces in working memory to bring them together and make them easier to handle. Some experts believe that a part of the brain called the neocortex retrieves information in a hierarchical way. And certainly, the organizational technique of hierarchy is fully a part of most outlining systems, as well as many computer languages.

When you write your Act II headlines, you tap into hierarchical power by bringing the structure itself from long-term memory and applying it to the organization of your slides. A hierarchy turns out to be a deep and memorable way to help you and your audiences get right to the heart of the matter.

THINKING LIKE A STORYBOARD

In this chapter, you will:

- Transform your script into a storyboard with preliminary backgrounds.
- Write out the words you'll speak during the presentation.
- Review the three guidelines for storyboarding.

When you complete the Beyond Bullet Points (BBP) Story Template, you have in hand a focused and coherent story that sets the foundation for all your slides. Your story is so clear that even if your technology fails during your presentation, you have the security of knowing that you can present using only a printout of the story template as your guide. But of course, you'll want to use graphics in your presentation, because research indicates that people learn better when you add graphics to your narration in a multimedia presentation.

In Chapter 4, you used a story thread to prepare new information for the eye of the needle of your audience's working memory, and in Chapter 5, you used the sharp tip of a triangle of hierarchy to determine the sequence and order of information along that thread. Now in this chapter, you will focus on the two strands of that story thread that represent the two essential elements you have to coordinate in any multimedia presentation— the visual and verbal channels, as described in Chapter 2.

You'll learn how to guide these visual and verbal strands through the rest of this book. Your challenge in this chapter is to set up your slides in specific ways that don't

split the attention of the audience or create redundancy. In Chapter 7, you'll explore the wide range of options you have to plan and sketch the graphics for your story-board; in Chapter 8, you'll add the final graphics based on the sketches you choose; in Chapter 9, you'll learn how to effectively narrate your visual storyboard during a presentation; and in Chapter 10, you'll see more examples of different types of presentations.

Expect that it will take some time to learn and apply the techniques described in these chapters, but as you develop your skills, the process will go faster, and this method will become a handy tool for rapid visual prototyping of creative concepts. As you build presentations over time, you'll develop a personal library of styles to review for inspiration on future projects.

WHAT WILL YOU SHOW, SAY, AND DO DURING EVERY SLIDE?

The prospect of managing everything you show, say, and do during every slide in a presentation can seem daunting at first. Even if you have written a clear and coherent set of headlines, as shown in Figure 6-1, how can you possibly fill all the slides you will create from the story template with graphics, narration, and interaction in a quick and efficient way? And at the same time, how can you seamlessly integrate all these complex elements during a live presentation? The answer lies in a different way of looking at PowerPoint—as a visual storytelling tool.

As mentioned in Chapter 3, if you were a filmmaker with a finished script, you'd probably hire a storyboard artist to sketch frames of selected scenes from your script. These initial sketches enable everyone on the production team to begin to see how the film will look so that they can start to turn the words from the script into spoken words and projected images. A storyboard is a powerful tool because it lets you see many frames from a story in a single view and consider how those frames relate to one another through a narrative. Without this important perspective, you would find it hard to see how the parts link to become a coherent whole.

You won't need to hire a storyboard artist to create your storyboard; instead, you'll adapt the basic techniques of creating a storyboard to your presentation to help you organize the visual and verbal pieces of your story. This approach will shift your thinking of a presentation from individual slides toward frames in a strip of cinematic film. By setting up a new presentation in this way, you'll use the storyboard not only to plan your words and visuals but also to present them to the audience using a single media document that works across projector, paper, and browser.

Delivering with Contoso by Pat Coleman		
Act I – The Compelling Setup		
The Hook	When a hurricane recently struck Florida, one company defied the odds	
The Relevance	You're looking for a reliable vendor to help you deliver results	
The Challenge	You've told us you're concerned about falling reliability, speed and flexibility	
The Desire	You'd like to choose the best vendor to help you turn the situation around	
The Map	Let us show you the 3 ways that Contoso can help you deliver what you need	
Act II – The Engaging Action		
Anchors (5 minutes)	**Explanation** (15 minutes)	**Backup** (45 minutes)
You'll improve reliability with Contoso	Your current vendor had a drop in reliability	Your vendor started the year with 80% reliability
		Over the year, your reliability dropped 10%
		The cause was a mix of tech and people issues
	Our operations team has delivered record reliability over the past 12 months	At Contoso we've never allowed our clients' reliability to fall below 90%
		Reliability is our first priority – and we integrate it throughout our operations
		We give clients like you access to a master reliability dashboard to monitor real-time data
	We can help you increase	Trey Research began last year at 80% reliability
		We helped them increase

FIGURE 6-1

Your completed story template.

PREPARING THE STORYBOARD

As you complete the story template in Chapters 4 and 5, you're also formatting your information in a specific way that prepares it for a storyboard. The concise headlines that communicate each act and scene in the story template are the same concise headlines that will communicate clearly to the audience on your slides. Writing headlines for both the story template and the slides is the powerful fulcrum that allows you to leverage PowerPoint software beyond bullet points into a new world of visual storytelling. This process embeds your script in a storyboard and ensures that everything you say and show maps back to the structure and sequence of a story. It also ensures that you have broken up your ideas into bite-size pieces so that working memory can easily digest them.

Although you're finished with the story template for now, it's a good idea to print a copy and keep it handy while you set up and work on your storyboard. The story template gives you the significant benefit of seeing your entire story on a single page or two, but when you import your headlines into PowerPoint, you will break the link between story template and storyboard. If you make changes to the headlines or the presentation structure later in your slides, it's always a good idea to update your story template so that it continues to serve as an organizing tool.

REFORMATTING YOUR STORY TEMPLATE MANUALLY

NOTE Once you learn how to reformat your story template manually, the process will take only a couple of minutes.

To prepare the headlines in your story template to become the headlines of your slides, you need to do some prep work on the story template.

1. First, save the Microsoft Word document.

2. Press Ctrl+A to select all the headlines in the template, and then press Ctrl+C to copy them.

3. Next, create a new blank Word document and save it on your local computer in a familiar folder, adding the word "Formatted" to the end of the file name.

4. Position the cursor in this new document. On the Home tab, in the Clipboard group, click the Paste button, and on the drop-down menu, click Paste Special.

5. In the Paste Special dialog box, select Unformatted Text, and then click OK. The resulting new document should look similar to Figure 6-2.

6. Delete the line containing the column headings and any extra text so that only your headlines remain.

7. Remove any extra spaces between words and add new line breaks where needed so that you end up with only one headline per line. Your final document should appear as shown in Figure 6-3.

8. After you save the document, close it.

Delivering with Contoso by Pat Coleman

Act I – The Compelling Setup

The Hook   When a hurricane recently struck Florida, one company defied the odds

The Relevance   You're looking for a reliable vendor to help you deliver results

The Challenge   You've told us you're concerned about falling reliability, speed and flexibility

The Desire   You'd like to choose the best vendor to help you turn the situation around

The Map   Let us show you the 3 ways that Contoso can help you deliver what you need

Act II – The Engaging Action

Anchors (5 minutes)   Explanation (15 minutes)   Backup (45 minutes)

You'll improve reliability with Contoso   Your current vendor had a <u>drop in</u> reliability   Your vendor started the year with 80% reliability

                        Over the year, your reliability dropped 10%

                        The cause was a mix of tech and people issues

            Our operations team has delivered record reliability over the past 12 months   At Contoso

FIGURE 6-2

Initial view after pasting headlines from the story template into a new Word document.

Delivering with Contoso by Pat Coleman

When a hurricane recently struck Florida, one company defied the odds

You're looking for a reliable vendor to help you deliver results

You've told us you're concerned about falling reliability, speed and flexibility

You'd like to choose the best vendor to help you turn the situation around

Let us show you the 3 ways that Contoso can help you deliver what you need

You'll improve reliability with Contoso

Your current vendor had a <u>drop in</u> reliability

Your vendor started the year with 80% reliability

Over the year, your reliability dropped 10%

The cause was a mix of tech and people issues

Our operations team has delivered record reliability over the past 12 months

At Contoso we've never allowed our clients' reliability to fall below 90%

Reliability is our first priority – and we integrate it throughout our operations

FIGURE 6-3

Word document with extra spaces between words removed, new line breaks added, and only one headline per line.

CREATING YOUR STORYBOARD

Now that you've reformatted your story template, the next step is to import your headlines into PowerPoint. You'll do that with the BBP Storyboard Formatter—a specially formatted PowerPoint file that takes care of some technical steps for you so that you don't have to take the time to apply them manually.

NOTE If you choose not to use the BBP Storyboard Formatter, manually apply the settings as described in the sections, "Tip 1: Set Up the Slide Master Manually" and "Tip 2: Set Up the Notes Master Manually," later in this chapter.

Download the BBP Storyboard Formatter file from the Resources page at www.beyondbulletpoints.com to a folder on your local computer.

Locate the BBP Storyboard Formatter on your local computer, and double-click it. Because the file format is a PowerPoint Design Template, as indicated by the .potx file extension, double-clicking the file will open a new presentation based on the template's formatting. Your PowerPoint file contains one blank slide and is now shown in Slide Sorter view. Next, to create your storyboard:

1. Name and save the new PowerPoint file on your local computer.

2. On the Home tab, in the Slides group, click the bottom of the New Slide button, and near the bottom of the drop-down menu, select Slides From Outline.

3. Then, in the Insert Outline dialog box, find and select the formatted story template in the Word document you just created—it should have the word *Formatted* that you added to the title—and then click Insert. (If you get an error message, you likely have your formatted Word document still open; in that case, return to the document and close it.)

This last click of the mouse (when you clicked Insert Outline) produces a result that amazes most people when they see it happen before them on the screen because it creates a PowerPoint storyboard. You have now created a single slide for each of the headlines you wrote in the story template, with each headline now placed at the top of a slide, as shown in Figure 6-4. It's a storyboard because you literally have a story embedded into your slides—the story you wrote in your story template, which now reads from one slide to the next when you view your slides in Slide Sorter view.

You'll unlock the tremendous power of your storyboard shortly, but first, take a tour to see what you're working with:

◼ If there are any blank slides in the presentation without headlines, delete them.

◼ At the lower right of the PowerPoint window on the status bar is a View tool-bar with three buttons. When you click them from left to right, you will see the storyboard in Normal, Slide Sorter, Reading, and Slide Show views.

◼ Click and drag the handle on the Zoom toolbar to the left to decrease the mag-nification of your current view and to the right to increase magnification. The indicator to the right of the Zoom toolbar displays the exact percentage of mag-nification. Click this value to open the Zoom dialog box and make more precise adjustments.

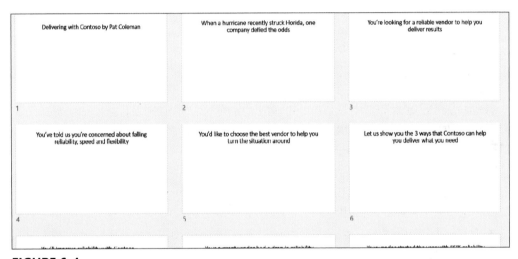

FIGURE 6-4

Slide Sorter view of all your headlines imported into the BBP Storyboard Formatter.

NOTE   After you master the fundamentals of the BBP approach, customize the settings of the BBP Storyboard Formatter according to your needs. Save the template to your local computer to make it easily accessible when you create a new presentation; for details, see the section "Tip 3: Install the Storyboard Formatter on Your Local Computer," later in this chapter.

CUING WORKING MEMORY WITH PRELIMINARY SLIDE BACKGROUNDS

One of the big benefits of using the story template is that you easily see how all your ideas relate to one another in the Word document. The story template is a particularly effective organizing tool for the Act II scenes because it shows you a visual hierarchy of your ideas. In each column, you write out the headlines in descending order of importance from top to bottom and add columns of information from left to right.

However, when you transform the story template into a storyboard, you lose the template's ability to show you the hierarchy of your ideas. Every slide you see in Slide Sorter view looks as though it carries the same visual weight, and each slide follows the next in an undifferentiated sequence.

To be able to quickly see your built-in informational hierarchy in Slide Sorter view and address the need to provide visual cues for working memory, apply custom layouts with special backgrounds that indicate the presentation's organization. These custom layouts will be only temporary while you sketch your storyboard. Later, in Chapter 8, you'll change these custom layouts or apply new ones apply a custom layout with:

Using the BBP Storyboard Formatter, you'll apply a custom layout with:

- an orange background to your map slide;
- a darker blue background to the anchor slides;
- a lighter blue background to the explanation slides; and
- a white background to the remaining Act I and backup slides.

FINDING YOUR SLIDES Keep a printout of the Word version of the story template handy as you locate the corresponding slides on the storyboard. If you have trouble finding slides because the slides are too large, or the headlines are too small, click and drag the handle on the Zoom bar to increase or decrease the magnification of the Slide Sorter view. Try counting slides to find the slides you're seeking. For example, once you have located an anchor slide, you know that an explanation slide follows directly after it, and you count three backup slides after that one to find the next explanation slide, and three backup slides after that to find the third explanation slide.

To color-code these slides in Slide Sorter view:

1. Click Ctrl+A to select all the slides in the presentation. On the Home tab, in the Slides group, click Layout, and on the drop-down menu, click the layout titled "Backup Sketches," as shown in Figure 6-5.

2. Now, select the map slide, click Layout, and on the drop-down menu, click the layout titled "Map Sketch."

3. Next, select the first anchor slide, hold down Ctrl, and click to select the second and third anchor slides.

4. Click Layout again, and on the drop-down menu, click the layout titled "Anchor Sketches."

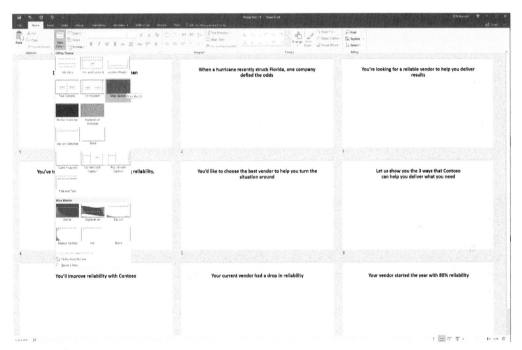

FIGURE 6-5

Applying the Backup Sketches custom layout to all the slides in Slide Sorter view using the custom layouts included in the BBP Storyboard Formatter.

5. Next, click the first explanation slide, hold down Ctrl and select the rest of the explanation slides, and then click the Layout button, and on the drop-down menu click the layout titled "Explanation Sketches."

NOTE If you choose not to use a storyboard formatter at all, follow the steps in the section, "Tip 5: Apply Slide Backgrounds Manually," near the end of this chapter.

Scroll through your slides as you read the headlines, and check them against the printout of your story template to make sure you have applied the layouts properly. If you made a mistake, select the slide, click the Layout button, and select the correct layout to apply it. Your storyboard should now look like Figure 6-6.

As you scroll through the slides of the presentation in sequence, the change in color of the backgrounds from orange to darker blue to lighter blue to white indicates you have made a transition to a new point that corresponds to Act I or the three columns in the storyboard. This transition should also be reinforced by your spoken words when you deliver the presentation.

Even though the shaded backgrounds are only temporary, already the contrast of the different shades of color calls attention to the three levels of hierarchy:

- The orange color calls attention to the most important map slide.
- The darker blue calls attention to the anchor slides.
- The lighter blue calls attention to the explanation slides.
- The white color calls attention to the backup slides.

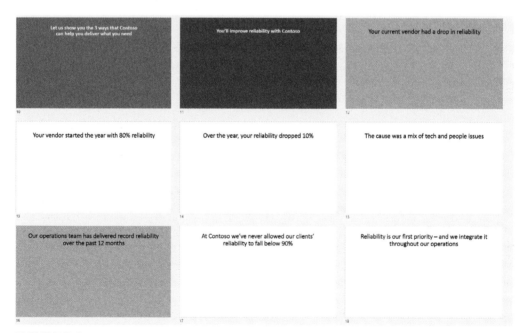

FIGURE 6-6

Slide Sorter view, showing the map slide with an orange background, the anchor slides with darker blue backgrounds, the explanation slides with lighter blue backgrounds, and the backup slides with white backgrounds.

Stick with these backgrounds for now so that you'll be able to sketch over the backgrounds as you work in the storyboard. In Chapter 7, you'll review and sketch a range of color backgrounds, layouts, and graphics to call attention to the different levels of information, and in Chapter 8, you'll apply them to the slides in their final form.

PRACTICING SCALING TO TIME

As you saw in Chapter 5, if you complete all three columns of Act II, you have enough anchor, explanation, and backup slides to fill about a 45-minute presentation. However, at the last minute, you might need to scale down your presentation from 45 minutes to 15 or even 5 minutes. Now, practice how easy it is to do that with only a few clicks of the mouse. Follow these steps in Slide Sorter view to scale the storyboard to time by hiding the slides you don't need to use in the presentation:

- If you're giving a 45-minute presentation, do nothing. All your slides will appear to your audience.

- To prepare a 15-minute presentation, hold down the Ctrl key and click the white backup slides throughout the presentation. With all the backup slides selected, right-click any backup slide, and then select Hide Slide. Now, only the Act I, anchor, and explanation slides will appear when you give the presentation; the backup slides will be hidden. View the result by pressing the F5 key to start the slideshow from the first slide. Press the Esc key to return to Slide Sorter view.

- To prepare a 5-minute presentation, complete the tasks for a 15-minute presentation, but in addition to selecting the white backup slides, select the light blue explanation slides, and then right-click any explanation or backup slide and select Hide Slide. Now, only the Act I and anchor slides will appear during the presentation; the rest of the Act II slides are hidden. Test the result by pressing the F5 key. Press the Esc key to return to Slide Sorter view.

When you use the Hide Slide feature, a slash appears across the slide number located below the lower-left corner of each slide thumbnail in Slide Sorter view. To reset the hidden slides to make them viewable again during a presentation, select the hidden slides, right-click any slide, and click Hide Slide again; the slash through the slide number will disappear. Keep in mind that hidden slides don't appear on-screen when you run a presentation, but they will be printed unless you clear the Print Hidden Slides check box in the Print dialog box.

When you hide the slides as you scale to time, you maintain a single presentation file that has the flexibility to accommodate different-length presentations. Because you created a hierarchy of ideas in Act II, you can scale your presentation up or down to time without losing the core integrity of the story—with only a few clicks of your mouse.

EDITING YOUR HEADLINES IF NEEDED

As you practiced scaling to time in Slide Sorter view, you might have noticed that some of the headlines extend beyond the two-line limit or have text that is unevenly balanced between the two lines. To fix that, you'll master the basics of editing headlines, described in the section "Tip 4: Edit the Headlines," later in this chapter. Scroll through all the slides, and when you find a headline that exceeds the two-line limit of the title area, edit it down to size. Sometimes, you reduce a headline's length simply by deleting a word or two, without affecting its meaning. At other times, you might have to revise and restructure the wording of a headline to make it fit.

To force a headline to break to the next line so that the two lines are evenly distributed, position the cursor after any word in a headline and then press Enter. Always stick with the two-line limit for headlines to maintain consistency in the presentation, to leave ample room for visuals, and to challenge yourself to be as concise as possible.

REVIEWING THE STORYBOARD

Congratulations! You have now officially moved beyond bullet points. Even before you've added a single visual, your PowerPoint file is embedded with a strong story, meaningful headlines anchoring every slide, preliminary backgrounds that indicate the presentation's structure, and a basic layout designed to hold graphical elements in the main area of the slides instead of bullet points.

Your new PowerPoint storyboard is inspired by the idea of a filmmaker's storyboard, but it's a much more sophisticated tool than its namesake. What you've created is the foundation for a complete, integrated, and coherent media document that manages both the words you speak and the visuals you show on-screen.

PLANNING FOR THE VERBAL CHANNEL BY WRITING DOWN WHAT YOU'LL SAY

No slide is an island because it always exists in the context of your spoken words. To create a coherent presentation, you need to plan each slide and the words you speak while you project the slide on a screen. Your primary objective in writing out your narration is to seamlessly integrate the soundtrack of your voice with the visual track of your slides so that you avoid splitting the attention of your audience between the two. To ensure that you properly manage what you say with what you show on-screen, click the View tab on the Ribbon, and in the Presentation Views group, click Notes Page. Scroll through all the slides in the presentation, which will each look like Figure 6-7. Starting in this view reinforces the concept that you're designing an experience consisting of both projected visuals and spoken words.

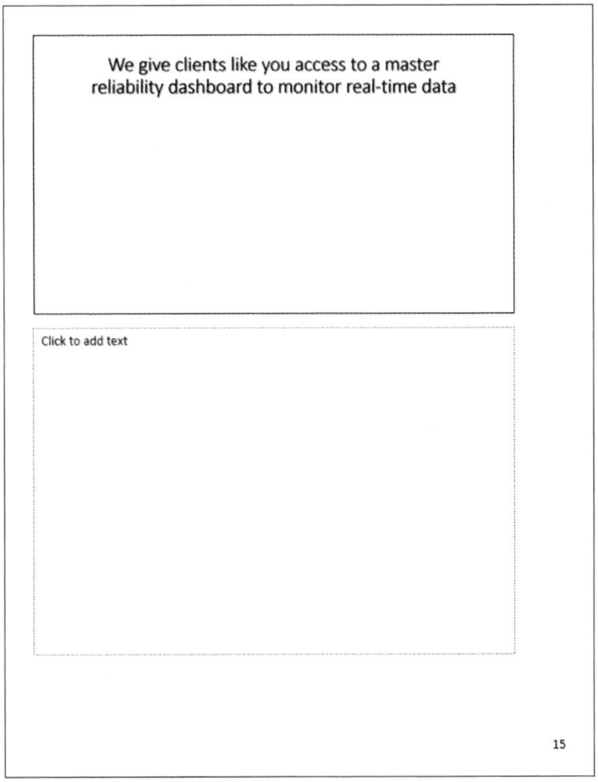

We give clients like you access to a master
reliability dashboard to monitor real-time data

Click to add text

15

FIGURE 6-7

Reviewing both projected visuals and spoken words in Notes Page view.

As described in Chapters 2 and 3, the top half of the page shows what you see on the slide, and the notes area below shows your spoken words. The headline of the slide does double duty in Notes Page view by summarizing the main idea that will appear on-screen during the presentation, and it also summarizes the meaning of the entire notes page. If you're used to having a great deal of written information on-screen, writing out your verbal explanation in the notes area gives you confidence that you will cover the bulk of the information through the verbal channel. In turn, this written, verbal explanation gives you the freedom to keep the visual channel simple, focused, and to the point.

To unlock the power of Notes Page view, review the slide headline in the top half of the page, position the cursor in the text box in the bottom half of the page, and then write out what you plan to say about this headline, as shown in the magnified view of the notes area in Figure 6-8. The text you write in the notes area represents what you'll say while the slide is displayed on the screen—normally for less than a minute. If you find that you have more to say and your narration extends past the limits of the text box, go back to the story template, and break up your ideas across more slides.

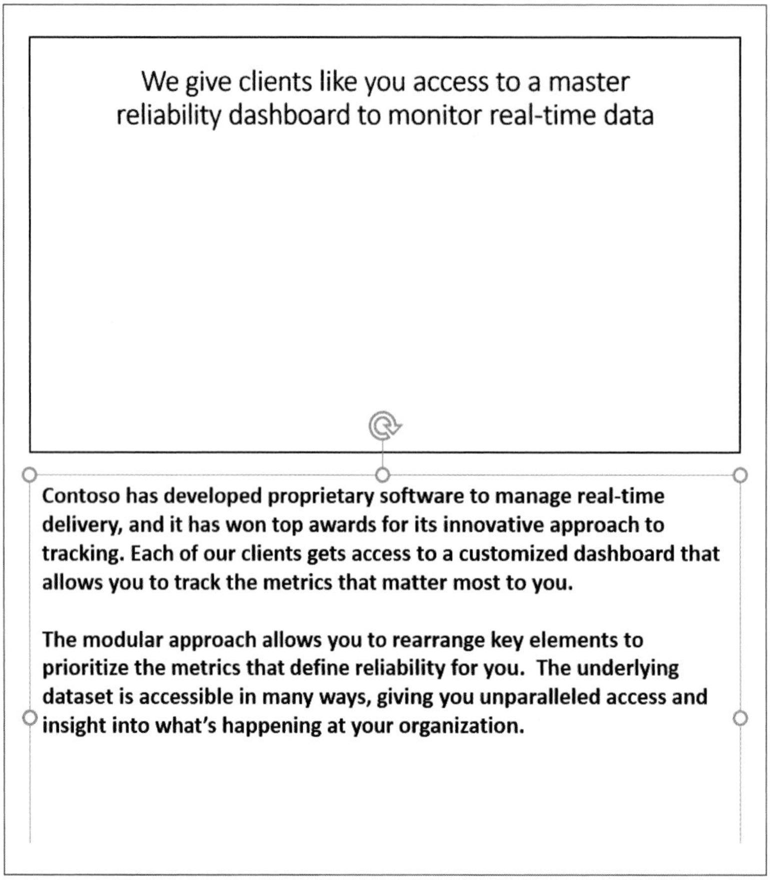

We give clients like you access to a master reliability dashboard to monitor real-time data

Contoso has developed proprietary software to manage real-time delivery, and it has won top awards for its innovative approach to tracking. Each of our clients gets access to a customized dashboard that allows you to track the metrics that matter most to you.

The modular approach allows you to rearrange key elements to prioritize the metrics that define reliability for you. The underlying dataset is accessible in many ways, giving you unparalleled access and insight into what's happening at your organization.

FIGURE 6-8

A magnified view of the notes area in Notes Page view, displaying an idea being described in complete sentences and paragraphs.

Fully writing out your ideas in the notes area fleshes out the ideas and increases your confidence in the topic. It also helps you to develop a close connection with the headline, which will aid you later when you speak. During the presentation, the headline will show the audience at a glance the idea of the slide. Also, the headline will prompt you to improvise on the detailed written explanation, with a relaxed voice that comes from knowing the topic so well.

If you're used to having text on-screen as a reminder of what to say, you also have full confidence in knowing that whatever you write in the notes area now is also viewable to you alone as the speaker in Presenter view.

A valuable byproduct of starting to design in Notes Page view is that at the end of the design process, you have well-designed slides and a useful handout. If you plan to share the presentation with your audience or others who were not present, it is important to write out what you'll say about the headline in complete sentences and paragraphs in the notes area. Doing so ensures that your handout is complete and accurate when you print out both the slide and textbox together. Don't worry about the formatting of Notes Page view now; you can adjust that in Chapter 8, and you'll also have the option to place additional graphics in the notes area if you choose.

NOTE You also have the option to add text to the notes pane when you are in Normal view by positioning the cursor in the notes pane below the slide view window and typing. A common mistake is to think that you're in Notes Page view when you use the notes pane in Normal view this way. The disadvantage to using Normal view to write out your notes is that you lose track of how each slide will look as a handout.

For a quick presentation for which you don't plan to print handouts, write short notes to yourself in the notes area of the slides of the storyboard. For now, spell out as much of your explanation as possible at this stage of the presentation. If you're pressed for time, write what you have at this point and then expand on your text in more detail later. Or use a digital recorder or smartphone to capture your thoughts as you're speaking about each slide and insert the transcribed text passages into the corresponding notes areas.

REMEMBER Start writing out your spoken words in the text area in Notes Page view so that you establish the complete context for what you'll say. Continue to add notes in this view, as well as in the notes pane in Normal view.

Now that you've prepared and reviewed the PowerPoint file, it's time to start planning the presentation's visuals with a few sketches.

PLANNING FOR THE VISUAL CHANNEL BY SKETCHING YOUR STORYBOARD

Just as a filmmaker would, you should start getting visual in your storyboard by sketching what you would like on each slide before you go looking for the actual graphics you'll use. Creating sketches of the slides accelerates the design process because it keeps you from getting distracted amidst the many visual possibilities you'll find when you search through photo and graphics libraries. A series of sketches also helps you to select a consistent style because you see all the slides together and can consider a design for all the slides at once.

NOTE If you've never sketched your PowerPoint slides before, this might seem like an extra step that you don't have the time to take. However, the investment you make in taking the time to sketch will save you time in the long run. Often, the frustration that comes from developing PowerPoint presentations, especially at large organizations, comes from endless revisions to graphics. When you sketch your slides first, you get everyone involved to sign off on the sketches to make sure they're what everyone wants. By getting agreement on the visual concepts now, you avoid frustration and inefficiency later.

You have two ways to go about sketching your slides—either on a computer or on paper. By far, the best way to sketch ideas for your slides is to use a computer that allows you to draw directly on the slides on the screen with a stylus. When you create your sketches in electronic format, you have a record of what you did that you email to others to review. Connecting your computer to a projector and projecting your slides on a screen as you sketch ideas with your team is a powerful way to tap into the collective visual intelligence of the group, and into your team's visual creativity.

If you have a computer that allows you to draw on the screen, open a slide in Normal view, click the Draw tab on the Ribbon, and try out the many options of pens, colors, and weights.

Read the headline of your slide, and think of the simplest way to illustrate it. Now, place the stylus on the screen below the headline and draw your illustration directly in the slide area as you would with a regular pen and paper, as shown in Figure 6-9.

FIGURE 6-9

Slide showing a sketch made directly on the screen using a stylus on a touchscreen.

Don't worry if you're not an artist. Just do your best to capture the general idea of what you're looking for, even if it means drawing the simplest stick figures, shapes, and arrows. In Chapter 8, you'll turn these simple sketches into professional, simple, and clear photographs, illustrations, and diagrams.

If you can't draw even a stick figure, just write the words to describe what you want on the screen. Don't try to make everything perfect at this point. Apply your creative side here, and you will likely find that you develop a sense of surprise, cleverness, and a visual sense of humor in your sketches to make sure the presentation doesn't get too stiff and impersonal.

In the Slide Thumbnails pane on the left, view the sketch you just drew in thumbnail size—the first illustration in the sequence of slides of your storyboard.

TIP   Even if you don't have a touchscreen computer, you can still sketch on any computer by using the Draw tools with your mouse. The limitation is that your sketching will not be as smooth or natural with a mouse as it is with a stylus.

If you don't want to sketch electronically, try using paper. To get started, print a copy of your slides by clicking File, Print, and under Settings, select one of the following options:

- The default Full Page Slides selection will print an individual copy of each slide. Tape these pages to a wall or assemble them in a loose-leaf notebook that you flip through as you sketch ideas for individual slides.

- The Notes Pages selection will print the notes pages. Assemble these pages in a notebook and sketch visuals in the slide areas or take notes to add to the notes areas later.

- The Handouts selection will print handouts according to the number of slides you want per page; click 1, 2, 3, 4, 6, or 9 to print the corresponding number of slides per page; and sketch on the thumbnail images of the slides.

When you have selected a format, click Print. (If you have any Hidden Slides and want to print them, under Settings select the Print All Slides dropdown and then select Print Hidden Slides.) Although the examples in Chapter 7 were all sketched electronically, you can apply most of the same techniques by sketching a paper storyboard.

TIP   To make sketching your paper storyboard more convenient by printing more than nine slides on a single page, see the section "Tip 8: Print Full-Page Storyboards," later in this chapter.

STORYBOARDING USING THREE GUIDELINES

Whether you have an electronic or paper version, as you review and work with your new storyboard, three guidelines can help you and your audience to stay connected to the big picture.

GUIDELINE 1: BE VISUALLY CONCISE, CLEAR, DIRECT, AND SPECIFIC

You wrote the headlines for your story template following the procedures in the section "Writing Headlines Using Three Ground Rules" in Chapter 3. Just as you strive to be concise, clear, direct, and specific with your words, you should strive to be the same with your visuals. Whether you use words or visuals to communicate, your singular goal should be to get across the most meaning in the most efficient way possible.

When you sketch your storyboard, use the simplest illustration possible without any excess detail. Not only does a simple illustration help you make your visual point quickly, but it also will guide you to avoid the extraneous detail that would otherwise clog the eye of the needle of working memory of your audience as described in Chapter 2.

As you sketch, always pay special attention to the wording of the headlines as you read through them in Slide Sorter view to reword them and tie them together more tightly. As you reword a headline on a slide, go back and edit the headline in the story template as well. If you find that you start making many changes to slide headlines, go back to the story template directly to work out the structural issues you are having before returning to the storyboard.

GUIDELINE 2: IN ACT II, SKETCH CONSISTENCY WITHIN COLUMNS AND VARIETY ACROSS COLUMNS

When you work with the storyboard, keep in mind that in Act II, *it's all about the hierarchy*. Act II of the story template is your disciplined guide that helps you make the tough decisions about whether to include or exclude ideas and automatically prioritizes for you every slide, from the most important to the least. When you apply preliminary layouts with color backgrounds to indicate the levels of importance of your slides, you see in Slide Sorter view how the hierarchy fits into the specific sequence of the slides of the presentation. And now you'll build on the rock-solid verbal foundation of Act II by using visual techniques to keep the hierarchy at the top of the minds of both you and your audience.

When you begin to sketch, the Act II structure will help you decide what you want to accomplish visually on your slides, as shown in Figure 6-10. As you learned in Chapter 5, you want the audience to remember your Map and Anchor slides above all others. If your audience walked away and remembered nothing else, these slides carry the most important information. You'll sketch on these slides the most memorable things you say, show, and do to make these points stick. Here, you'll use striking photographic icons, illustrations, or visual elements from your motif.

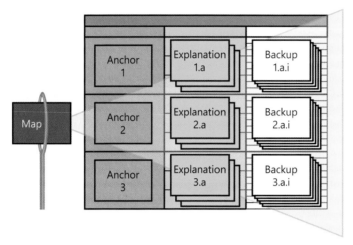

FIGURE 6-10

Act II hierarchy, indicating the relative importance of the slides.

Next, you'll sketch the second-most important explanation slides, which the audience will likely remember. Here, you might use diagrams, charts, or other illustrations. And then you'll sketch the third-most important backup slides, which the audience may not remember in detail. Here, you'll include graphs, charts, screen captures, and other visual elements.

As you sketch the slides that correspond to the three columns of Act II, you want to keep a consistent look regarding similar layout, style, and placement of headlines and graphics within each column, as shown in the slides that correspond to the headlines from the Explanation column in Figure 6-11. By sketching the slides from a single column together, as you'll do next in Chapter 7, you avoid concentrating exclusively on only single slides; instead, you focus on what is happening *across* slides. This makes sure that you approach the design of any slide by its context and relationship to other slides within its column, not as individual slides in isolation.

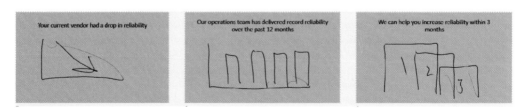

FIGURE 6-11

Telling a visual story across three slides from the Explanation column.

In addition to sketching consistency on slides from within the same column of Act II, you also want to sketch variety *across the columns* of Act II of the story template. You don't have to worry about how you'll do this; it will happen automatically because of the way you approach the sketching process in Chapter 7. However, it's important to know what's happening regarding consistency as you sketch your storyboard. For example, the explanation slides shown earlier in Figure 6-11 will not appear in direct sequence in the storyboard because they will each appear directly before each of their corresponding backup slides.

However, you do still want to tell this visual story across these explanation slides even when they are broken up by the backup slides, as shown in Figure 6-12.

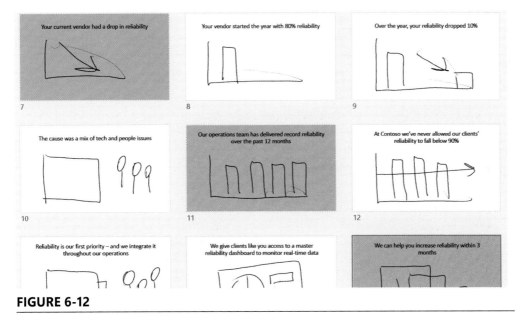

FIGURE 6-12

Telling the story across each of the three slides from the Explanation column, even though they are separated in sequence by the slides from the Backup column.

In the sequence of slides, as they appear in this example, you introduce the first explanation slide and then follow the idea with its three backup slides. You then present the second explanation slide and follow the idea with its three backup slides. This back-and-forth technique is helpful to your audience because with the first explanation slide, you summarize what you are about to tell them, and then with the backup slides, you do the actual telling. As you write out the narration in the notes area on the explanation slides, you likewise should summarize the backup slides to follow.

Think of the slides as cognitive stepping stones that are guiding and supporting the working memory of the audience along their paths of understanding.

GUIDELINE 3: SKETCH OUTSIDE THE SCREEN, TOO

You have in your PowerPoint file a powerful planning tool, with each slide representing one idea that you will convey at one point in the presentation as summarized by the headline. You will probably add graphics to most of these slides to illustrate the headlines, but you don't have to limit yourself to showing information on a slide exclusively with a graphic; you have many other media tools and techniques at your disposal.

For example, use a physical prop that you hold in your hands or pass around to audience members to communicate an explanation slide, as shown in Figure 6-13. You might switch to a different software application on your desktop to communicate the headlines across three backup slides. Or you might use a brief video clip to illustrate each of your three anchor slides.

The storyboard will guide you as you decide whether to use different media. You will specifically choose to include different media based on the slide's headline and its location within the Act II hierarchy. For example, you wouldn't use your most memorable video clip on a backup slide because you don't want your audience to remember the backup slides over the anchor slides; you would integrate and use the clip through the anchor slides instead.

Even when you use other media, your storyboard will still be the foundation that guides the entire experience. On the slides where you use other media, in most cases, you'll keep just the headline on the screen to keep the meaning of what you're doing clear and in the context of the overall presentation. Or you may use a photo as a physical prop to ensure that everyone sees it clearly. You'll see an example of this technique shortly in Chapter 7.

THREE GUIDELINES FOR STORYBOARDING   Inspired

by a filmmaker's storyboard, your PowerPoint storyboard helps you manage both the words you speak and the images you show. Follow these three ground rules to keep your storyboard coherent:

1. Be visually concise, clear, direct, and specific.

2. In Act II, sketch consistency within columns and variety across columns.

3. Sketch outside the screen, too.

FIGURE 6-13

Holding a physical prop while displaying a photo of it on the screen.

BBP CHECKLIST: PREPARING THE STORYBOARD

Does your storyboard:

- Include backgrounds that cue the anchor, explanation, and backup slides?

- Provide you with the ability to quickly scale your presentation up and down to time?

- Contain notes in the notes area of what you'll say during each slide?

Now that you have an operational storyboard, here are 10 advanced things to do with it.

10 TIPS FOR ENHANCING YOUR STORYBOARD

Your storyboard is a versatile tool to prepare and plan both your spoken words and your projected visuals during the presentation. Once you've mastered the basics, try using these 10 tips to enhance the storyboard.

TIP 1: SET UP THE SLIDE MASTER MANUALLY

To create your own Storyboard Formatter, follow these steps to set up the basic formatting you'll need to start sketching the storyboard:

1. Open and save a blank PowerPoint presentation, and as described earlier in this chapter, import the formatted story template headlines into PowerPoint following the New Slide, Slides From Outline sequence.

2. In Slide Sorter view, on the Home tab, in the Editing group, click Select, Select All, and then in the Slides group, click Layout, Title Only.

3. On the View tab, in the Master Views group, click Slide Master. In the Slides pane on the left, click the Office Theme Slide Master (the big thumbnail).

4. In the slide in the workspace, right-click the Title placeholder, and on the formatting minibar, select Calibri for the font (or a different font if you prefer), select 32 for the font size, and make sure that Centered is selected.

5. Right-click the Title box again, and on the shortcut menu below the formatting minibar select Format Shape.

6. In the Format Shape task pane select Text Options, then choose Text Box; on the Vertical Alignment drop-down menu, choose Middle Centered; in the Autofit area, select Do Not Autofit.

7. On the Slide Master tab, in the Close group, click Close Master View to return to the previous view of the slides.

TIP 2: SET UP THE NOTES MASTER MANUALLY

Just as the Storyboard Formatter uses the Slide Master to set the formatting for all the slides, the Notes Master sets the formatting for all the notes pages. By making a few adjustments to the Notes Master, you'll be able to use the notes pages to plan both your slides and your spoken words effectively.

To format the Notes Master, follow these steps:

1. Continue working on the same PowerPoint file you started in the section "Tip 1: Set Up the Slide Master Manually," and on the View tab, in the Master Views group, click Notes Master.

2. Review and make any changes to the Notes Master that you wish. For example, on the Notes Master tab, in the Placeholders group, check or uncheck any Notes Master placeholders, including Header, Date, Footer, and Page Number.

3. On the Notes Master tab, in the Close group, click Close Master View to return to the previous view.

TIP 3: INSTALL THE STORYBOARD FORMATTER ON YOUR LOCAL COMPUTER

To make the BBP Storyboard Formatter available on your local computer every time you create a new PowerPoint file, save it in your PowerPoint Templates folder by following these steps:

1. Double-click to open the BBP Storyboard Formatter that you saved to your computer earlier in this chapter.

2. Click File, Save a Copy, and then click the drop-down arrow and choose PowerPoint Template from the list of file types.

3. PowerPoint automatically selects the location on your local computer where the default PowerPoint template is stored. To create a new presentation, click File, New, and then either the Custom or Personal tab.

TIP 4: EDIT THE HEADLINES

PowerPoint provides two ways to edit your headlines:

■ Click the View tab and, in the Presentation Views group, click Normal. In this view, click in the title area of the slide, insert the cursor, and then start editing.

■ View the presentation in Outline format. Click View, Presentation Views, Outline View to see a list of headlines and, to the left of each headline, a number and a small icon of a slide. Click in the text of the headline you want to edit. As you make changes to a headline on the Outline pane, the corresponding text in the title area of the slide to the right is updated. Drag the vertical line at the right side of the Outline pane to increase or decrease its size to accommodate the width of the headlines. The Outline pane is useful for reviewing all the headlines of the slides in a list that you read from top to bottom. Print this outline later to use as speaker notes.

TIP 5: APPLY SLIDE BACKGROUNDS MANUALLY

If you do not use the BBP Storyboard Formatter, you will not be able to use the built-in custom layouts to format the anchor, explanation, and backup slides, but you can still format them manually. To quickly do this, follow these steps:

1. In Slide Sorter view, right-click the Map slide, click Format Background on the shortcut menu, and in the Format Background pane, click Fill and then select Solid Fill.

2. On the Color gallery, click More Colors, select dark blue, and then click OK. Make sure that the Transparency bar slider is set to 0 percent.

3. Click the first Anchor slide, and then hold down Ctrl and click to select the second and third anchor slides.

4. Now right-click one of the slides, click Format Background on the shortcut menu, and in the Format Background pane, click Fill, and then select Solid Fill.

5. On the Color gallery, click More Colors, select medium blue, and then click OK. Make sure that the Transparency bar slider is set to 0 percent.

6. Next, click the first explanation slide, and then hold down Ctrl and select the rest of the explanation slides.

7. Now, right-click one of the slides, click Format Background on the shortcut menu, and in the Format Background pane on the Fill tab, select Solid Fill.

8. On the Color drop-down menu, click More Colors, select light blue, and then click OK. Make sure that the Transparency bar slider is set to 0 percent.

Do nothing to the Act I and Backup slides.

Be sure to change only the background colors for now and otherwise leave the slides blank except for the headlines. If you were to include logos, other slide backgrounds, and other graphics on your storyboard at this point, they would constrain your design decisions and interfere with the way you will use backgrounds in this chapter to purposefully cue the working memory of your audience.

TIP 6: SET UP CUSTOM LAYOUTS AND THEMES MANUALLY

The BBP Storyboard Formatter includes built-in layouts that you apply to your anchor, explanation, and backup slides. These were built using the custom layouts feature in PowerPoint, which is described in more detail in Chapter 8. You'll be able to modify the current custom layouts at that point, or add new ones and apply them to your slides.

TIP 7: THE BBP STORYBOARD SKETCHPAD

Visit the Resources page at *www.beyondbulletpoints.com* to download a blank BBP Storyboard Sketchpad to print and use to sketch ideas for the Act I and Anchor slides, as shown in Figure 6-14.

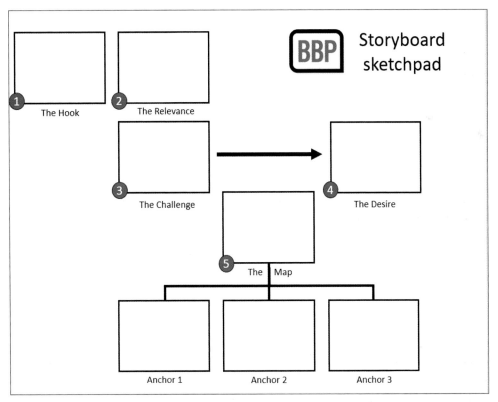

FIGURE 6-14

The BBP Storyboard Sketchpad.

TIP 8: PRINT FULL-PAGE STORYBOARDS

Although PowerPoint allows you to print up to nine slides per page on a handout, an add-in for PowerPoint called the Handout Wizard allows you to print many more slides per page. This is particularly useful if you plan to sketch your storyboard on paper. For example, fit groups of 20 slides from your storyboard on 8½-by-11-inch sheets of paper by using the Handout Wizard to arrange them five slides across and four slides down. Fit even more slides per page if you use 11-by-17-inch sheets of paper. The add-in places all the slide thumbnails on a single PowerPoint slide that you then print. For more information about the Handout Wizard add-in, visit www.skphub.com/how/install.htm.

TIP 9: CREATE NESTED STORYBOARDS

What if you're not certain which of two stories you want to present until you're standing in front of the audience? The section "Tip 4: Multiple Stories and Multiple Templates" in Chapter 4 explored the possibilities of developing two related story templates in parallel. Both stories presumably relate to the same topic, so they could share the same Hook slide as the starting point for whichever story you choose to present from that point forward.

To do this, create a separate PowerPoint file from each story template, and then copy and paste all the slides from the second presentation to the right of the last slide in the first presentation. This creates a "nested" storyboard in which the second story sits in the same file as the first. Note the number of the slide that begins the Relevance slide of the second story.

When you present the Hook slide, ask the audience a question such as, "Do you prefer Option 1 or 2?" Based on their responses, if you decide to stay on path 1 with the first story, you advance the slides as usual. However, if you decide to take the alternative path 2, type the number of the relevance slide of the second story and press Enter to go directly to that slide and begin that story instead.

The drawback of this approach is that you might have more than a hundred slides in the file to manage, so when you try it out, you'll need to balance the flexibility of a nested storyboard against the management challenges that large storyboards create.

TIP 10: REHEARSE WITH ONLY YOUR HEADLINES

Before adding sketches and graphics to all your slides, which you'll do in Chapters 7 and 8, it's a good idea to rehearse with only the headlines on the slides. You might be more comfortable rehearsing alone at this stage, or you could rehearse with your team if you prefer to get some early feedback.

7

THE MAGIC OF SKETCHING YOUR GRAPHICS FIRST

In this chapter, you will:

- Sketch the Act I, map, anchor, explanation, and backup slides.
- Consider the full range of graphics you could use.
- Consider the full range of other possible media tools and techniques.

When you put stylus to screen or pencil to paper to sketch your slides, it's a revolutionary moment. Think of the way you use PowerPoint according to the conventional approach. You open up a slide with a predesigned background, type a category heading such as "Our Company" in the title area, and then type a list of facts about the company below, maybe adding a small photo of your company building to spice things up.

However, now you are doing something completely different. As described in Chapter 6, you've printed out copies of your slides, and you have the paper version of your slides before you. There are no words to type anywhere. The headline on the slide summarizes your point, and the off-screen notes area holds the words you'll speak aloud. With just a clear headline on the printout of the slide before you, the only thing left to do now is tap into your innate visual thinking skills to illustrate the headline.

WHAT DO I SKETCH ON EACH SLIDE?

Sketching puts you in a different frame of mind, especially if you spend most of your day working with words and numbers. Your blank storyboard, as shown in Figure 7-1, is your opportunity to communicate in new and effective ways.

Even if you've never sketched before, just take it one slide at a time. This chapter guides you through the sketching process and shows you a range of specific sketches to draw on any one of your slides or across several of them. The sketches in this chapter relate to the specific example from the story template, but they also work on many types of presentations. Be patient as you practice your new visual thinking skills. As you tackle the first few slides, your creativity will start to flow, and you'll get the hang of sketching in no time.

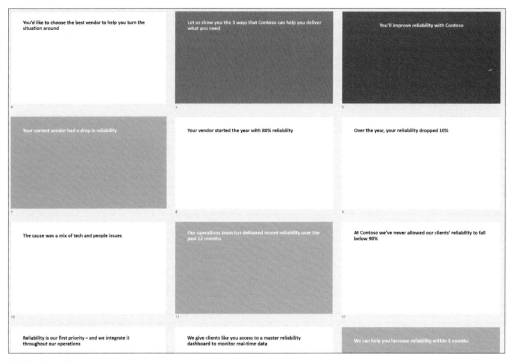

FIGURE 7-1

This chapter will guide you through the process of sketching every slide in your storyboard.

Just as you wrote the verbal essence of your presentation in the story template, your focus now is to sketch the visual essence in the storyboard. Again, don't worry about the artistic quality of the sketches; they are only temporary placeholders for the graphics you'll add to each slide later.

So let's get started at the start, by reviewing a range of sketching possibilities for your Act I slides.

SKETCHING THE ACT I SLIDES

As you saw in Chapter 5, the first five slides of your presentation accomplish the crucial work of orienting the audience to your story and making the experience personal and relevant to them. When you import your headlines into PowerPoint, an additional slide is inserted in front of these five slides; a title slide is automatically created from your title and byline, as shown in Figure 7-2. Now, you will sketch illustrations for the Title slide along with the Act I slides to powerfully complement the clear and coherent flow of ideas you set in motion at the beginning of your story.

Arrange the printouts of the Title and Act I slides in front of you. If you're using a touchscreen computer, review the slides to sketch in Slide Sorter view first, then click on an individual slide to sketch it in Normal view, and then return to Slide Sorter view to review your work.

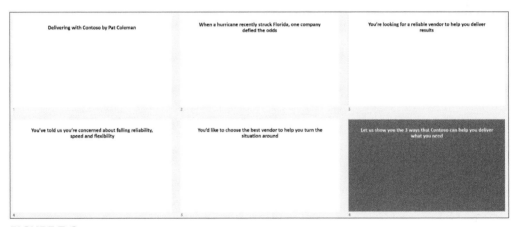

FIGURE 7-2

The Title and Act I slides in the storyboard.

SKETCHING THE TITLE SLIDE

The Title slide will be the first thing to appear on the screen as you begin your talk, so it should intrigue the audience and set the visual tone of the presentation to come. In this instance, as shown in Figure 7-3, sketch a transportation vehicle to illustrate "delivering," as indicated in the title, "Delivering with Contoso."

FIGURE 7-3

A sketch of a Title slide (upper left) and three sketches of a possible Speaker Introduction slide: one with only the logo of your organization, another with three small icons, and a third with only a question mark.

ADDING A SPEAKER INTRODUCTION SLIDE

One of the most overlooked parts of the presentation experience is what happens directly before you start speaking—your introduction to the audience. A good speaker introduction raises an audience's interest in the topic of the presentation and establishes the speaker's authority to give the talk in the first place.

To make sure your presentation gets off to a solid start, plan the way you'll be intro-duced by adding an optional speaker introduction slide. In Slide Sorter view, position the cursor to the right of the title slide in the presentation, and on the Home tab of the Ribbon, in the Slides group, click the bottom of the New Slide button, and then select Blank in the gallery.

What you sketch on this new speaker introduction slide depends on who will be intro-ducing you. If someone else from your organization will introduce you, sketch your organization's logo on the slide, as shown on the upper right slide in Figure 7-3. In this case, only the logo will appear on-screen while that person introduces you. If you're an expert in your field, sketch a photo of the cover of a report or book you've written.

In the notes area of this slide, write the introduction you would like the person who introduces you to read. Keep it brief and informal, and include your relevant creden-tials for the topic of the presentation. This isn't about boosting your ego. To be in the right frame of mind to listen to the presentation, the audience needs to know that you're the right person to be giving this talk. When you meet with the person who will introduce you, provide a printed Notes Page version of this slide to show what will be displayed on the screen along with the script of the introduction you would like that person to read. Ask the person doing the introduction to read it verbatim; many a presenter has gotten off on the wrong foot when they were introduced with incorrect facts, inappropriate comments, or off-color humor.

If you will introduce yourself at the start of your presentation, sketch three visual icons that symbolize who you are in the context of the presentation. For example, as shown on the lower left slide in Figure 7-3, sketch the logo of your organization, which will appear as you describe what you do there. Next, sketch the shape of the state of California, which will appear while you describe your upbringing in the state to your California audience. Finally, sketch the cover of your favorite book or movie, which will appear as you describe how that book or movie shaped who you are today. These three simple images will prompt you to speak naturally, unlock your personality, and connect with your audience. When you add graphics later, animate the images so that they appear in sequence as you click your remote control.

If you're speaking to a small group or conducting a workshop, consider inserting an additional introductory slide asking your audience members to introduce themselves. To illustrate that slide, simply sketch a question mark, as on the lower right slide in Figure 7-3. When the question mark appears on- screen, ask the audience members to introduce themselves and state one thing they would like to accomplish at the event. As each person speaks, use a flip chart or a touchscreen computer to write the names and responses on paper or the screen. This approach demonstrates to the audience that you will listen to them, that you agree to accomplish certain tasks over the course of the presentation, and that you have created a record of the conversation. Review the same flip chart or screen again at the end of the presentation to make sure you covered everything.

SKETCHING THE HOOK SLIDE

Now, you'll sketch the hook slide, which orients the audience to the context of the presentation.

PICTURE A STRONG START

As you probably remember from Chapter 4, the first five slides work their magic by appealing primarily to emotion. To enhance your appeal to emotion, add a full-screen photograph to the slide. If that's the way you want to go in this example, sketch a photo of a hurricane to accompany the headline, as shown on the upper left slide in Figure 7-4.

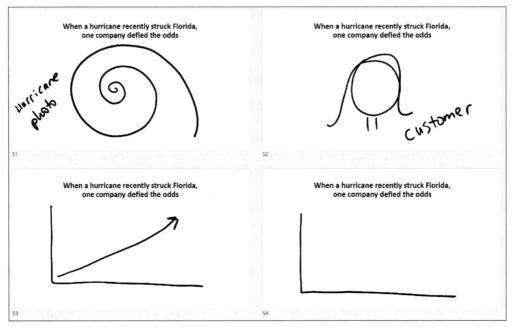

FIGURE 7-4

Four ways to sketch the same hook slide: a photograph of a hurricane, a photo of a customer, a chart, and only the axes of the chart (the line will be drawn by hand).

> **TIP** To explore more than one sketch option for any slide in your storyboard, select the slide in Slide Sorter view, and then click Ctrl+D to duplicate it. Try a different sketch on the duplicated slide, or create several slides and compare them side by side before you decide which sketch you like best.

START WITH AN ANECDOTE

An effective way to start strong is to tell an anecdote—a brief story—while you display a simple graphic. In this case, the anecdote should communicate the point of the headline of the slide. Be sure that your story lasts no more than a minute or two because you have many more slides to present. To illustrate your anecdote, think of the topic of your story; perhaps it is about one of your potential client's customers who faced a challenge that the client solved. In that example, sketch the photo of a customer on the slide, as shown on the upper right slide in Figure 7-4.

When you advance past the Title slide to the Hook slide, say something like, "I know you're expecting me to start with bullet points, but I'm going to start with a story instead. Let me tell you about one of your customers you may not know yet..." Your spoken words and the simple graphic work together to create a sense of surprise, focusing attention on you and what you say next—a good example of a strong way to start.

START WITH A CHART

When you decide what to sketch, choose the visual elements that are the best fit for an audience. For example, if you're presenting to executives in the financial industry, sketch meaningful visuals they are more accustomed to seeing—charts and graphs. When you sketch a chart that everyone in the audience instantly recognizes (as in the example shown on the lower left slide in Figure 7-4), you quickly connect with the audience because you're speaking the same visual language.

START WITH A SIMPLE LINE

To make the chart concept even more powerful, integrate other media into the hook slide to increase engagement and make the experience more interesting. For example, sketch only the two axes of a chart on the slide, as shown on the lower right slide in Figure 7-4. When you show the chart axes, say something like, "I know you all are familiar with what is happening in our business environment." After a pause, position the stylus on the screen of your touchscreen computer and draw a line traveling upward and then downward as you say, "Things have been good, but now they are turning in another direction." Because people don't usually write directly on-screen during a presentation, this technique is sure to be memorable and catch everyone's attention. If you don't have a touchscreen computer, do something similar by drawing the chart axes on a flip chart before your talk and then placing the chart near the podium. When you're ready, move to the flip chart and draw a similar line there.

START WITH A VIDEO

Using a video is a great way to capture everyone's attention at the start of a presentation, especially when you present to large groups. If you have the resources to license or produce a brief video clip to illustrate the headline on the hook slide, sketch a note to indicate you'll use a video on that slide.

SKETCHING THE RELEVANCE SLIDE

Next, on the relevance slide, sketch something that engages the audience and puts them in the middle of the action. If you sketched a photograph on the hook slide, as shown earlier on the upper left slide in Figure 7-4, use the same sketch on this slide and add your audience's logo, as shown on the upper left slide in Figure 7-5. When you arrive at the slide during the presentation, you might improvise on the headline and verbally say, "In the midst of any storm, you need a partner who can help you deliver results."

Similarly, if you sketched a chart on the hook slide, as shown on the lower left slide in Figure 7-4, use it again on the relevance slide. Sketch your logo over the chart to illustrate that your audience needs a partner, as shown on the upper right slide in Figure 7-5. Carrying over the same graphical element from the preceding slide helps to tell the story visually across the two storyboard frames. Your verbal explanation will keep the story flowing, too, as you transition between the two slides by saying something like, "We all agree that you have results you need to deliver." Advance to the relevance slide, and say, "And you need a partner who can help you do that."

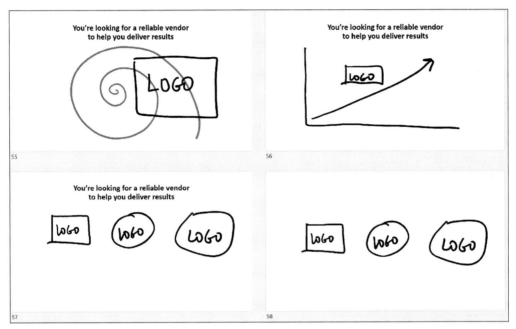

FIGURE 7-5

Four ways to sketch the relevance slide: using the hook slide's photograph and updating the headline, using the hook slide's chart and adding a logo, showing several vendors' logos, and using the logos but hiding the headline.

CREATE A SIMPLE VISUAL PROMPT WITH A PHOTO

If you're feeling bold, sketch the logos of all the vendors interviewing for this contract on the relevance slide, as shown on the lower left slide in Figure 7-5. This visualizes the broader context and relevance of this presentation to your audience, who will see not only your presentation but that of your competitors. By acknowledging that reality, you present yourself as a peer of your audience who really understands where they are, rather than as solely one of many people interviewing for the contract.

HIDE THE HEADLINES

To unlock even more visual power from the three logos in the last example, hide the headline, as shown on the lower right slide in Figure 7-5. When the headline is not visible on the screen, you increase the audience's reliance on you to explain why you are showing this image. To sketch this slide, simply draw a line through the headline. Or go ahead and take care of this now: in Normal view, click on the outer edge of the headline box and drag it off the slide into the blue area above the slide, or change the font color to match the background. The headline now will be hidden from the audience when you show the slide in Slide Show view. When you're working on the slide in Normal view and have dragged the headline off the slide, you'll still be able to view the headline above the slide area.

TAP INTO THE POWER OF PAPER

Although you use a projector to show your slides on-screen, consider what paper does for you, too. Especially for an audience that likely wants to see detailed data, quickly establish credibility by referring to a detailed, printed handout when you display one of the Act I slides. Here say something like, "We crunched the numbers and they're all here, but out of respect for your limited time, we've pulled out what we thought would be most relevant to your situation, which will be the focus of this presentation." Print a handout of your slides, spreadsheets, or whatever other format your data is in. Unless your audience requests them or you think it's appropriate to provide the handouts early, wait until the presentation ends to provide handouts, so you keep the focus on your topic and avoid them becoming a distraction.

SKETCHING THE CHALLENGE AND DESIRE SLIDES

As described in Chapter 4, the challenge slide engages the audience by describing a challenge they face, and the desire slide motivates the audience by affirming what they want in light of the challenge. This gap between challenge and desire forms the dramatic tension you propose to resolve in the rest of the story. Just as the wording you choose for the Challenge and Desire headlines spells the difference between hitting or missing the mark with your audience, what you choose to sketch here will make a difference, too.

Because these two slides are so critical to the entire presentation, sketch them as a pair, as shown in Figure 7-6, as you carefully consider how to connect with the emotions of the audience and confirm that they care about the problem that exists in this gap between the challenge and desire.

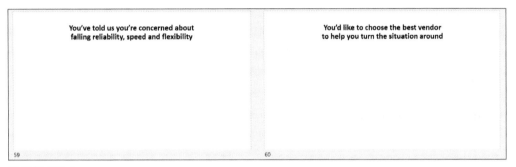

You've told us you're concerned about
falling reliability, speed and flexibility

You'd like to choose the best vendor
to help you turn the situation around

59   60

FIGURE 7-6

It's critical that you hit the mark of the challenge and desire slides, both verbally and visually.

USE AN "EMOTIONAL" CHART

Just as with the hook slide, it might be a good match for your audience to use a chart or graph on these two slides. Sketch a line graph showing the organization's declining reliability, speed, and flexibility on the challenge slide, as shown on the upper left slide in Figure 7-7. On the desire slide, sketch an upward arrow showing improvement, as shown on the upper right slide in Figure 7-7. Although charts are normally considered purely objective displays of information, this chart is sure to stir up emotions if the audience members are unhappy with the numbers shown in the challenge and would like to get to the desire. The use of this particular chart in this context makes an emotional connection with this audience, although in other contexts and to other audiences, the same chart might not work.

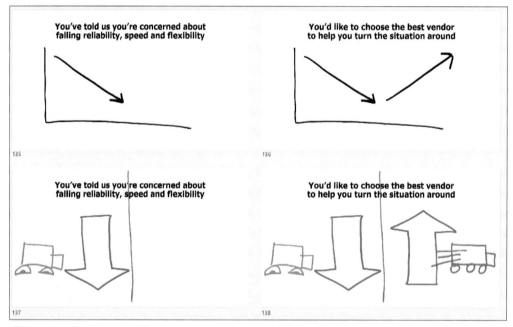

FIGURE 7-7

Two ways to sketch the pair of challenge and desire slides. Top row: Sketch a chart on the challenge slide showing declining performance and then sketch a line showing improvement on the desire slide. Bottom row: A split-screen layout starts with a photo with a downward-facing arrow on the challenge slide; a second photo includes an upward-facing arrow on the desire slide.

DOUBLE YOUR IMPACT BY SPLITTING THE SCREEN

Emphasize the dramatic tension that exists between challenge and desire by sketching two contrasting photographs in juxtaposition. Sketch a line down the middle of both the challenge and desire slides to indicate you are going to place two photos side by side. To the left of the line on the challenge slide, sketch the photograph you would like to represent challenge. For example, sketch a photograph of a transportation vehicle with a flat tire, along with a downward-facing arrow, as shown earlier on the lower left slide in Figure 7-7. The photograph of the vehicle brings the reality of the situation into the room on the slide, and the addition of a downward-facing arrow indicates declining performance. Sketch the same graphic on the left of the desire slide, and then to the right of the midline, sketch a contrasting photograph. In this case, add another photograph of a vehicle in motion, except this time featuring an upward-facing arrow. When you show the slides in sequence, the challenge slide introduces the first photograph as you explain it, and then on the desire slide, the second photo appears directly next to the first. This pair of contrasting images communicates the tension between challenge and desire more powerfully than words ever could.

INTERACT AT THE CHALLENGE AND DESIRE SLIDES

Of all the places in your storyboard where you plan to interact with your audience, the challenge slide is a particularly good one. When you interact with your audience here, open a conversation to get the critical information you need to confirm you are on track. If you hear from your audience that you are off-track with your challenge slide, adapt your verbal narration or follow a different track through the material. (See "Tip 9: Create Nested Storyboards" in Chapter 6 for more information about creating a range of possible pathways through a presentation.)

TAKE A POLL

To engage your audience using the challenge slide on the upper left in Figure 7-7, try one of the oldest and simplest techniques to prompt interaction: ask a question. Sketch a question mark on the chart. The challenge headline is "You've told us you're concerned about falling reliability, speed, and flexibility." When you show this slide to a smaller group, ask an open-ended question such as, "What sort of impact have you personally felt?" and then have a conversation about it. When you show the same slide to a larger audience, ask the question, "How many of you agree?" and then hold up your hand to signal the audience to raise their hands. Quickly count the number of hands and tell the audience the results of the poll as you move on to the next point, saying, "It looks like about two-thirds of you agree. Well, today we're going to talk about..."

Taking a quick poll like this makes the audience feel like they're part of the conversation and also gives you a gauge of where the audience stands in relation to the topic. Vary this technique with larger audiences by providing the audience with interactive polling devices, which some companies build specifically for PowerPoint. When you ask the audience a question, the results of the poll are displayed directly on your challenge slide in the form of a chart that summarizes the polling results. The same thing can be accomplished using Twitter and other social media tools.

INTRODUCE THE THEME

So far, you've focused on numbers and charts to start off strong with your audience. Another way to go is to sketch out a theme as it plays out over the challenge and desire slides. If you chose to incorporate a theme through the headlines of your story template, now you'll extend this recurring theme from your written words to the sketches of your slides.

For example, if you use a puzzle theme in the story template, the challenge headline might read, "The pieces of our strategy from the past no longer fit together, and you're feeling the impact." The desire headline might be, "You'd like to find a new way to put the puzzle together." As shown in Figure 7-8, sketch 3 puzzle pieces on the upper left challenge slide to visually refer to the "pieces." Sketch the pieces coming together on the upper right desire slide to "put the puzzle together."

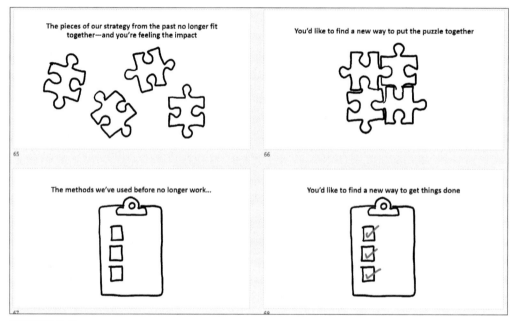

FIGURE 7-8

Two ways to sketch the pair of challenge and desire slides. Top row: Introduce the theme of scattered puzzle pieces, and then show the pieces coming together to form a picture. Bottom row: The challenge slide shows a clipboard with empty checkboxes, and the desire slide shows the checkboxes selected.

An alternative theme might have a challenge headline that reads, "The methods we've used before no longer work..." and a desire headline that reads, "You'd like to find a new way to get things done." As shown in the bottom row in Figure 7-8, sketch the clipboard with empty checkboxes on the challenge slide, and then sketch check marks in the same boxes on the desire slide.

Later, add simple animation to the elements on the challenge and desire slides because these slides serve the important function of capturing the audience's attention in Act I. In the examples on the top row in Figure 7-8, sketch a note to animate the puzzle pieces to appear separately on the challenge slide and then come together to form the picture on the desire slide. On the slides in the bottom row, make the checkboxes appear on the clipboard on the challenge slide, and then make the check marks appear one by one on the desire slide.

UNLOCK INFORMATION WITH A VISUAL PROMPT

To use interaction to obtain useful information from your audience, sketch a simple photo object that relates to your topic on one or both challenge and desire slides, and then use the photo to prompt conversation about specific topics. For example, if your challenge headline reads, "What worked in the past isn't working anymore, and you're feeling the impact," sketch graphics that indicate the various possible impacts. For example, sketch a dollar sign for money lost or a clock for wasted time. Hide the headline on the slide, and when the graphics on the slide appear, say, "There are many ways the situation is changing. What are the ones that are most important to you?"

LINK THE ACT I SLIDES WITH A VISUAL STORY

To tie together tightly the slides in this example, sketch a single unifying image across all of Act I to make it a backdrop. Figure 7-9 shows how to do this. The title slide includes a sketch of a logo, the hook slide shows a hurricane photo to set up the anecdote, and then the relevance slide shows the hurricane with the Contoso logo indicating you're an established problem-solver. The challenge slide uses a chart indicating declining performance, and the desire slide adds an upward arrow indicating the desired point—improved performance. The final map slide adds the Contoso logo next to the improved results, which ties together the familiar visual elements with the core message of the presentation.

This is a good example of how your slides are no longer like pieces of paper filled with lists of facts. Now, your slides are like frames in a filmstrip, moving at a pace of about one frame per minute, with your voice providing the soundtrack to a clear and compelling story. Although to the audience, your presentation is a single smooth and seamless experience.

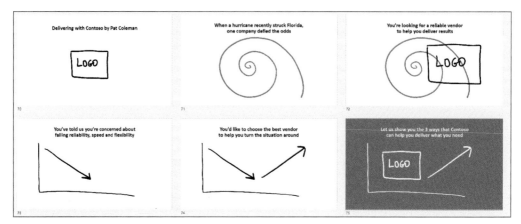

FIGURE 7-9

Telling a visual story across all the Act I slides.

TIP Build the same sort of visual story across the frames of Act I by sketching a single photograph, copying it to each slide, and then sketching additional elements on each slide. If you present using a touchscreen computer, sketch graphical elements directly on the photograph for more impact.

To increase the visual impact of these Act I slides, sketch a note on the slides reminding you that you plan to hide the headlines so that only the graphics are visible to the audience. As described earlier, in the instances when you present slides without headlines, the simple graphics make the audience rely on you to describe the slides' meaning, which creates an engaging interdependence between speaker and audience. This is an effective technique to use in your Act I slides while you make an emotional connection with your audience. Later, on the Act II slides, you'll usually want to keep your headlines visible to your audience to guide their attention through more complex types of information.

Although in this example the map slide shown in Figure 7-9 was sketched as part of the group of Act I slides, be sure you visually integrate it with the important anchor slides, as you'll do next.

TOUCHSCREEN SKETCHING TIPS
The best way to sketch a visual story across slides is to work backward from the last slide to the first.

1. For example, in the sequence of slides shown in Figure 7-9, first sketch all the elements you want to include on the lower right map slide.

2. Hold down the Ctrl key while you click to select the Ink objects you want to include, and then right-click and select Copy.

3. Go to the preceding slide, right-click and paste the Ink objects, and then on the Pens tab, click Eraser and move the mouse pointer over the parts of the sketch you don't need.

4. Then copy this sketch, and follow the same steps as you work backward through the slides.

Designing the last slide in the sequence first ensures that the final slide is organized and composed in a way that works. If you were to build from the first slide to the last, you would probably end up making changes to the last slide's layout. Working backward through the sequence also saves time because you don't need to sketch the same elements on the different slides in the sequence. Unfortunately, inking on your touchscreen computer works only in Normal view and not in Slide Sorter view, so you'll need to switch back and forth between the two views to see how the story is flowing visually across slides.

SKETCHING THE MAP AND ANCHOR SLIDES

Your next job is to sketch the most important group of slides in the presentation—the map and anchor slides. If you're working on paper printouts, gather these slides. If you're using a touchscreen computer, to see the anchor slides together, zoom out in Slide Sorter view, and then locate the anchor slides. Drag each one in sequence so that they follow the map slide, as shown in Figure 7-10. When you've finished sketching, you'll drag these slides back to their original positions. You don't have to do this every time you sketch, but it is helpful as you're honing your storyboarding skills. It's important that you see and work with these four slides together as a visual package because when each slide appears in its sequence in the storyboard, it should cue the audience that these are the most important slides in the presentation.

The Map headline summarizes the Anchor headlines, and in turn, the Anchor headlines summarize the Explanation headlines, and the Explanation headlines summarize the backup slides. Because the Map headline sits at the top of the informational hierarchy, as described in Chapter 5, it is really the verbal summary of the entire presentation. Likewise, what you sketch on the map slide should be a visual summary of the anchor slides and the entire presentation. If you had only one slide to show, this one would be it.

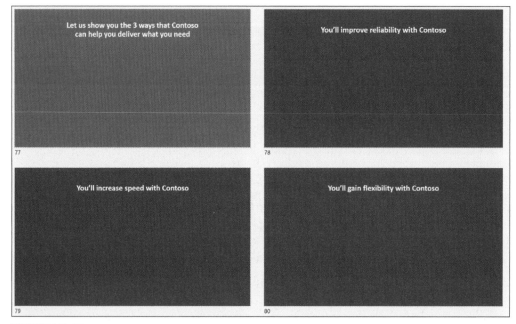

FIGURE 7-10

The orange map and dark blue anchor slides should be the most visually memorable in the storyboard.

Because this group of slides formed by the map and three anchor slides is so important, sketch them using the most creative, memorable, and powerful techniques you can create. If you have a marketing background, apply the most powerful "branding" techniques you know—the set of techniques to visually distill a message and integrate it into an experience. The only difference here is that you're applying them to the highest level of ideas in your presentation.

Following are a range of techniques to "brand" the top level of your thinking on your map and three anchor slides. These sketching ideas are some of the basics; as you become comfortable with sketching, try out your own ideas, or invite a graphic designer to give you a hand.

TRIPLING YOUR IMPACT WITH THREE PANELS

A simple yet effective visual technique is to sketch full-screen photographs to illustrate each of the anchor slides. Full-screen photographs are a good fit on the map and three anchor slides if they function to make the ideas of the headlines memorable. In the example shown on the upper right slide in Figure 7-11, the first anchor slide refers to "reliability," so the sketch of the photograph is a vehicle driving through snow. The second anchor slide, on the lower left, refers to "speed," so that sketch illustrates an odometer. The third anchor slide refers to "flexibility," so the sketch is of a driver who can adapt to changing circumstances.

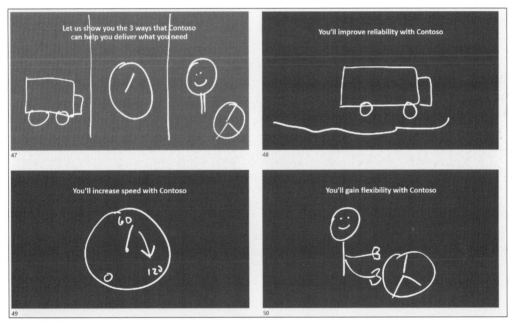

FIGURE 7-11

Sketches of the map slide with a three-panel layout and the anchor slides with full-screen photographs.

Now that you've sketched three photographs on the anchor slides, use these elements to sketch a triptych, or a single slide with three vertical graphical elements placed side by side. To create a triptych on the map slide (upper left), draw two vertical lines on the slide to create three panels, and then sketch in each of the three panels a key visual concept from each of the three photographs that were sketched on the anchor slides. As you present them in sequence, these sketches on the map slide form a tight, crisp visual package and provide a preview of the material you're about to cover.

> **TIP**   When you're brainstorming a visual concept, and you are looking for more ideas,
> type the concept into a search engine. When you get the results, click the Images tab to view
> what other people have done to illustrate the concept.

ADDING IT UP WITH ICONS

Another approach related to the three-panel photographs is to sketch simple icons
that represent the essence of your idea in a basic visual form. For example, add a sketch
of "1-2-3" on the map slide that illustrates you'll cover "Three ways that Contoso can
help you deliver what you need." Then sketch a simple icon that illustrates the headline
of each anchor, as in Figure 7-11, except now create a "build" of the three icons across
the slides. Sketch a truck on the first anchor slide, copy it to the second anchor slide in
addition to a speedometer. Next, copy both sketches and add them to the third anchor
slide in addition to a fleet of trucks, as shown in Figure 7-12.

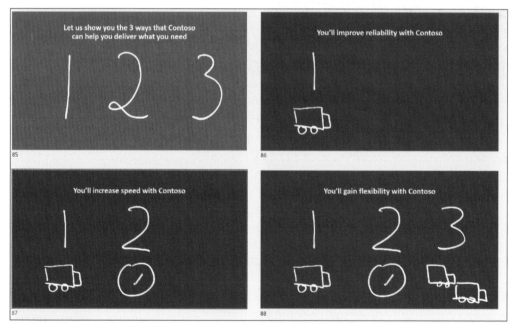

FIGURE 7-12

Map and three anchor slides with icons in a diagram format.

As shown here, you build a simple three-step diagram out of the icons by adding the numbers 1-2-3 above each icon.

PROPPING IT UP

A classic technique in oral presentations is to show a physical prop and explain how the object relates to the presentation. The map and three anchor slides are a good place to integrate a prop, especially when you tie in that prop with your theme. For example, hold up a numbered puzzle piece when you present each anchor slide to carry through a puzzle theme. Or better yet, pass out to your audience their own numbered puzzle pieces to hold. They will literally carry the main message of the presentation out of the room in their hands, and undoubtedly in their long-term memories too. If you plan to use a physical prop, sketch a photograph of it on the map and three anchor slides. During the presentation, you'll show the photo of the prop on the screen while you display the prop physically in the room.

USING VIDEO, SOUND, OR MOTION GRAPHICS (SPARINGLY)

If you plan to use video, audio, or motion graphics in your presentation, these forms of media stand out so significantly from your slides that you want to use them carefully and strategically. Before you use them, consider the research study described in Chapter 2 that found when you remove extraneous information from a multimedia presentation, you increase learning.

Remember, in Act II, it's all about the hierarchy in your storyboard. Your measure of success is whether your audience recalls and applies the information shown on your anchor slides. If you plan to use video, sound, or motion graphics to illustrate the Anchor headlines, go ahead and sketch these elements on the anchor slides. Be very careful about using these types of media in another part of the presentation if you don't use them on your anchor slides. You would be unsuccessful in your presentation if the audience remembered your trendy video on the backup slides but not the message of your anchor slides.

BLACKING OUT THE SCREEN
Consider fading to black to empha-size the anchor slides. Visuals projected on a screen are spellbinding, but when you break that spell by blacking out the screen, you focus the audience's attention completely on you and your ideas at a specific moment. This creates an abrupt shift in the presentation with dramatic effect that works well to emphasize important points.

The best way to black out a screen is to change the background of your slide to black: Right-click the slide, and then select Format Background, and in the Format Background pane, click Solid Fill and in the Color gallery, click Black. Make sure the Transparency control is set to 0 percent. Making the background of any slide black in your storyboard ensures that when you review the presentation in Slide Sorter view, you see exactly where among the sequence of slides you will fade to black and what happens on the slides immediately before and after.

An alternate way to black out a screen without changing the background of your slides is to use the B key. When you present your slides in Slide Show view, press the B key on your keyboard, or the appropriate button on your remote control, to turn the screen to black. Then, as all eyes turn to you, you'll emphasize the anchor verbally. When you've finished, press the B key again to return to the same slide. (Alternatively, press the W key to turn the screen to white.)

RAISING INTEREST WITH YOUR LAYOUTS

A striking way to set up your map and three anchor slides is to use a distinctive layout to make them stand out among all the other slides in the storyboard. In Chapter 6, you set up a preliminary darker blue background on the anchor slides when you set up the storyboard. Change those placeholder backgrounds to something more striking. For example, use a split-screen layout on the anchor slides. This layout style, shown in Figure 7-13, is a quick and easy way to set up these slides for sketches, and it's a particularly good fit for using icons as described earlier in this chapter.

In Chapter 8, you'll explore PowerPoint features to set up and apply different layouts to the different levels of the storyboard. For now, if you want to quickly set up these slides to see how they look when you sketch on them in split-screen layout format, go to Normal view for the first anchor slide. On the Insert tab, in the Illustrations group, click Shapes and then select Rectangle. Position the cursor in the upper right of the slide, click and drag until the rectangle fills half the screen, and then right-click the box and add a white fill. Then click and drag the headline to the left and click and drag the sizing handles to fit the headline, as shown on the upper right slide in

Figure 7-13. Copy and paste the rectangle into the other two anchor slides and adjust the headlines. On the map slide, add a horizontal white rectangle to the middle of the slide to distinguish this slide from the anchor slides, as shown on the upper left slide in Figure 7-13. Once you have the temporary layouts in place on the map and three anchor slides, sketch on the slides as usual.

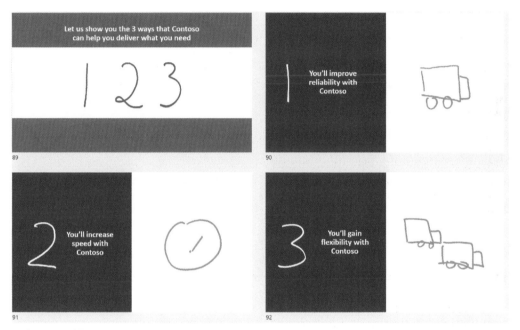

FIGURE 7-13

Sketches of the map and three anchor slides with a split-screen layout on the anchor slides.

KEEPING THE THEME FLOWING

Your sketches will start to strengthen your visual story if you have used a theme throughout your story template. For example, carry the puzzle theme from the Act I slides to the map slide, as shown on the upper left slide in Figure 7-14. Beginning with the third anchor slide on the lower right, sketch three puzzle pieces together with the numbers *1-2-3*, then put the first two puzzle pieces on the second anchor slide on the lower left, and then put the first puzzle piece on the first anchor slide on the upper right.

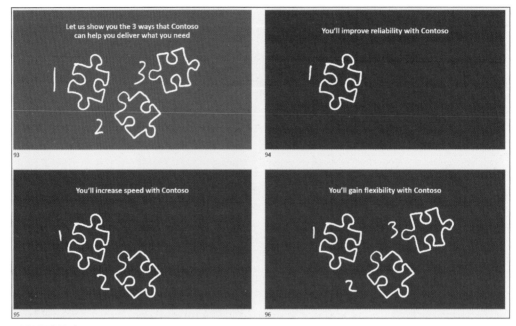

FIGURE 7-14

Sketches of the map and three anchor slides with a puzzle theme.

The photos in this example might be full-screen photos or simple photo objects with the backgrounds cut out. Or if you want to get really creative, bring the puzzle theme and the photos together by sketching each photo inside a puzzle piece.

PAUSING AT THE END OF EACH ANCHOR SECTION

Just as the challenge and desire slides are good places to ask questions and prompt dialogue, other good places to do that are just before the second and third anchor slides. To plan for audience interaction at these points, go to Slide Sorter view after you sketch your anchor slides, select Anchor 1, and then press Ctrl+D to duplicate the slide. Drag the duplicate Anchor 1 slide to just before the Anchor 2 slide. Now select Anchor 2, duplicate it, and drag the duplicate to just before Anchor 3.

After you present the explanation and backup slides that follow Anchor 1, you'll see the Anchor 1 slide again, and there you'll pause to ask your audience for questions. When you've finished, advance to the Anchor 2 slide. Pause again after the Anchor 2 slide, and then advance to Anchor 3. You also might choose to duplicate these slides in Chapter 8, after you've added graphics to visually reinforce the anchor slides at the end of the first and second Act II scenes.

PRESENTING WITH MORE THAN ONE SPEAKER

Some organizations feature multiple speakers during a presentation; if you plan to do that, put each of three speakers in charge of one of the three anchor sections. Hand over the microphone to the next speaker when it is that person's turn to present the assigned section of anchor, explanation, and backup slides. The change of speaker adds emphasis to each of the anchor slides, but because the presentation is constructed from a single underlying story template, the audience members experience a single story that makes sense to them. Sketch a note on each anchor slide of the name of the assigned speaker if you plan to do this.

Next, you'll explore a visual way to link the rest of the slides to come—by sketching a navigation bar.

SKETCHING AN OPTIONAL NAVIGATION BAR

Tie together the slides of the presentation even more tightly with a visual navigation bar at the bottom of the screen. In the conventional PowerPoint approach, the space at the bottom of a screen usually contains the presenting organization's logo. Sketch your own organization's logo to illustrate the point of any single slide in the storyboard if the headline calls for that, or sketch the logo on the Introductory slide, as described earlier. However, don't place your logo on every slide because it sends the wrong visual message that every slide is all about you when it is really all about the audience.

A good way to use the small space at the bottom of the explanation and backup slides is to visually cue your audience to the organization of, and current location within, the presentation. For example, if you use a puzzle theme through the presentation, add a small horizontal bar at the bottom of the subsequent explanation and backup slides after you sketch the first puzzle piece on the first anchor slide. Then sketch a small puzzle piece throughout these slides, as shown in Figure 7-15. You'll learn how to set up and apply navigation bars using custom layouts in Chapter 8.

After you add a second puzzle piece to the second anchor slide, add a similar puzzle piece to the navigation bar through the rest of the explanation and backup slides in this section, as shown in Figure 7-16. Then, after you add a third puzzle piece to the third anchor slide, add three similar puzzle pieces to the navigation bar through the rest of the Explanation and backup slides in that section.

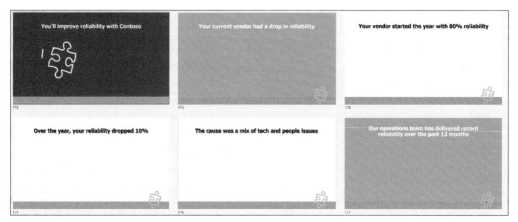

FIGURE 7-15

The lighter blue explanation slides and white backup slides now include a navigation bar with a single puzzle piece.

As the audience views the slides in sequence, the navigation bar appears the same, until you reach the slides in the subsequent anchor section, when they see a new puzzle piece appear, which cues them that they are in a new section.

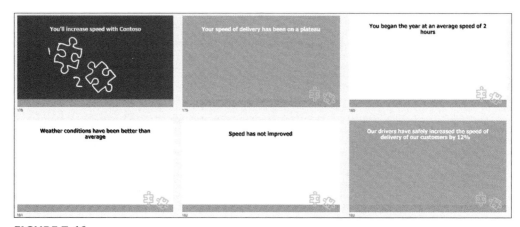

FIGURE 7-16

The second anchor slide, the explanation slides, and backup slides with a navigation bar with a second puzzle piece added.

SKETCHING THE EXPLANATION SLIDES

Your next job is to sketch the second-most important slides in the presentation—the explanation slides for each scene of Act II. In Slide Sorter view, zoom out to locate the lighter blue explanation slides, and then drag each one to follow their corresponding anchor slide to see them together, as shown in Figure 7-17. When you've finished sketching, you'll drag these slides back to their previous positions. As with the map and three anchor slides, it's important that you see and work with these four slides together as a package, just as each anchor headline summarizes the explanation headlines to come, each anchor slide should visually summarize its explanation slides.

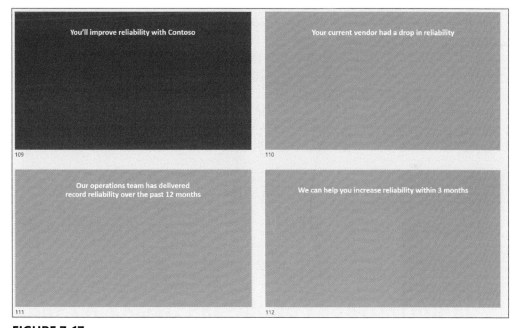

FIGURE 7-17

The first darker blue anchor slide and its corresponding lighter blue explanation slides.

Look at the sketch you created for the anchor slide, and then read your explanation headlines and imagine how to sketch the story forward across these slides. Sketch a single visual story across the explanation slides if it's possible. But it might be that the explanation slides are independent facts that are tied together only by the preceding anchor slide and not to one another. If the explanation slides stand alone as independent ideas, sketch a standalone illustration for each one and use other techniques to visually tie the explanation slides together, such as using a similar split-screen layout or a navigation bar running through the explanation slides, as described earlier.

TIP If you have difficulty sketching the explanation slides, sketch the backup slides first and then return to the explanation slides. This approach is helpful because the explanation slide summarizes the backup slides to come, and if you sketch the backup slides first, use them to come up with a visual summary for the explanation slide.

SKETCHING A VISUAL ORGANIZER

Earlier in Figure 7-8, the sketch of a clipboard with checkboxes served to carry an idea across the challenge and desire slides visually. Try a similar concept using checkboxes to organize your ideas across your explanation slides visually. On the upper left in Figure 7-18, the anchor slide features a sketch of a clipboard with three checkboxes to illustrate the three points you'll make. Sketch the first explanation slide (upper right) with only the top box checked to illustrate the first explanation headline, and then on the second explanation slide (lower left), add a second checkmark to illustrate the second explanation headline. On the third explanation slide (lower right), add a third checkmark to illustrate the point you'll make on the third headline.

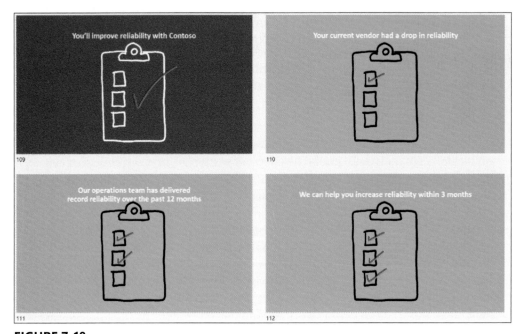

FIGURE 7-18

Sketches of an anchor slide and explanation slides using a checklist to tie them tightly together visually.

As they appear in sequence, the anchor slide introduces the simple visual concept of the clipboard with three checkboxes. The first explanation slide introduces the concept of the first item with a check mark, the next slide builds on the preceding one and adds a second check mark, and then the third slide builds on the preceding slide and adds a final check mark. When each explanation slide is dragged back to its position in the storyboard, it introduces another layer of meaning to the visual checklist story and at the same time ties together the backup slides that follow.

SKETCHING HEADLINE-ONLY EXPLANATION SLIDES

When you deliver a 15-minute version of your presentation, you will spend the bulk of time on your nine explanation slides that back up your three anchor slides. But when you deliver a 45-minute version of your presentation, you won't spend much time on the explanation slides because they only serve as a quick summary of what is to come in the backup slides. If that's the case, and if you're pressed for time to find graphics, plan to use the headline alone. Sketch a downward-facing arrow that notes you will move the headlines down to the center of the slide, as shown in the upper right slide in Figure 7-19.

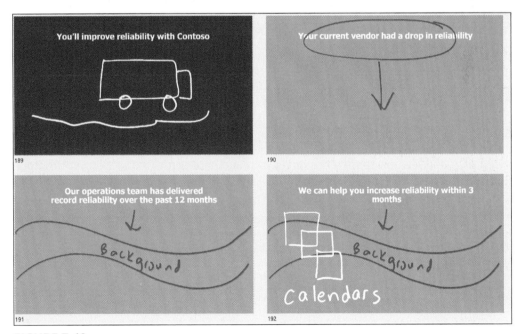

FIGURE 7-19

Sketches of an anchor slide and explanation slides that show headline only, headline with a background, and headline with a background and graphic.

If you think a headline alone will be too stark, sketch on the slide a shape you would like to add to the background, as shown in the lower left slide. And if you have the time to find a graphic, sketch a small graphic to add to the background shape that illustrates the headline of the explanation slide, as shown in the lower right slide—in this case a stack of three calendar pages to illustrate the headline that references three months.

USING A SCREEN CAPTURE   For a quick illustration, consider sketching a screen capture. Anything viewable on a computer screen can be captured and displayed on a slide, including pictures of your desktop, Web pages, documents, and more. For example, use a screen capture to convey more detailed quantitative information available in other documents. Each dollar amount or other piece of quantitative information included in a headline is likely derived from a spreadsheet or another data source that reflects the detailed analysis that produced it. You could probably spend an hour discussing the details of any single figure, but if you did that, you wouldn't have time to cover any of the other points in the presentation.

Instead, sketch a screen capture of a close-up of a spreadsheet that you will add to the slide, and when you display the slide, explain that the detailed data is contained there. Sketch a note on the slide that you will also bring printouts of the spreadsheet providing the detailed financial analysis and explanation that support the headline. Now the headline communicates the main idea you want to get across, the tightly cropped screen capture of the spreadsheet indicates you have a backup for your point, your verbal explanation conveys what you intend, and the printouts hold the detailed information you will have readily available.

When you've finished sketching the explanation slides, in Slide Sorter view, drag each slide back to where it belongs in the sequence of the storyboard. Now look at the storyboard and see how these slides guide your audience across the sections of the storyboard—with an anchor slide, explanation slide, and then backup slides all carrying the visual story forward.

SKETCHING THE BACKUP SLIDES

Your last job is to sketch the third-most important slides in the presentation—the backup slides that follow each explanation slide. In Slide Sorter view, zoom in to see a set of explanation and backup slides together, as shown in Figure 7-20. It's important that you see and work with these four slides together as a package because when you write out an Explanation headline in Act II, it summarizes the backup headlines that come next. Similarly, each explanation slide should be a visual summary of the backup slides.

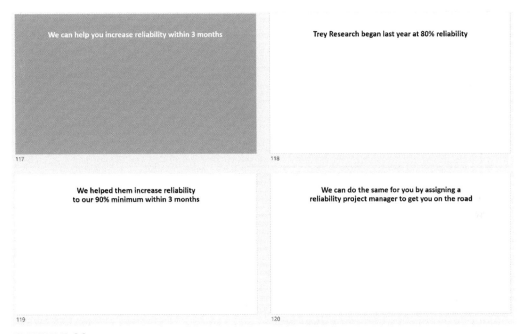

FIGURE 7-20

A lighter blue explanation slide and the following three white backup slides.

Look at the sketch of the explanation slide, and then read the following backup head-lines and imagine how to sketch the story forward across the backup slides. Sketch a single visual story across the backup slides if it's possible. But it might be that the backup slides are independent thoughts that are tied together only by the preceding explanation slide; in that case, sketch standalone illustrations for each backup slide.

EXPLAINING IDEAS BY BUILDING A DIAGRAM

A common problem in conventional PowerPoint presentations occurs when a diagram or chart is too complex to be understood—or at least not understood all at once on a single slide. If your audience is new to the information in any diagram or chart, you will easily overwhelm the limited capacity of their working memory and impair learn-ing if you show too much at once. You address the underlying root of this problem by breaking down anchor headlines in the story template into smaller pieces as you write the explanation and backup headlines, which later become the foundation for indi-vidual slides that appear on-screen for less than a minute while you narrate each slide.

Because you have used this approach, instead of explaining a great deal of information in a diagram on a single slide for many minutes, explain the same information in smaller pieces for less than a minute each, across a series of slides. Doing so ensures you present new information evenly over the sequence of slides of any explanation, showing and saying only the correct information at the correct time to ensure you do not overload or split the attention of the working memory of your audience between what you are saying and showing at any moment.

Building a visual story across the corresponding series of backup slides is an effective way to illustrate your ideas. For example, sketch on your explanation slide a few calendar pages to show you can improve reliability in three months, as shown on the upper left slide in Figure 7-21. Then carry through the story across the three backup slides. On the first backup slide, shown on the upper right slide, sketch a chart showing the starting point of reliability. On the second backup slide, sketch the improved situation on the chart, as shown lower left; and then on the third backup slide, sketch a photo of the person in your company that would help make the improvement happen, as shown lower right.

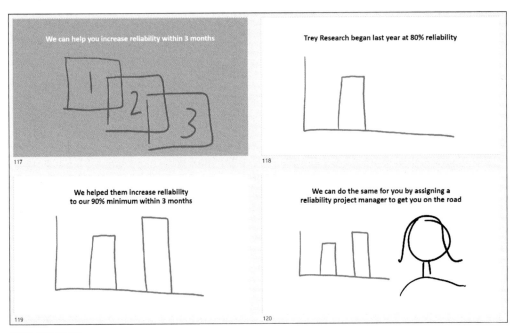

FIGURE 7-21

Sketches of an anchor slide and explanation slides explaining backup detail across the slides.

MY DIAGRAM DOESN'T FIT! If you have a diagram you've used in other presentations and you'd like to fit it into your new BBP presentation, go to the story template and figure out where the pieces of the explanation of the diagram fit into the overall story. If the diagram contains information that is new to the audience, you need to break it up into smaller pieces to ease the new information through the working memory of your audience. As you use the story template to explain the diagram, think of the three main parts of the diagram and describe them in the anchor headlines. Then complete the story template as before, breaking up each anchor piece into smaller pieces in the explanation headlines and then breaking each explanation sub-piece into smaller pieces in the backup headlines. When you return to the storyboard to revise the storyboard headlines, you'll have laid the groundwork for a series of slides that explains the new information in the diagram piece by piece, slide by slide—rather than all at once.

When you apply the same approach to other types of diagrams, you will make sure that you properly synchronize the verbal and visual channels of working memory, as described in Chapter 2. When you present your slides this way, you also align with the research-based *temporal contiguity principle* described in Richard E. Mayer's research, which is based on studies that show that people understand information better when animation and narration are presented together rather than animation first and narration second.

BUILDING A CHART ACROSS A SERIES OF SLIDES

After you have broken up an idea into smaller pieces across a set of backup headlines in the story template, build a chart across the corresponding series of backup slides to illustrate quantitative information. With the sequence of headlines in place in the storyboard, you'll know what you want to communicate before you start building the chart. Again, this is where the wording of the headlines in the story template will define what you sketch. Build a chart across a series of backup slides if the headlines contain a specific quantitative explanation, such as "The industry average returns are 20 percent" and "Your average returns are 10 percent" and then "We can help you close the gap." If your headlines don't explain a chart, but you would like them to do so, return to the story template to see how to revise the headlines to make the chart work.

TIP If you find that your headlines don't quite map to the sequence in which you want to present information, return to the story template and adjust the headlines there first. Then return to PowerPoint to edit the headlines accordingly.

COMPLETING THE BACKUP SLIDES

You should be getting the hang of things by now because you've already sketched many of the elements that you also sketch on the backup slides. Here are some of the techniques to use to sketch the backup slides:

■ **Use a chart, graph, or diagram.** As in the previous levels, sketch graphics for your backup slides, such as a chart, as shown on the upper right slide in Figure 7-22, or a diagram that illustrates the headlines as shown on the lower right slide.

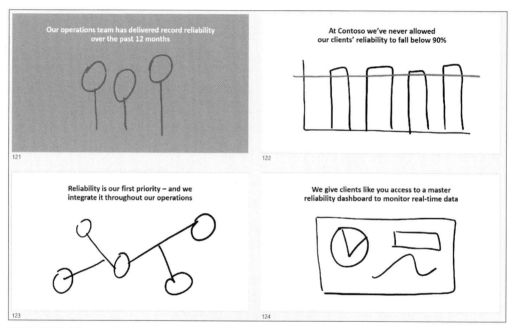

FIGURE 7-22

An explanation slide with a photo and backup slides with a chart, a diagram, and a screen capture.

■ **Use photos, screen captures, or other graphics.** As with all the other slides you've sketched so far, consider the use of photographs to illustrate a point, such as the photo of the team shown on the explanation slide on the upper left slide. If a photo alone doesn't work, consider a screen capture such as shown on the lower right slide in Figure 7-22.

SWITCHING TO OTHER MEDIA

Plan to switch out of PowerPoint into another software application to demonstrate an activity that you plan to cover in your backup slides. For example, an instructor would switch over to Excel to demonstrate how to use one of its features, or to Word to show how to edit a document. During the presentation, when you arrive at an explanation slide, verbally explain the point of the headline. Then switch over to the other application to demonstrate the points you covered on the backup slide. Then return to the PowerPoint slide when you're finished. Before the presentation, hide the backup slides because you will cover those points during the live demonstration.

SWITCH BETWEEN APPLICATIONS DURING A PRESENTATION

Hold down the Alt key and press the Tab key, and then press the Tab key again until you select the corresponding software application that is open on your desktop, and then release the Alt key. After you've shown what you need to illustrate the headline, press Alt+Tab again until you select the software application you want to use next.

With this technique, you're using PowerPoint as the foundation for managing what's happening on-screen. As always, the headlines of the slides establish the ideas you want to communicate at any and every point in the presentation.

Similarly, switch over to other non-PowerPoint media to provide variety in the presentation, including:

- Flip chart, whiteboard, or chalkboard
- A document projector
- Video clips, audio, or motion graphics
- A physical prop
- Paper handouts

ADAPTING YOUR SKETCHES TO YOUR PROFESSION

As you're thinking about what other sketches to include on your backup slides, review the optional Act II headings in the section "Tip 3: Tailor Your Act II Column Headings to Your Profession," in Chapter 5. For example, if you're a market researcher, your backup slides will probably include sketches of screen captures that illustrate your analytical tools, brief video clips from focus groups, and of course charts, graphs, and diagrams. If you're an attorney, your backup slides will contain sketches of your specific evidence, such as screen captures of your "hot documents," photographs, short clips from video depositions, and scientific drawings. If you're selling a software product, your backup slides will include sketches of the various sections of your product demonstration.

SKETCHING YOUR STORY TEMPLATE

It might take some time to learn the new skills of sketching your slides across frames and levels. If you're having a tough time figuring out how to sketch diagrams, charts, and other explanation or backup slide elements, leave PowerPoint for a few minutes and review a printed copy of your story template. Read through the headlines from top to bottom in the explanation column, and sketch directly over the column how you want to illustrate each explanation slide. For example, create a diagram, as shown in Figure 7-23. Then read through the headlines in the Backup column, and sketch how to illustrate each backup slide. For example, use a diagram, chart, or video clip. Here, it might be easier to see that the sketch of each explanation slide should be a summary and introduction of the adjacent Backup headlines to the right.

Explanation (15 minutes)	Backup (45 minutes)
Your current vendor had a drop in reliability	Your vendor started the year with 80% reliability
	Over the year, your reliability dropped 10%
	The cause was a mix of tech and people issues
Our operations team has delivered record reliability over the past 12 months	At Contoso we've never allowed our clients' reliability to fall below 90%
	Reliability is our first priority – and we integrate it throughout our operations
	We give clients like you access to a master reliability dashboard to monitor real-time data
	Trey Research began last year at

FIGURE 7-23

Sketch what you want to illustrate directly on a printout of the story template.

TIP   Sketching directly on the story template connects you back with the verbal story you wrote and helps you see what you're trying to accomplish from a different perspective. To sketch directly on the story template while you work with a team, place a screen capture of the story template on a slide and mark it up with with the Drawing and Pen tools while it is displayed on a screen in the room.

Keep this technique in mind when you're writing the story template for the first time and as you go forward with your sketches in the storyboard.

BBP CHECKLIST: SKETCHING THE STORYBOARD

Do your storyboard sketches clearly show

- Where your Act I, anchor, explanation, and backup slides are?
- How you tell your story across frames, at each level of the storyboard?
- Which graphics you'll use?
- Where you will use interaction, props, and other media?

READY, SET, SKETCH!

Now that you have a range of techniques in mind, sketch every slide in the entire storyboard first, even if you already have some finished graphics that you know you want to use. Doing so helps you avoid getting caught up in the visual details of individual slides that prevent you from spending time on the rest of the slides. After you have a sketch for every slide in place, you'll review the entire storyboard in Slide Sorter view in Chapter 8; this review allows you to assess how much time you have to add graphics, where you need to spend your time first, what resources you have to get things done, and who to ask for help if you need it.

The more you practice sketching your storyboard, the more skilled you'll become. Just as with writing the story template, it helps to bring in other people to collaborate with you on the storyboard. If you're using a touchscreen computer, project the storyboard on a screen and sketch together; if you're using paper, tape printed copies of individual slides on the wall and collaborate that way. And just as you do when you verbally edit the story template, look for ways to visually edit, tighten, and improve your storyboard.

When you have a fully sketched storyboard in hand, it's time to turn the sketches into finished graphics as you complete your final storyboard in the next chapter.

8

GETTING GRAPHICS, QUICK AND EASY

In this chapter, you will:

- Review the three guidelines for adding graphics.
- Apply custom layouts to the different sections of the storyboard.
- Add graphics to your storyboard.

Turning words into visuals can be a daunting task for anybody, especially if you're used to putting mostly bullet points on your slides. Fortunately, you've already done significant work to prepare the way for this moment; you have in hand a storyboard that includes all the slides in your presentation, and each slide includes a sketch that indicates the specific graphic you want to add.

WHICH GRAPHICS DO I ADD TO EACH SLIDE?

Like completing the story template, adding final graphics to your storyboard is both easy and hard. It's easy because all you need to do is use your sketch as a guide to "fill in the blank" below the headline on each slide with the graphic that the sketch describes. But it's also hard because you have a potentially unlimited range of graphics and styles to choose from, and you must find the ones that are the best match for both you and your audience. Especially if working with graphics is a new skill for you, this project might feel daunting right now. However, think of approaching this task

just as you would any other project—by first assessing the current state of the project, then figuring out what needs to be done, and then planning for how you're going to accomplish that. This chapter will help you through the process of adding graphics to your storyboard step by step, helping you to break up the project into smaller, more manageable tasks that will make your work quick and easy.

DEFINING YOUR DESIGN CONSTRAINTS

Every graphic design project has constraints—as much as you might want to take your time creating a work of art, the reality might be that you have only until this afternoon or tomorrow to create a visual story masterpiece. It's important to know up front what limits you're facing so that you can plan your project accordingly. Do that by asking a few questions:

■ **What is the scope of the project?** Look at your presentation in Slide Sorter view, as shown in Figure 8-1, to get a sense of the number of graphics you'll need to find. You should first identify where you will *not* need graphics and eliminate those slides from your count. For example, if you're giving only a 15-minute version of your presentation, you will hide the backup slides, as described in Chapter 6, and focus your efforts on the other slides you need. Likewise, if you'll be switching over to another software application to present the ideas on some of the backup slides, you won't need to add graphics to those slides either because you'll hide those slides as well.

■ **How much time do you have?** Next, determine how much time you have to get the job done. If your presentation is a report you need for this afternoon, you'll have to do your best with the resources at hand; however, if it's a presentation for a new product launch in three months, you obviously have more time to invest and to bring other people in on the project. Consider whether you have any additional deadlines before you need the final version of your slides, such as getting marketing or legal approval. All these factors will determine whether you have a couple of hours, a day, a couple of days, a week, a month, or longer to get the project done.

■ **Where can you get graphics?** This chapter will show you a wide range of ways to get graphics for your slides, but one of the most useful resources you'll use is a stock photography Website. These sites feature a database to search to locate photographs, illustrations, motion graphics, and video. Always properly obtain a license or otherwise get permission to use graphics if you do not already hold the rights to use them. Stock photography Websites are set up to make the licensing process fast and easy, often charging just a few dollars per photo.

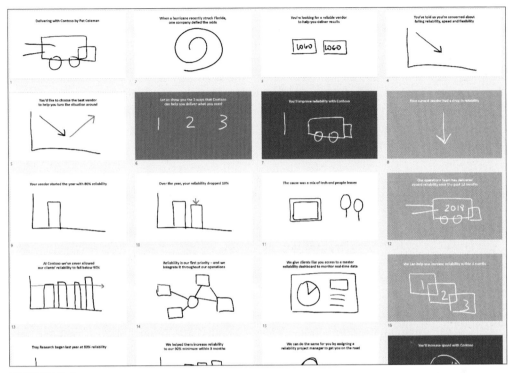

FIGURE 8-1

Review the fully-sketched storyboard.

- ■ **What's your budget?** If you have a budget of $0, you will be limited to only free graphics, screen captures, and any graphics you create yourself. If you have a budget of $100, license 10 photographs from a stock photography site for an average of $10 each; if you have $500, hire a freelance graphic designer for five hours at $100/hour; and if you have $10,000, commission a video that you integrate into your anchor slides and elsewhere throughout the storyboard.

- ■ **What other resources do you have available?** If you have the skills, create original illustrations yourself in another software program, or shoot your own photographs and edit them with image editing software. If you don't have these skills, consider other people to ask for help, such as an in-house design team or your coworkers.

Whatever constraints you have, you don't need design training to produce effective results with your new storyboard. This chapter will introduce and demonstrate some new tools and basic design techniques to start applying to your presentations today.

ADDING GRAPHICS USING THREE GUIDELINES

The most important thing to keep in mind when you add graphics to your storyboard is that you're not just designing *slides*; you're designing a complete *experience* that manages the visual and verbal channels for the working memory of your audience. It's easy to become absorbed in the details of fonts, graphics, and animations on the slides while losing track of your spoken words and how the entire experience helps the audience to understand your message. To make sure you stay on track, keep three guidelines in mind while you're working with graphics.

GUIDELINE 1: SEE IT IN SECONDS

In Chapter 7, you sketched your storyboard across adjacent backup slides and sketched across anchor and explanation slides to keep intact the presentation's levels of hierarchy. This process ensures that when you view the entire presentation in Slide Sorter view, you see exactly how you manage the attention of your audience *across time*. Within that context, you then focus on the individual slides to see how to best manage your audience's attention in any particular *moment of time*, both visually and verbally. The best place to understand the design of your slides is in its complete context of screen and narration—that is, in Notes Page view. As illustrated in Figure 8-2, the Notes Page view composition is built on three levels of information hierarchy.

The top of the information hierarchy is the on-screen headline, which summarizes the point you make at this moment; the second level of the hierarchy is the on-screen graphic, which visually explains the headline; and the third level of the hierarchy is the off-screen narrative explanation in the notes area, which further explains both the headline and the visual element with your spoken words. Although you'll be working on individual slides in Normal view, you should frequently return to Notes Page view during the process of adding graphics to view the slides in the context of their verbal narration.

Keeping in mind how your voice will seamlessly integrate with the graphics you add to each slide, look at Figure 8-3, which shows the built-in hierarchy of the default layout for your slides in Normal view. When you display any layout on the screen, you want your audience's eyes to go first to the most important information on the slide—the headline that summarizes your point. The headline communicates the topic clearly to the audience, reminds you as a speaker what you want to say, and keeps both parties focused on a specific topic.

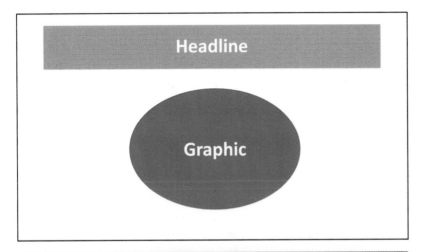

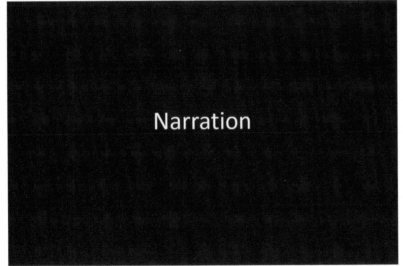

FIGURE 8-2

Complete information hierarchy seen in Notes Page view.

Next, you want your audience's eyes to move to the second-most important element on the slide—the graphic. Whatever graphic you add here should illustrate the head-line and help your audience see your point by using the power of the visual channel of working memory. The graphic should pack as much meaning as possible into visual form and still be simple enough to be quickly digestible.

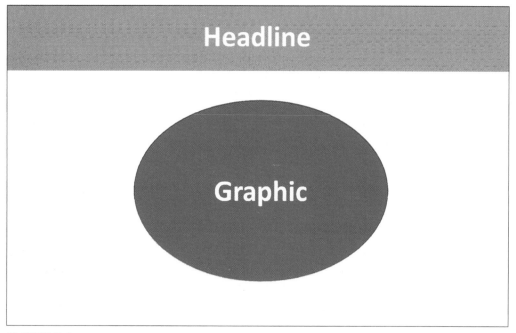

FIGURE 8-3

Slide hierarchy seen in Normal view.

On the default slide layout when you first import your headlines into PowerPoint slides, the position for the graphic is centered on the screen, where it is easy to see and understand. Customize this slide layout according to what you sketched for each hierarchical level of the storyboard. If you do adjust some of the slide layouts later, keep them simple and include white space to give your audience visual breathing room to easily process the new information.

Although the basic layout for the slides is simple in style, it is sophisticated in its effect because the audience scans the headline and graphic and quickly understands the idea. This "verbal-visual reading" of the slide should get your point across in seconds so that the working memory of your audience can then pay attention to you and what you're saying. The goal is to help your audience quickly digest the slide; even if you display the slide for only a few seconds and then black out the screen, your audience should be able to articulate the main point of that single slide as you intended. After the slide initially sets the stage this way by quickly conveying the meaning of the headline, the slide shifts in function to a reinforcing backdrop while you verbally explain the point in more detail over the next minute or less.

GUIDELINE 2: ALIGN THE AESTHETICS WITH THE AUDIENCE

Life would be easy if you could choose any graphics to add to your slides, but there is the matter of aesthetics—how your audience thinks your graphics look. You might personally prefer the style or composition of a particular graphic, but in truth, what you think doesn't matter as much as what your audience thinks. For better or worse, your aesthetic choices can present a major obstacle to communication if you don't get them right. If people are paying attention to what they see as your ill-advised choice of graphics, they're not paying attention to your message. Not only is effective learning at stake, but also your credibility. In the days before visual aids, you established credibility through your verbal introduction, your ideas, your authority, and your physical appearance. Now, with slides, you have an additional need to establish *visual* credibility. Without visual credibility, you and your presentation will be perceived as amateurish and lacking substance.

Because the beauty of a graphic is in the eye of the beholder, you really need to know the beholder of your presentations—your audience. As you research your audience to determine how to focus your presentation across the first five slides of Act I, you also want to find out as much as possible about their aesthetic preferences as well. If you've been in a particular profession or industry for a while, you probably already have a sense of what is perceived as acceptable aesthetics. For example, if you're presenting to corporate executives, you'll take your aesthetic cues from a company's marketing materials, annual report, and office environment. But if you're presenting to a jury, you'll take your cues from the juror questionnaires, popular culture, and the local area. Choose the graphics appropriate to the group so that your graphics do not stand in the way of your message. As a secondary consideration, you also need to be personally comfortable with the aesthetics to deliver the material confidently and naturally.

Although the general aesthetic preferences of your audiences and their cultures might vary, you'll want to generally choose a minimalist style because adding anything extraneous places an unnecessary cognitive load on the working memory of your audience. That said, even if something is simple, it can be an aesthetic mismatch with your audience.

As you search stock photography databases for graphics that are a good aesthetic match with your audience, scan through as many as time will allow so that you get a full sense of the spectrum of possibilities. For example, the headline from the storyboard shown on the upper left in Figure 8-4 reads, "You'd like to find a new way to get things done," and the sketch from Chapter 7 indicates that you'd like to use a clipboard image. When you visit a stock photography Website and search for "clipboard," you'll get thousands of results, which presents you with thousands of potential graphics you could use for this slide. Many of the graphics here might work—or possibly, none of them will.

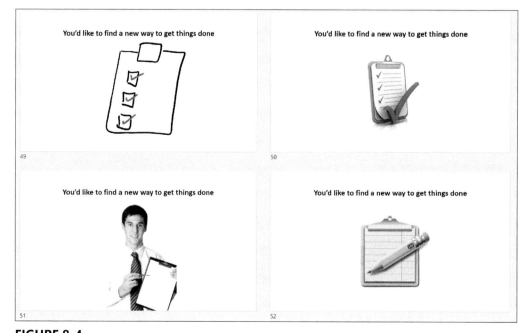

FIGURE 8-4

Aesthetic mismatches for a clipboard.

TIP The general guidelines for choosing graphics are to keep things as simple and unadorned as possible, and when in doubt, take it out. Review the graphics with other people on your team and gather their opinions to get a range of perspectives to help you choose which graphics work best aesthetically for both you and your audience.

When you're searching for an aesthetic match between a graphic and your audience, your focus should not be on whether you think a particular graphic is good or bad, but rather on whether a specific graphic will do the job of communicating the point of a specific headline to your specific audience. Scrolling through the search results reveals that many of the graphics probably are an aesthetic mismatch for the audience of the sample presentation in this book. For example, the clip art example of a clipboard on the upper right of Figure 8-4 is done in a cartoon style that might make your message come across as not being as serious as the topic at hand. The clip art example on the lower right is a mismatch because the image features a large pencil and comes across as too playful and not aligned with the aesthetic style the audience expects.

Using a photograph of someone holding a clipboard is in the realm of possibility, but this example on the lower left will distract attention away from the point of the headline and prompt thoughts in the viewer's mind such as, "Who is this person" or "I'm not a fan of his tie." Again, this is not about whether these example graphics are good or bad because they all would work perfectly well in some other contexts, just not for this audience.

TIP An important consideration when you're using graphics from commonly used sources is to be careful not to use images you've seen used in many other presentations. If an image is perceived as trite or overused, it will distract from your headline as well.

Although none of these examples from the search results may be an aesthetic match with the audience, there are others that could work. For example, instead of a paper-based clipboard originally sketched on the upper left in Figure 8-5, you could choose an electronic clipboard in the form of a touchscreen tablet. The example of the photograph on the upper right is simple enough to serve as the basis for a graphic in the presentation. A design constraint of this chapter includes not working with photo manipulation software, but you can still do simple things to make this image work if all you have is a preexisting photograph such as this one. Add three square boxes using PowerPoint drawing tools to create the checkboxes (lower left), and then add the check marks (lower right).

FIGURE 8-5

A closer aesthetic match of a clipboard for the audience.

The final slide on the lower right is a closer aesthetic match with this particular audience than the clip art and photo examples shown earlier in Figure 8-4. A professional designer might do an even better job with this slide. However, accepting the constraints of doing it yourself and using only existing photographs and PowerPoint drawing tools, you can adapt and improvise like this to make the best of what you have.

NOTE Choosing an unpolished aesthetic style can be a savvy and sophisticated strategy at times. If everyone presents the same slick, polished, and flawless style, everyone's presentations will look the same. If you choose something simple to contrast with the norm, you could break through the visual boredom and succeed at making a memorable impression. There is, of course, a risk that using a technique like this might not work if your audience expects the same aesthetics as they see everywhere else. So you need to be confident that you can make this choice work for both you and your audience.

Your innate taste, talent, and skill come into play when you find, create, or add graphics. You might find you are naturally good at choosing graphics that align with the aesthetics of your audience. But you also might discover that your talents lie elsewhere; if so, it's best to enlist the help of your coworkers or designers to help you find the best graphics for the job, or use professionally designed graphics.

GUIDELINE 3: DEFEND YOUR FOUNDATION!

At this stage in crafting your visual story, you've worked hard to create a strong foundation all the way from the words and structure of your story template through to your sketches. But if you're not careful to defend the foundation you've built, you might break the mechanisms that make this method work so well, and things can start to unravel quickly.

The main temptation is to add more to a slide than what you need to make your graphical point. But as Chapter 2 explains, research indicates that the more extraneous information you add, the more you increase the load on working memory and decrease learning. Every bullet point you add back to the slide, every additional color, and every extra visual detail can potentially clog the eye of the needle, the limited capacity of your audience's working memory to process new information. Keep subtracting from—not adding to—your slides. If you find yourself continuing to add more to a slide to make your point, most likely there's a problem with the structure and sequence of your ideas, and you should return to the story template to address the section of the presentation where the slide originates.

Although you might be able to control your own inclinations to add more visual detail to your slides, the biggest risk to your solid presentation foundation is from others who pressure you to keep adding information. For example, you might choose a simple illustration for a slide, as shown on the upper left in Figure 8-6—a stock photo of a hand drawing a simple arrow from Point A to Point B to illustrate the headline "Our algorithm predicts the best route to take."

Perhaps you then invite your boss over to your desk to ask for his opinion. He thinks you should really emphasize the vehicles driving the routes, so he asks you to add a photo of a van and underline the word *route*. Then he says that he wants you to clarify the headline by adding the words *accurate quantitative-based*, which extends the headline from one simple line to two more complicated ones (upper right). Not sure whether the slide is exactly right, he calls his boss over for her opinion. She says that you should emphasize the quantitative nature of the tools referenced in the headline by changing the word *quantitative* to uppercase and then adding a photo of a map (lower left). Then the chief information officer happens to walk by and says that the slide looks unbalanced and that you should add a photograph of a GPS device the driver would have (lower right).

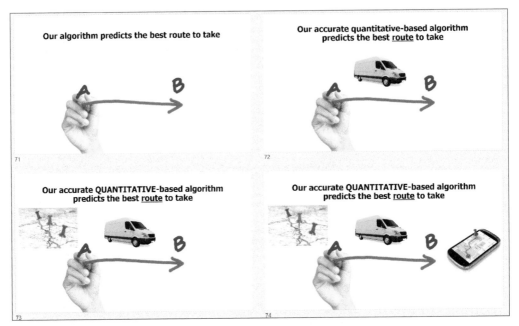

FIGURE 8-6

A graphical foundation as it is eroded over time.

Compare the original simple and clear slide, upper left, with the final result, lower right. In spite of everyone's good intentions to make the slide better, the combined additions made it worse. As the old saying goes, "If you emphasize everything, you emphasize nothing."

The headline on your slide already sits in the most prominent position on the original slide (upper left), so there's no need to embellish it to make it stand out; there is an easy flow as the audience sees the headline, looks at the graphic and listens to the speaker. The emphasis on individual words disrupts easy reading of the headline (upper right) and creates unnecessary visual competition about where to look first. The same happens when you add the other two photographs at the lower right; they have transformed what was once a clear and easily viewable slide into a distracting hodgepodge. The audience can no longer easily see the meaning of the entire slide in seconds. The group process has broken the solid foundation of clarity and rendered the slide ineffective.

Not only does breaking the foundation impact an individual slide, but it also disrupts the sequence of slides. It's easy to get lost in the individual slides instead of seeing the big picture of the story template. For example, for your visual story work, you should have the same font style and size of headlines on all your slides to ensure that each slide is easy to read and links together visually. Within the hierarchy levels of your storyboard, you should have consistent placement of headlines as each slide flows visually from one to the next.

You break the consistency in the approach *only for specific reasons*—for example, when you disrupt the flow of ideas to indicate that the next idea is more important than the others, as determined by the story template. But in this example, other members of your organization broke the consistency *for no reason*—the unnecessary details added to the headlines do nothing to help the big picture of the presentation and instead hurt it. The situation can get even worse if you start adding new slides to your storyboard and rearranging them without reflecting the changes in the story template. Soon, the internal pacing and flow of the presentation begin to unravel, too.

The graphical way to fix the problems shown in Figure 8-6 is easy: remove everything except the minimum number of visuals needed to illustrate the headline, as in the original slide (upper left). But the organizational fix will take a bit more work. People's urges to add extraneous detail are most often related to habit or myths, such as thinking that the more you add, the more people will learn; or that you need to add pizzazz to catch someone's attention; or that it's more important to entertain people rather than helping them retain and apply new information. To protect your hard-earned foundation, stand firm on your research-based grounding from Chapter 2 as you help other people understand that "less is more" is more than a slogan—it's a strategy and proven tactic for getting optimum results in your presentations.

THREE GUIDELINES FOR ADDING GRAPHICS Adding graphics is the crucial last step in designing the storyboard. Follow these three guidelines to make sure you get the graphics right:

1. See it in seconds.

2. Align the aesthetics with the audience.

3. Defend your foundation!

STARTING THE PRODUCTION FLOW

Aim for a first rough draft of your storyboard, not a finished product. Don't spend too much time on any single graphic; you could easily spend all day on one slide and get nothing else done. Instead, put something on the slide for the first draft, even if it's not exactly what you're looking for, and come back to work on the imperfect things later. Work in a sequence that will make most efficient use of your time, beginning with getting others to help you.

NOTE This book assumes you know the basics of PowerPoint, such as using drawing tools and inserting, resizing, and cropping photographs. If you need a tutorial or a refresher on how to use the software, some basics books are available, such as Joan Lambert's *Microsoft PowerPoint 2016 Step by Step* (Microsoft Press, 2015). To review the basics of working with photographs, see "Tip 2: The Photo Basics: Size, Crop, and Compress" later in this chapter.

DELEGATING THE GRAPHICS TASKS

If you have coworkers who can help you find or create graphics to add to your storyboard, get them started first so that task is underway while you do your work. A good way to provide these coworkers with the information they need is to save a new version of the PowerPoint file with another name, and delete all the slides that your coworkers won't need to see. Or you could add sections to the file, name the sections with your coworkers' names, and then put the slides you want from them into those sections as needed and send them a copy of it. When your coworkers open the file, they'll have the specific slides you assigned to them, and if you ask them to view the slides in Notes Page view, they'll see the headline that summarizes your point, the detailed off-screen narration, and the sketch you added to the slide in Chapter 7. They can replace the sketch with a graphic, and when they email the file back to you, insert the new slides, copy and paste the entire slides, or copy and paste just the graphics from the slide area.

If you have the resources to have graphics custom-made, assign those tasks in the same way, providing the designer with the slides. See "Tip 4: Design for Your Designer" later in this chapter for additional advice about working with designers.

GETTING THE GRAPHICS YOU ALREADY HAVE

Next get the things done on the project that you can do quickly, to reduce the scope of the project. For example, if you already have on hand 10 preexisting graphics out of the 40 you need, adding them now to the storyboard means that you're 25 percent done, which will give you a better handle on the situation.

The first place to go to get graphics is your existing presentations, if you have any. If you build a library of visual stories over time, it will help your production process go faster each time because you'll build presentations from scratch less and less. If you don't have previous presentations, you might have some graphics in other slides that are simple and illustrate the point of a headline. However, if they are overly complex, or otherwise don't align with the simple foundation of your storyboard, don't use them.

GETTING GRAPHICS AT STOCK PHOTOGRAPHY WEB SITES

If you're a good photographer, take your own photographs using a digital camera to use on your slides; otherwise, visit a stock photography Website. Search for graphics based on keywords you enter into a search box, such as "clipboard." You'll then see a search results screen similar to the one shown in Figure 8-7.

TIP   It's worth the time to learn how to use advanced search tools at these sites to narrow your search based on specific parameters, such as color, vertical or horizontal orientation, or popularity ratings. When you're looking for photos that have white or transparent backgrounds, include the term "isolated" in your search terms. When you see a photo that's close to what you want but not an exact fit, click on it to examine the photo details page, where you might find related images or access to the artist's portfolio. If you're unsure whether you want to license the photo but want to hold open the option for doing so later, set up a lightbox—a temporary holding area for the photos you might use.

As you consider where to get graphics, you probably have more readily available graphics than you think, especially if you work in an organization—for example, many marketing departments have libraries of photographs that are already licensed for use in presentations. In every case, make sure the photographs are optimized for presentation use at screen resolution—print resolution produces much larger file sizes that unnecessarily expand the file size of your presentations and can make them more difficult to use.

FIGURE 8-7

Search results for "clipboard."

CREATING THE GRAPHICS YOU CAN

PowerPoint includes a range of drawing tools that you might already know how to use, such as creating shapes, lines, arrows, callouts, charts, and graphs. Add any of these elements as a simple graphic on a slide, or use the drawing tools to add other graphical elements, such as callouts, to existing photographs.

APPLYING FINAL SLIDE LAYOUTS TO YOUR STORYBOARD

In Chapter 6, you applied preliminary sketch layouts to the anchor, explanation, and backup slides so that you could see them clearly in Slide Sorter view and practice scaling your presentation to time. These visual cues indicate to your audience's working memory which slides are more important than others as you present them in sequence. In Chapter 7, you reviewed different ways to sketch these slide layouts to build on this foundation and keep the hierarchy of the presentation clear. You'll now apply a finalized version of these important layouts.

You have several options for your final layouts: use predesigned versions that are included in the BBP Storyboard Formatter you used in Chapter 6, have a presentation designer create layouts for you, or design layouts yourself manually. Whichever approach you choose, the layouts should adhere to the following guidelines to ensure you cue your audience to the type of Act II slide they are looking at, as shown in Figure 8-8:

- When you apply the anchor slide layout (left), it should call attention to these slides first out of all your slides. In this case, the anchor layout features a solid aqua color box that fills two-thirds of the top of the slide.

- The explanation slide layout (middle) should call attention to these slides second out of all your slides. In this case, the explanation layout features a gold horizontal bar, centered vertically to hold the headline.

- The backup slide layout (right) should provide a simple foundation for the bulk of your slides. This example of a backup slide layout (right) includes a thin tan horizontal strip at the bottom of the slide, leaving the rest of the slide clear and open for a simple graphic.

FIGURE 8-8

Example custom layouts for the anchor, explanation, and backup slides.

The completed anchor, explanation, and backup slides from the example presentation shown in Figure 8-9 demonstrate how both layout and color work together to indicate the relative importance of these slides. As shown in this example, by applying these layouts to the corresponding slides in your presentation, you preserve the powerful information hierarchy in your story that you created in Act II of the story template.

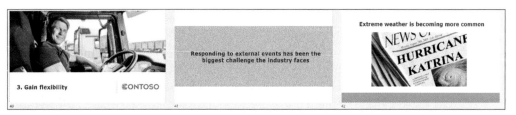

FIGURE 8-9

Custom layouts applied to sample anchor, explanation, and backup slides.

APPLYING, REVIEWING, AND REFINING THE LAYOUTS

Choose a layout set from the BBP Storyboard Formatter, and apply it to the corresponding slides in your presentation:

1. In Slide Sorter view, press Ctrl+A to select all the slides in the presentation.

2. On the Home tab, in the Slides group, click the Layout button to display a drop-down gallery of layouts. Scroll through the layouts and choose the Backup slide layout to apply it to all of your slides.

3. Hold down the Ctrl key again while you select each of the anchor slides, click Layout, and then click the anchor slide layout.

4. Hold down Ctrl while you select the explanation slides, click Layout, and then click the explanation slide layout.

5. Last, click the Title Slide and apply the Title Slide layout, and then hold down the Ctrl key while you click the Act I slides and apply the Act I slide layout (if you have one) or the Title Only slide layout (if you don't).

After you finish applying layouts, the slides of your storyboard should appear as shown in Figure 8-10. Now that you have custom layouts in place, you have a foundation for the graphics that you'll add to individual slides next.

FIGURE 8-10

Examples of anchor, explanation, and backup slides with the corresponding custom layouts applied.

CUSTOMIZING LAYOUTS

Customizing layouts for your anchor, explanation, and backup slides will give you tremendous flexibility as you get to know them better and find ways to make your graphical work easier and faster. The great thing about custom layouts is that experimenting is easy. If you create a layout you don't like, or that doesn't work, or if you make a mistake, it's easy to return to the layout in Slide Master view and make changes there that will automatically update the corresponding slides built from the layout. If a slide does not update after you change the layout, select the slide, and on the Home tab, in the Slides group, click the Reset button. When you have a set of custom layouts you like, copy and paste them from the Slide Thumbnails in Slide Master view to other presentations, and save them to use again later.

ADDING GRAPHICS TO THE MAP AND ANCHOR SLIDES

When you apply custom layouts to your storyboard, you now have a graphical foundation established for all of your slides. The next step is to add graphics to the map and anchor slides you sketched in Chapter 7, shown in Figure 8-11.

FIGURE 8-11

Original sketches of the map and anchor slides.

The map slide sketch (upper left) features three icons to reinforce the three anchor points. As you learned in Chapter 7, if you had only one slide to show in a presentation, this one would be it because it both visually concludes Act I and visually summarizes the anchor slides to come.

Each of the three anchor slides features an expanded photograph from the map slide, and the headlines have been shortened, which increases their impact by focusing on each of the three main benefits described on the three anchor slides: reliability, speed, and flexibility.

In Figure 8-12, anchor layouts have been applied to these slides, along with the final graphics, with the aqua box replaced by a photograph.

FIGURE 8-12

The map and anchor slides with graphics added.

PREPARING SLIDES THAT DON'T REQUIRE GRAPHICS

Now that you've taken care of the most important slides in the presentation, the next thing to do is take care of the slides that don't require graphics. The storyboard sketches in Figure 8-13 show four examples of these slides:

- Blacking out a screen on an Act I slide (upper left)
- Displaying a physical prop (upper right)
- Switching to another application on an explanation slide (lower left)
- Using only a headline and no graphic on an explanation slide (lower right)

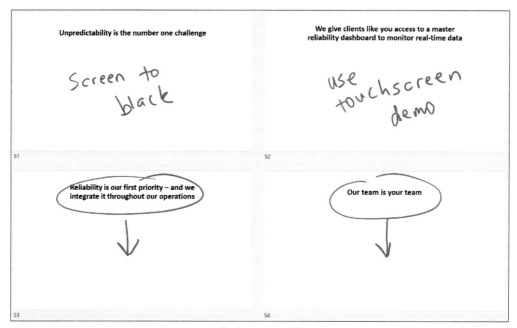

FIGURE 8-13

Sketches of slides that use techniques other than graphics.

As described in Chapter 7, black out the screen, as shown in Figure 8-14 (upper left), by right-clicking and formatting the background color as black, or by inserting a black rectangle to fill the screen. Drag the headline outside of the slide area so it will not appear on-screen, or change the color to match the background. If you plan to use a physical prop, drag the headline down to the middle of the screen (upper right) or black out the screen so the focus will be on you and the prop rather than the slide.

To switch to a different application on the screen when you get to a slide, center the headline (lower left) to introduce your activity as you switch applications. If you are pressed for time and would like to include a headline-only on a slide, apply the explanation slide layout and leave the slide as it appears (lower right).

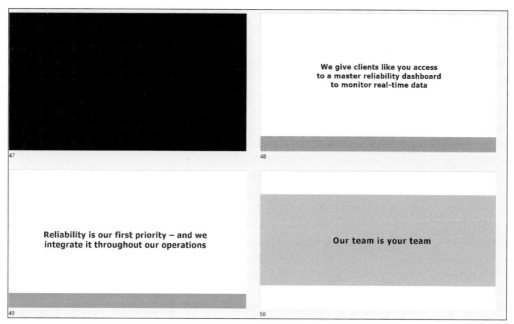

FIGURE 8-14

Completed slides, without graphics.

ADDING GRAPHICS TO THE ACT I SLIDES

Now, start at the beginning of the presentation and add the graphics to your Act I slides that you sketched in Chapter 7, shown in Figure 8-15.

In the completed example shown in Figure 8-16, the photo of the hurricane on the hook slide (upper left) is the visual prompt for an engaging anecdote. The relevance slide features the Fabrikam logo (upper right) to establish that the presentation is all about the audience —the Fabrikam executives. The challenge slide (lower left) features a downward arrow indicating the core challenge of falling reliability, speed, and flexibility. In the desire slide (lower right), an upward arrow affirms the upward direction the audience wants to achieve when faced with the challenge they just heard.

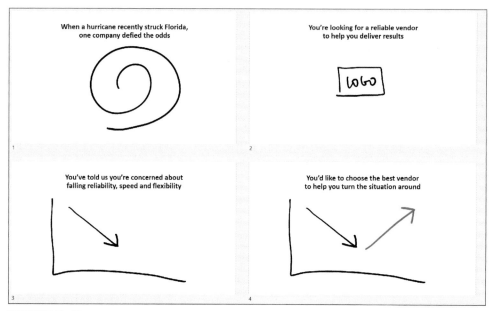

FIGURE 8-15

Original sketches of the Act I slides.

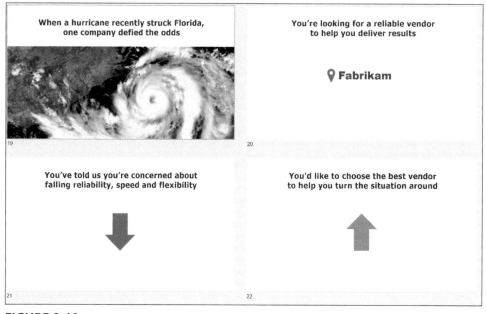

FIGURE 8-16

The Act I slides with graphics added.

In your Act I slides, an effective technique is to click and drag the headlines off the slide area when you work in Normal view or change the color of the font to match the background, so the headlines are not visible to your audience when you display the slides as in Figure 8-17. This increases the visual impact of the Act I slides as they do their important work of making an emotional connection with your audience and making your audience reliant on you to explain what the images mean.

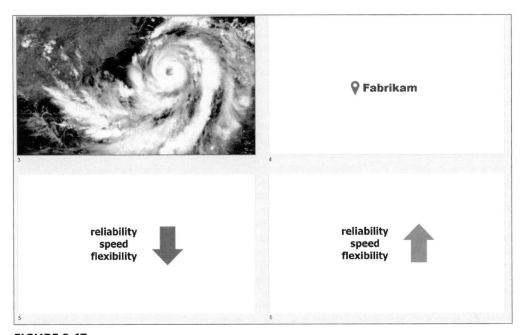

FIGURE 8-17

The Act I slides without headlines visible.

ADDING GRAPHICS TO THE EXPLANATION SLIDES

As described in Chapter 7, the sketches of your explanation slides might guide you toward adding a photograph, logo, diagram, chart, or other illustration on the individual slides. Figure 8-18 shows an anchor slide with graphics you've already added (upper left) and the sketches of its three related explanation slides.

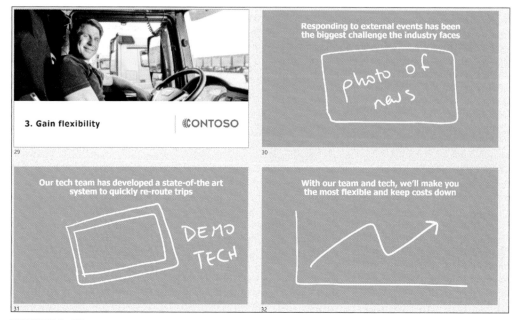

FIGURE 8-18

Anchor slide with graphics added and original sketches of the related explanation slides.

Locate and add graphics that correspond to these sketches on each of these slides, as shown in Figure 8-19. Notice that these slides are telling a story, slide by slide, as they explain the initial anchor slide. In turn, each explanation slide will visually introduce and summarize its subsequent backup slides. You would apply a similar technique of building a visual story step by step if your story template and sketches call for the use of a diagram or chart on the explanation slides.

ADDING GRAPHICS TO THE BACKUP SLIDES

For a 45-minute presentation, the bulk of your work when adding graphics involves the backup slides. As described in Chapter 7, you might have sketched photos, charts, or screen captures to add to these slides, as shown in Figure 8-20.

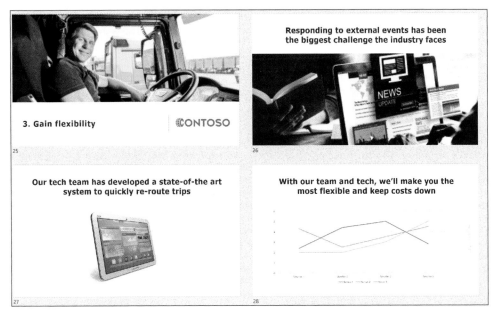

FIGURE 8-19

The explanation slides with graphics added.

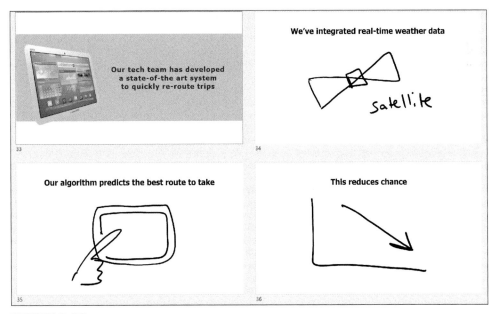

FIGURE 8-20

Explanation slide with graphics added (upper left), along with original sketches of the related backup slides.

If you use images from a stock photography Website, these slides might look like the slides on the upper right and lower left in Figure 8-21 after you have added the graphics you found.

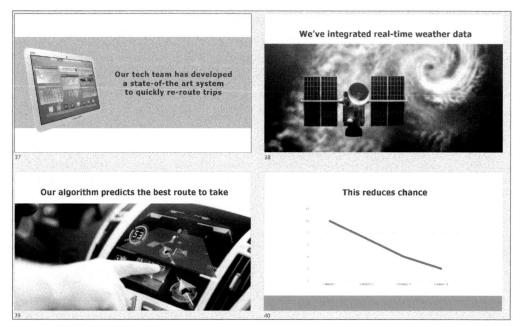

FIGURE 8-21

The backup slides with photographs and a chart added.

TIP   One of the simplest and most overlooked sources for graphics is your computer screen. To create a shot of your screen, press Print Screen (usually labeled PrtScn on your keyboard), and then on a slide in Normal view, right-click and choose Paste to place the image on the slide. Alternatively, choose Insert, Screenshot and choose from the pulldown options for any screens you have open. Commercial screen capture programs such as SnagIt (*www.techsmith.com*) allow you many more options for customizing your shots, such as adding a subtle drop shadow.

If you sketched a chart on a backup slide, it might look like the slide on the lower right in Figure 8-21 in its final state. Although many of the guidelines and much of the writing and research related to charts deals with displaying them on paper, PowerPoint charts are usually projected on a wall with a live presenter explaining them. Because there is the added element of a synchronized verbal explanation in the live presentation environment, charts designed on a slide can generally be simpler than those displayed on paper without a live presenter.

With the visual story you've crafted, you're certain that the main point of a chart is fully explained by the headline because you always clarify your point in the form of a headline before you select the chart to explain it. If someone were not present to hear your narration, you would provide that person with a handout of a Notes Page version of the slide that includes the headline, chart, and off-screen notes area explanation. Displaying the chart over a series of slides that are mapped to a sequence of headlines, as described in Chapter 7, helps to introduce the new information in smaller pieces at an appropriate pace for the audience to understand.

TIP   To keep a chart free of clutter and focused on the data at hand, simplify its formatting by removing excess lines, graphical treatments, colors, and grids. Avoid adding unnecessary ornamentation or special effects that inhibit the audience's ability to understand information, as described in Chapter 2. Strive for a minimalist style that allows the numbers to speak for themselves. When you need to show your numbers using a chart, consider consulting one of the books that can help you to display data effectively.

CREATING THE ACT III SLIDES

As you'll recall from writing your story template in Chapters 4 and 5, you never got around to writing Act III of your story—the resolution. You will quickly take care of the end of your story now with a couple of mouse clicks.

A classic way to end a story is to back out the way you came in. End your visual story the same way by holding down the Ctrl key while you select your challenge and desire slides along with your map slide. With these slides selected, press Ctrl+D to duplicate the three slides. Now drag these duplicated slides to the end of the presentation, following the last backup slide of Act II. If you haven't already done so, here, you may differentiate these slides graphically from their Act I counterparts by hiding the headlines so that they don't appear on the screen, as shown in Figure 8-22.

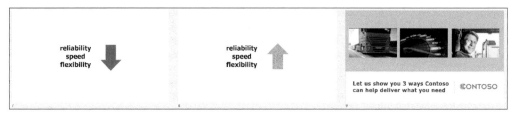

FIGURE 8-22

The challenge, desire, and map slides duplicated as the closing Act III slides, with the headlines hidden.

When you reach the challenge slide in the closing Act III of the presentation, say something like, "You'll remember we started today by looking at the impact you feel because the old way is not working anymore [advance to the desire slide] and the desire to find a new way that works. Well [advance to map slide], today we've shown that by changing your way of thinking in three ways, you'll get the results you want...."

These familiar images connect back to the emotional core of the story and visually reinforce the messages you want your audience to remember. Just as you start strong visually and verbally, these same slides can help you end strong visually and verbally. Change the order of the slides, if appropriate, and otherwise adapt, innovate, and improvise verbally. Whatever you plan to say in your strong ending here in Act III, be sure to make the appropriate updates in the notes area of the corresponding slides that you duplicated.

FINE-TUNING AND FINISHING UP

Now that you have the first draft with a graphic on every slide, go back and review what you have with an eye toward refining your presentation.

ADDING GRAPHICS TO THE TITLE AND CLOSING CREDITS SLIDES

In a film, the opening title sequence establishes the mood and tone of the story to come. Achieve a similar effect by adding graphics to the Title Slide. Apply the same style to the Title Slide that you did to the other slides in Act I. For example, if you use the photographic design technique for the Act I slides, use the same style for the Title Slide. Then apply the same technique you use for the Title Slide to a closing slide that will remain on-screen when you finish your presentation. You may want to include your organization's name, your contact information, a Web address, or a simple image that conveys the theme of the presentation.

REVIEWING AND ADDING GRAPHICS TO THE NOTES PAGES

The notes pages should balance equally the amount of space you dedicate to the slide you show on-screen and the amount of space you dedicate to the notes area, which holds the ideas you explain with your narration. In the example in Figure 8-23, the black line around the slide placeholder was changed to white to open up the white space on the printed notes page. The Slide Master and Notes Master both have white backgrounds, and because neither the slide nor the notes areas are bounded by lines, the headline of the slide summarizes the idea of the entire printed page. However, if you used layouts with color bars, those will appear and will affect the layout accordingly.

To preview how the notes page version of any slide will look when printed, click File, Print and under Settings, click the drop-down menu that says Full Page Slides and select Notes Pages.

When you finish making adjustments or adding graphics to all the slides, return once again to Notes Page view of each slide to review the notes areas and make sure your written words are clear and concise. Begin with the first notes page: read the headline, review the visual, and then read the notes area to make sure everything flows smoothly. When you've read the last line in the notes area, scroll down to the next notes page and make sure it reads smoothly as a continuation of the story from the previous notes page. It's a good idea to print the entire document as notes pages at this point to check the wording and flow.

Our tech team has developed a state-of-the art system to quickly re-route trips

Our engineers at Fabrikam worked around the clock to develop state-of-the art technology that will re-route trips at the first sign of changes in weather, traffic or natural disasters. Using location-based technology and predictive artificial intelligence, we are able to predict changing conditions with 90 percent accuracy, giving us the information we need to avoid problems.

The key components of the technology include:
- App-based tool that can be accessed by laptop, tablet or phone
- Current location-based GPS technology based on location of vehicles
- Integration into online mapping technologies
- Back-end platform using commercial routing tools

With the app in hand, drivers are able to quickly get alerts and updated routing information unavailable through other means. Our platform is quickly becoming the industry standard as we lease it to other companies – although Contoso would have access to the master dashboard and have the ability to use features only available to our own customers.

We're glad to offer a tech demo for your engineers at the earliest availability.

28

FIGURE 8-23

Notes Page view.

REVIEWING AND FINALIZING THE STORYBOARD

Congratulations on completing your visual story! Your final presentation should look something like the one shown in Figure 8-24.

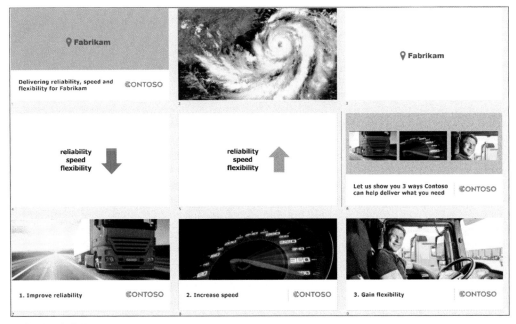

FIGURE 8-24

Completed storyboard with graphics added to all the slides.

After you've reviewed the complete presentation, have someone with fresh eyes take a look at the presentation to verify that you didn't miss anything, make a typographical error, or misstate something. When you prepare the presentation for review, plan to send it as notes pages for review, not only of what appears on-screen but also of the information covered in the notes area.

TIP   Saving your PowerPoint file in PDF format allows you to send a version of the presentation electronically in a form that does not allow others to alter it. To save a presentation as a PDF file:

- Click File, Export.

- Select Create PDF/XPS Document, and click the Create PDF/XPS button.

- In the Publish as PDF or XPS dialog, click Options and in the Publish What drop-down menu, choose Notes Pages.

- Click OK and then click the Publish button to create the PDF

BBP CHECKLIST: ADDING GRAPHICS TO THE STORYBOARD

Do your final graphics

- Clearly illustrate each headline in the simplest way possible?

- Show consistency within levels of the presentation hierarchy and variety across levels?

- Keep your slides free of any extraneous visual information?

- Align with the aesthetics of your audience?

You've come a long way since you started on the road to crafting your visual story in Chapter 1, and the example presentation in this book should help you start applying the approach in this book to your next presentation. Next, Chapter 9 will provide some guidelines and tips to consider when you deliver your visual story to an audience, and Chapter 10 will show you a range of presentations to review for additional inspiration.

As you get familiar with adding graphics, take a look at these 10 tips for improving on the basic techniques described in this chapter.

10 TIPS FOR ENHANCING YOUR STORYBOARD

Once you've prepared and planned both your spoken words and your projected visuals, try using these 10 tips to enhance the storyboard.

TIP 1: CLIP YOUR IDEAS

A great way to keep a fresh supply of creative visual ideas is by keeping a clipping file. Whenever you see an interesting layout, photograph, illustration, graph, or other visual idea in a newspaper, magazine, book, or other printed material, cut it out or copy it and place it in a folder in your file cabinet. Or for an electronic clip folder, create a folder in Microsoft OneNote or another note organizer and use the clipping tool to save an electronic image of the item. The next time you're stuck, refer to your paper or electronic file folders for creative inspiration.

TIP 2: THE PHOTO BASICS: SIZE, CROP, AND COMPRESS

You might find that a photo you choose to add to a slide doesn't fit or that it is too large a file for a PowerPoint presentation. To fix these problems, apply one of the three most important techniques you'll use to work with photographs: sizing, cropping, and compressing.

When a slide fills only a portion of the screen, it communicates only a portion of its visual potential. To increase its communicative power, resize the photo to fill the entire screen. To do that, click the photo, and drag one of the round sizing handles that appear at each of the four corners to enlarge the photo to fill the entire slide area. Be careful not to drag a square sizing handle on one of the sides of the graphic, or you'll distort the photo as you resize it. You always want to preserve the image's original proportions so that your audience doesn't notice any distortion.

Review the picture to make sure that it's crisp and clear at its current size. If it isn't, find another image. Never use a photo that is unfocused, grainy, blurry, or otherwise unclear because you'll distract from your message and diminish your visual credibility. People are used to seeing sharply focused photographs in professional media, and if you don't deliver the same in your slides, they'll think less of the presentation, no matter how good the story is.

After you resize a photograph and verify that it's clear and focused, you might find that it extends over the edges of the slide. If so, crop the image to keep only the portion you want in the slide area. Click the picture, and on the Picture Tools Format tab, in the Size group, click Crop, which will turn the sizing handles into cropping handles. To crop one side of the photograph, drag the cropping handle on that side toward the center of the photo to eliminate the part of the photo you don't want to keep.

The last tool to apply is Compress Pictures, available on the Picture Tools Format tab in the Adjust group when you click a picture. It's not uncommon for a single high-resolution photograph to be hundreds of megabytes in size, unnecessarily bloating the

PowerPoint file. This huge image file can create problems when you try to email the PowerPoint file or share it with other people. Solve this problem before it happens by making sure that the photographs are compressed to the smallest size needed for them to appear clearly on-screen. Select the picture, click the Compress Pictures button, click the options you want and select the target output you prefer—the lower the PPI (pixels per inch), the smaller the file size.

TIP 3: TRY THREE TREATMENTS

You don't know what you have until you see it, and that's especially true with graphics. That's why you should create a range of options for yourself before you decide what to do with the design of your slides. When a professional design firm starts a job for a client, it's common practice to present the client with three design options. This gives designers a free hand to express their creativity by trying three completely different treatments. It gives clients a range of options from which they can select based on what works for them. For both parties, it provides a way of stepping back from the emotional attachment anyone has to the different designs and gives a point of reference and comparison that can be used in deciding which design direction to take.

This time-tested method will serve you well when you design your PowerPoint storyboard. Select the sketches for the anchor slides from the presentation you've created, and try three completely different design treatments. Show the design treatments to your team, and test them on people unfamiliar with the presentation and ask for feedback. When you're satisfied with a design that will work for the audience, extend that design across all of the slides in the presentation.

TIP 4: DESIGN FOR YOUR DESIGNER

If you have the resources, invite a professional presentation designer to help you design your slides and storyboard. Bring the designer in early—if possible, while you write the story template—so that the designer can absorb and learn from your thinking process. Working with the designer from the start avoids the frustration that graphic designers feel when someone hands them a presentation with the instructions to "make it pretty," and the designer cannot clarify the structure. In that scenario, no one is happy.

Instead, the story template places responsibility for the clear structure of the story squarely on the presenter. The resulting storyboard shows the designer the order in which you want the ideas to appear and how you'll reinforce the message through the presentation. Discuss how the anchor, explanation, and backup slides form the hierarchy of a presentation, and explain that you want the backgrounds and layouts of these slides to cue the audience's working memory to the presentation's organization.

Always walk through the slides in Notes Page view to make sure the designer can see the relationship between the projected image on-screen and your spoken words.

When everyone agrees, ask the designer to provide you with three completely different visual treatments of key slides in a test file that you select from Acts I and II. Then compare the treatments and choose the elements and styles that are the best fit with you and your audience. Ask questions to be sure you understand why the designer is proposing a particular treatment. Through your interaction, you're sure to spark new creativity and understanding that will set the stage for a well-designed presentation. Because the designer doesn't have to take on the unnecessary job of figuring out what you want to say and in what order, you'll accelerate the design process and avoid possible confusion. Instead, the designer is freed up to do what a designer does best—designing. Using this approach develops a smooth process that's sure to result in a PowerPoint presentation that gives everyone involved a rewarding communication experience.

TIP 5: CREATE A LAYOUT LIBRARY

If you have colleagues who are also using BBP, consider pooling your resources to create a BBP design library. If your organization uses Microsoft SharePoint, create a collaborative Website for people who are willing to share their PowerPoint files. For example, create document library folders labeled "Anchor Layouts and Slide Examples," "Explanation Layouts and Slide Examples," and "Backup Layouts and Slide Examples." Anyone who created a presentation using one of those design techniques would then post it in the corresponding folder. You and the members of your team would no longer have to begin presentations from scratch; instead, you'd have a library of ideas ready for you to check out.

TIP 6: BUILD A CHARTS LIBRARY

Many individuals and organizations use a relatively limited range of diagrams and charts to explain the information that relates to their work. Instead of formatting diagrams and charts from scratch every time, design a single set of commonly used graphics that carry a clear and consistent design according to the best design principles. Whether you design the set of charts yourself or hire a professional information designer to help, standardizing the way you display quantitative information saves you time formatting and ensures that you maintain the integrity of the data you display.

TIP 7: CONSIDER COLOR

Consider the importance of color when designing the layouts for the levels of your presentation. According to widely accepted principles of color theory, some individual colors such as red or high-contrast combinations of colors such as black and white call attention to themselves before others.

Your choice of colors should always align with the hierarchy of your ideas. If you consider integrating your organization's colors into your custom layouts, be careful when you do that, because those colors might conflict with your goal of guiding the working memory of your audience. For example, you might use red in your company colors, but using a red element on your explanation and backup slide layouts will call attention to that element instead of the headline and the graphic, which will erode the way your slides are working to guide the attention of the audience.

You might run into resistance from others in your organization when choosing colors to indicate the hierarchy of importance of the ideas in your presentation. If that is the case, defend your foundation by holding a meeting to convey the importance of verbal and visual hierarchy in communicating effectively to an audience, showing BBP and non-BBP versions of the same presentation to demonstrate how you aim color to guide the audience's attention.

TIP 8: CALL OUT ADDITIONAL INFORMATION

To add a label to a graphic, on the Insert tab, in the Illustrations group, click Shapes, and then in the Callout group, select the style you want. After you add the label to the slide, modify it by adding text and adjusting the formatting as you would with any PowerPoint shape.

TIP 9: SKETCH IT ALL, LIVE!

If you are a good storyboard sketcher, consider something completely different and present your PowerPoint slides with only the headlines and no graphics added at all. When you present live, use a tablet PC to sketch a graphic to illustrate each headline as you go along. It will be a deeply engaging and interesting experience for the audience, plus you can save the sketches you made with the PowerPoint file and send the illustrated file to everyone who attended.

TIP 10: DEVELOP A SINGLE ILLUSTRATION, SLIDE BY SLIDE

If you're feeling particularly ambitious, try developing a single illustration across the entire presentation. You'll have to plan this carefully in the story template, but the basic idea is that you introduce one piece of the graphic, one slide at a time, as you verbally explain each piece, until everything in the illustration comes together into a single graphic at the end of the presentation. This technique helps you explain the big picture to your audience.

DELIVERING YOUR VISUAL STORY

In this chapter, you will:

- Remove distractions from the presentation environment.
- Rehearse the delivery of your visual story.
- Deliver a dynamic presentation.

The root of the word inspire—from Latin: *spirare*—means "to breathe," and that's one of the core objectives of this book—to inspire you with the confidence and tools you need to breathe deeply and relax more when you present. Most of the elements that contribute to your confidence are built into the process you've been following every step of the way. Now, when you've finished creating your presentation, it doesn't hurt to revisit them before you deliver your story live.

Although your slides look dramatically different from conventional slides, the real fruit of your labor is your confident understanding of what you want to say and how you want to say it. And when you open your slides, you now have a sophisticated media toolkit that blends your clear ideas and story with the delivery technology.

Now it's time to use that toolkit to bring your story to life.

DELIVERING YOUR PRESENTATION USING THREE GUIDELINES

The term *production* refers to the point when filmmakers capture live action on film. Film directors spend a great deal of time setting up scenes and filming the action many times so that they'll be able to use the best performances in the final cut. But you don't have that luxury in your slide production because you're presenting in a live environment, which means you typically get only a single shot at engaging the audience. Managing the complex mix of elements in a live presentation is challenging, but you already have firm control over the projected media, spoken words, and printed handouts in your presentation. As you use your slides to deliver your presentation, a set of guidelines can help keep the experience in balance.

GUIDELINE 1: STEP INTO THE SCREEN

In conventional presentations, often a small screen sits to the side of a presenter, where it is a nonessential visual aid that could be turned off without much impact on the presentation. In contrast, when you display your presentation on a large screen behind you, the audience should perceive you as inside the screen, as if it were a stage backdrop or a giant television. You are a living, engaging presence in your visual story, and you provide the critical audio track that ties everything together. When you step in front of the large screen, you create a hybrid medium that did not exist before. The projected screen makes your abstract thoughts visible, your body keeps the presentation grounded, and your voice guides and informs the experience.

After investing so much time in creating your visual media, you need to ensure the screen and its placement are appropriate to your presentation. Many conference rooms place focus on a chandelier or other architectural element rather than on the media experience you need to produce. Make sure you communicate what you need to the meeting or event planner. Never allow a screen to be placed on the opposite side of the room from where you are speaking. This setup will cause a split-attention effect that places an unneeded extra cognitive load on the audience by forcing them to continually look back and forth between you and the screen as they work to reconcile the two visual sources of information. Instead, make sure the screen is directly behind or just off to the side of you so that the light from the data projector does not shine in your eyes.

GUIDELINE 2: REMOVE THE DISTRACTIONS

It's easy to lose your focus on the message when there are endless things you could do to fine-tune your slides, such as adding more graphical elements, animations, and special effects. One of the major advantages of keeping your slides simple, which you did in Chapters 6, 7, and 8, is that it keeps you from being distracted by unnecessary details and keeps the audience from being distracted because too much is happening on the screen. Removing distractions leaves you in control of the media instead of having the media control you.

You use presentation software well when people don't even notice you use the tool at all. The last thing you want is for someone to compliment you on your slides; that would mean the medium called attention to itself instead of your ideas. The most important outcome of the presentation is that the audience understands the meaning you intend to communicate. When you finish the presentation, you want the audience to talk about your special ideas, not your special effects.

GUIDELINE 3: MANAGE THE FLOW

It's important to align your presentation with your unique personality so that you make an authentic connection with the audience. For example, when you spend the time to carefully write the story template in your own words, you develop a deep confidence in your story that frees you to improvise your narration and tailor your words to your audience instead of being chained to reading bullet points in the conventional approach. All this leads to a more relaxed and comfortable approach that will make the audience feel more relaxed and comfortable too.

A presentation is not a free-for-all, however, so it's important to improvise within the constraints of a specified form. This fundamental principle is applied in many arts, including jazz, in which musicians improvise only after they've mastered the fundamental techniques of the musical form. Similarly, improvise on the constraints defined in the guidelines presented throughout this book once you've mastered the basics.

THREE GUIDELINES FOR DELIVERING YOUR PRESENTATION
Your single storyboard helps you manage your spoken words, projected visuals, and printed handouts. Follow these three guidelines to ensure that the rest of the live presentation experience is engaging:

1. Step into the screen.

2. Remove the distractions.

3. Manage the flow.

GETTING READY

Up to now, you've focused on crafting a visual story that minimizes distractions that would otherwise overload the limited capacity of the working memory of your audience. You remove unnecessary information from the presentation by narrowing the focus of the story template. You keep extraneous information out of the slide area by following the storyboard and design ground rules. And you keep both graphics and narration focused on the headlines. After you've removed distractions from the slides, it's time to focus on removing distractions from the environment in which you'll present.

PREPARING THE ENVIRONMENT

The physical environment in which you present is just as important as the story you tell. The quality of your hard work is diminished if the room is physically uncomfortable, if there are distracting noises, if you don't have an electrical outlet within reach of the projector, or if the room looks just plain shabby. Just as you have a personal responsibility for the story template, you also have a responsibility for the physical experience of the environment in which you present. Use your leadership and diplomacy skills to work with facilities managers or meeting planners to ensure that everything is in order.

If you have access in advance to the room where you'll present, visit it to plan for your needs. Review the options for configuring the physical space, and rehearse the presentation in the actual environment if that's possible. If you're not able to visit the physical location in advance, contact someone familiar with the room to find out about the room setup.

At a minimum, both you and your audience should be physically comfortable in the environment. Establish a base of operations when you present, such as a podium, and claim the physical freedom to move around the room comfortably as you speak. If you use a touchscreen computer to deliver your visual story, place it on a podium or a low table out of the line of sight of your audience, and make sure that the projector cable and a power source are within reach.

When you're comfortable with the physical environment, turn to the technology you'll use to project the presentation.

TIP Lighting the room properly for a PowerPoint presentation can be a challenge. On the one hand, you want people to see the screen clearly, but on the other hand, you don't want the room to be so dark that people start to doze off. The latest models of data projectors and monitors have brighter displays that allow the audience to see the images on the screen clearly without turning down the room lights.

When you visit the room where you'll present, try out the projector and stand at the back of the room to review things from the perspective of audience members sitting there. Adjust the lighting so that everyone in the room can see the slides and see you clearly too. Ask a facilities manager to help if the lighting controls are not readily accessible or if you need additional lighting.

CHECKING THE TECHNOLOGY

Stories rely on a strong beginning to set the tone and direction of the rest of the narrative. Although you have a strong beginning built into Act I of the story template, the presentation actually begins when the eyes of the audience turn to you and recognize you as the speaker. You're not off to a strong start if what they see is you connecting the projector cable to your computer, focusing the image on the screen, and searching for your PowerPoint file amid the clutter of your computer's desktop screen. Audiences can be tolerant of these sorts of distractions, but don't count on that. That's why you need to prepare for your technical needs in advance.

When you survey the room where you'll present, take the time to perform all the steps required to set up the technology for the presentation. Plug the projector or monitor into the computer, power up the equipment, and open the PowerPoint file. Make any technical adjustments you need, and then resize the image to fit the screen and focus it. If you use a remote control device to advance the slides, try it out to make sure it works properly. Test the internet connection if you need one, and review any online materials you'll show on the projector during the presentation. If you plan to display Web pages, make a backup copy of them on your local computer if possible, in case you have problems with the internet connection.

If you're not able to set up the equipment and rehearse in the room in advance of the presentation, at a minimum set up the equipment before the presentation with enough time available to resolve any technology issues that might arise.

PREPARING FOR POSSIBLE PROBLEMS

Even if something goes wrong, you're still able to produce a solid presentation experience. For example, if your speaking time is unexpectedly cut from 45 minutes to 15 or even 5 minutes, quickly scale the presentation to the reduced time by hiding slides, as you did in Chapter 6. If your computer crashes and you have no way to recover it, cover all the presentation points by using a printout of the story template, storyboard, outline, notes pages, or slides. If the projector bulb burns out and you have no spare, your simple slides might be clear enough to be seen on the computer screen by a small audience at a table.

Your thorough preparation will enable you to carry out the presentation with confidence, no matter what problems come your way. If the presentation is particularly critical, such as the opening statement at a high-stakes legal trial or a keynote presentation to a large group at an important conference, arrange for your associates to run a second presentation in parallel as a backup, and connect both computers to a switch. If something unexpected were to happen, you could switch to the second presentation without distraction.

REHEARSING

In the past, you might have waited until you had finished creating the slides before you rehearsed the presentation for the first time. But as you've been crafting your story step by step, you're really rehearsing through the entire process. You get comfortable with your story when you write the story template in Chapters 4 and 5. You become acquainted with the flow and sequence of the story when you prepare the storyboard and narration in Chapter 6. And you become familiar with the visuals on-screen when you sketch the storyboard and add graphics in Chapters 7 and 8. Through each of these steps, you mentally rehearse the core of the presentation and address a number of possible distractions, such as becoming too reliant on the slides to remind you of every detail you want to present.

During a presentation, all eyes are on you, and people will watch for cues that indicate your enthusiasm and interest in a topic. If you speak in a monotone and appear disinterested, you shouldn't be surprised if the audience mirrors your lack of enthusiasm. Instead, vary your voice to emphasize important points, and pause for effect when you want a particular point to sink in. You've been working hard on your story, so let your confidence and enthusiasm come through your voice, as well as through your facial expressions. As you rehearse, you're sure to run into rough spots or things you want to change in the presentation, so keep a piece of paper handy for jotting down revision notes to yourself as you go. Then return to the presentation to make any final changes to the slides.

Ask someone on your team to attend your rehearsal and give you honest feedback about the presentation, because you're better able to improve with the help of an outsider's perspective. Some people are inclined to mention only good things, so ask your evaluators not only to confirm what you do well but also to suggest specific ways to improve. It's a good idea to ask for a range of opinions because each viewer will give you advice from a different perspective. Take account of whatever feedback you get, and make adjustments as needed.

USING NOTES

The presenter view feature in PowerPoint is a great asset to a presenter and provides helpful tools to remind you of what to say. The notes pane provides your notes about what to say, and a thumbnail of the next slide gives you a visual cue of the point to come.

TIP   One of the most common verbal distractions is the use of filler words like *um*, *uh*, *I mean*, and *you know*. Most people aren't even aware that they use these words—even some of the most experienced speakers. To reduce distracting verbal fillers, record yourself when you speak and count the *ums*. Or ask someone you know to count the number of filler word occurrences while you speak. The surest cure for this distracting habit is becoming aware that you do it in the first place.

Although you should be intimately familiar with the presentation at this point, keep a set of speaker notes on the podium in the form of a printed story template or storyboard outline. Don't use the complete notes pages as speaker notes. The written text in the notes area might tempt you to read from the page, and you'd need to physically flip from one page to the next, which would be distracting. Instead, when you print your key presentation documents, consider using as speaker notes the story template, a text outline of the storyboard, or thumbnail images of the storyboard:

■ To print the story template, open the Microsoft Word document that contains your story template. If you made any changes to the headlines in the storyboard, update the document to reflect those changes, and then print the document.

- To print a text outline of the storyboard, click File, Print, and in the Settings area, click the drop-down arrow next to Full Page Slides, and select Outline.

- To print thumbnail images of the storyboard, click File, Print, and in the Settings area, click the drop-down arrow next to Full Page Slides, and under Handouts, click either 6 Slides Horizontal or 9 Slides Horizontal.

- To print handouts from notes pages, click File, Print, and in the Settings area, click the drop-down arrow next to Full Page Slides, and select Notes Pages. Another option is to print the individual slides one per page, but you should have enough material with just the thumbnail images of the storyboard and the notes pages printouts.

- While you're at it, print any additional handouts you'll reference during the presentation, such as diagrams or flowcharts, spreadsheets, and detailed charts and graphs.

Once you've printed all of the documents, assemble them in a folder so you have them in a single place for reference.

> **TIP** To customize your speaker notes using thumbnail-size images of the storyboard, go to the View tab, and in the Master Views group, select Handout Master and make adjustments there such as adding your company logo.

PROMPTING A DIALOGUE

When you make the audience the main character of your story in Act I of the story template, the story is *all about them* instead of *all about you*. So rather than the presentation being a performance in which you're the star who entertains an adoring crowd, you're part of the supporting cast in the service of the audience. This is a shift from seeing the primary function of slides as *speaker support* to a new view in which your slides serve as *audience support*.

A presentation isn't a one-way street; it takes the interaction of presenters and audiences to create a dialogue. You just happen to be the first one to speak, and because you're the presenter, you're the one who is in charge of getting the interaction started.

BEING AUTHENTIC

The dialog you create with the presentation begins with you. After all, the audience is granting you their time to listen to what you have to say. An audience is more likely to give your presentation a fair hearing if they know you're authentic. You communicate your authentic personal credibility in a number of ways, beginning with the introduction you planned in your storyboard in Chapter 7, continuing with the clarity of your ideas and the crispness of your message, and then carrying through with the visual credibility of your slides and the verbal credibility of your narration.

Adding your name to the byline of the story template when you begin writing the script establishes your personal responsibility for the presentation process from start to finish. The biggest benefit of being so closely involved is that the presentation eventually becomes an extension of who you are.

As you work on focusing the story in Act I and distilling your ideas to three main points in Act II, you become increasingly confident in your message. And making creative choices for the design of the storyboard makes the presentation start to feel like an extension of your personality.

One of the biggest obstacles you can impose on yourself when you speak in public is the idea that you need to be someone you're not. This problem becomes magnified if you're handed a generic PowerPoint file with the same look everyone else uses. Although these presentations might look slick on the surface, they often lack the heart and soul that only the personality of a unique human being can bring.

You break out of this trap by using the new visual story you created, which should reflect your character and personality in the choices you make for the story and visuals. Then expand on that personal beginning by delivering a presentation that expresses your original voice. Audiences always prefer a presentation that's imperfect and a little rough around the edges—but still authentic—over a perfect and flawless presentation that has no soul.

When you present, never be afraid to be yourself, because that's what people really want you to be.

WORKING CONFIDENTLY WITH YOUR SLIDES

For many people, the thought of public speaking inspires fear, not confidence. The fear often comes from speakers not being comfortable with their story, themselves, or their level of preparedness. You remove the elements that create fear by securing a strong story, extending your personality through the story, and rehearsing thoroughly along the way. Your confidence comes shining through most clearly in the way you use the projected slides you designed.

After working with the PowerPoint file in Notes Page, Normal, and Slide Sorter views, you should be very comfortable with the material. When you advance to a new slide in the presentation, that slide's headline will prompt you for what to say next. The headline also addresses the audience in a conversational tone, making them feel relaxed and helping them to easily understand what you want to convey at that point.

Next on the slide is the graphical element. One of the benefits of your new simplified design approach is that the slides are free of bullet points and excess clutter; instead, you show a meaningful headline illustrated by a simple graphic. The goal of simple slides like these is to inspire interdependence between you and the audience. By showing less on-screen, you pique the audience's curiosity.

Next, you answer the audience's questions about the slide with your spoken words, which you developed fully in the written explanation of each slide in the notes area. You explain the meaning of the headline and graphic to the audience in your own natural voice.

These three basic elements—headline, graphic, and your voice—work together to create an implicit dialogue that engages the audience. When you finish the thought at hand, you advance to the next slide and repeat the process in a steady flow that naturally continues the dialogue.

As you deliver your visual story, you'll gain the focused attention of the audience through your relaxed approach, interesting narrative, and engaging visuals. Scan the room as you speak, making direct eye contact with audience members in every part of the room.

HANDLING Q & A

If you've done your work well in the story template, you anticipate questions by tailoring the presentation to the audience and addressing the questions they're wondering about as you complete each of the acts and scenes. However, having a Q & A session is important. Even if you've covered everything, people who are making decisions will still want to ask questions so that they feel like they've participated in the experience. Depending on how you planned it into your storyboard, you might open up the floor to conversation from the very start in Act I, or at the end of the first and second Anchor sections, or both. Or you might conclude your prepared remarks and then invite audience comments. In some instances, you might even want to purposely leave a few questions unanswered so that the audience will be sure to ask them and engage you in the Q & A. If you're speaking to a large audience and take a question, restate the question before you answer it to make sure everyone in the room hears it.

If someone asks a question about a particular slide, refer to the printed storyboard for the corresponding slide number (if you don't already know it), and then in Slide Show view, type the number of the slide and press Enter to go directly to that slide. If you want to show a slide that relates to a general question from one of the Act II scenes, type the number of whichever Act II slide corresponds with the question and press Enter. If you have extra material that didn't fit into the Act II slides, but you think you might still be asked about it, add the extra slides to the end of the presentation and refer to them if some questions relate to them.

> **TIP**   As an advanced technique, use the PowerPoint storyboard on-screen as a navigational aid. While you are in Slide Show view, right-click any slide and select See All Slides, which gives you a view similar to the Slide Sorter view. This creates an interesting visual, and because you know the storyboard so well, when someone asks a question about a slide, click the slide to go directly to it.

KEEPING CONTROL OF YOUR STORY

Because of your confident and relaxed approach to visual storytelling, you might find that people ask you questions during the presentation or offer stories of their own experiences. This is a good sign that the audience is feeling comfortable with your speaking style, and it is perfectly fine if that's the way you planned the presentation in the storyboard. The downside is that these queries can also cause you to head off on a tangent that throws off your timing and story structure. Handle questions graciously by quickly answering them or by acknowledging them and, if necessary, making a note and saying that you'll answer them during the Q & A session at the end of the presentation. If you don't know the answer to a question, admit that you don't know, and offer to follow up on the matter later.

It's essential to stay on course with your story; if you don't, you can easily lose control of the situation. The goal of your visual story is to create a compelling narrative that's tailored to the audience and anticipates their questions so that they're completely absorbed to the very end. If you missed the mark and your story wasn't a good fit for the audience, get as much feedback as possible and spend time later reviewing the story template to improve the next story you write. Pay particular attention to the Act I scenes to ensure that the story engages the audience fully.

At a minimum, present the 5-minute version of the presentation described in Chapter 6, which includes all of Act I and the Anchor slides, which together form the essential structure of your story.

PREPARING FOR DIFFERENT CONTEXTS

For most audiences, a large screen is ample for projecting a presentation; for large audiences, the screen needs to be big enough for the people in the back row to see the slides clearly. A large audience size usually prevents you from getting feedback while you're presenting, but that doesn't prevent the experience from being an implicit dialogue, as described earlier in this chapter.

For an audience of one or two people, give the presentation using a laptop with a large screen, printouts of the slides, or even a handheld computer. In each of these cases, you lose the power of a large projected image, but you gain regarding a more casual and conversational approach and the immediacy of starting right away with little or no need to deal with technology setup.

HANDING OUT HANDOUTS

Many presenters find it best to provide handouts after the presentation to prevent distractions. On the other hand, many audiences ask for handouts because they like to make notes on paper during a presentation. Try both approaches to see what works best for you and your audiences. One compromise is to print and hand out in advance a one-page version of the story template so that the audience has a basic road map of where you're going. Mention at the beginning of the presentation that you'll provide comprehensive handouts at the end, and at that point provide sets of handouts in the form of printed notes pages.

SENDING YOUR NOTES PAGES (NOT YOUR SLIDES)

If you can't present in person, you obviously miss out on the kind of communication that happens only in a live environment. But that doesn't have to stop you from presenting when you're not physically present; you just need to configure the PowerPoint presentation differently.

When you add graphics to the presentation in Chapter 8, you know that your new slides don't make much sense unless you look at them in Notes Page view. The same holds true if you send your slides to someone who couldn't attend the presentation in person, so don't send just the slides; send the notes pages instead.

Handouts in the form of notes pages offer quick reading as a printed document. Readers quickly understand the main idea of the document by skimming headlines and visuals from page to page, and they can also spend more time reading the narrative detail in the notes area if they want.

An effective way to send notes pages is in PDF file format, as described in Chapter 8. When you email the notes pages in this format, the audience has access to all of the information you want to present, but they do not have access to the original file where you keep the graphical materials and editable text you might not want to make available.

PRODUCING AN ONLINE PRESENTATION

Your new visual story will work well in an online context because the same engaging story structure is there. The same simple visuals that support interdependence with your spoken words are there, too, as well as the same evenly sized pieces of information, the same even pacing, and the same even flow.

BBP CHECKLIST: DELIVERING YOUR PRESENTATION Before and during the presentation, do you

- Prepare the environment, check the technology, and properly rehearse in advance?
- Use your physical presence and voice to bring the experience to life?
- Engage your audience both implicitly and explicitly?

AND NOW, PRESENTING...

You should now be ready to present to your audience. With your thorough preparation, you're sure to persuade the audience with your focused, clear, and engaging story.

Now that you've seen why and how visual storytelling works, it's time to get started on your own presentations. As you begin, use this book to guide you through the process step by step. Find others in your organization who are willing to help. As you apply the approach and get good results, you'll quickly create momentum that will propel clearer and more effective communications throughout your organization. As you start to live a life beyond bullet points, there's no turning back; you're on your way to a much more engaging way of presenting.

10 TIPS FOR ENHANCING YOUR DELIVERY

You now have a flexible and robust system for bringing your ideas to life using PowerPoint. Before you give a presentation, review the following 10 tips to find ideas to spark your imagination or inspire you to try something new.

TIP 1: THE LIVING BRAND

In the conventional bullet points approach, it's common for presenters to place a logo on the Slide Master, which means that the logo will appear on every slide in the presentation. There's no problem with including a logo in the introductory and con-cluding slides, but a problem arises when the logo is on every single slide. Based on the research realities in Chapter 2, adding a logo to every slide amounts to extraneous information that does not further the focus of the specific point being made in the headline. Eliminating the logo from the Slide Master increases the amount of screen real estate available for presenting information and opens up the many creative options that an empty screen allows.

Beyond those reasons, in a live presentation context, the concept of a visual stamp on a slide diminishes in importance because all eyes are on you, and you are actually *living the brand*. The high quality of your ideas, the compelling story, the interesting visuals, and the high level of engagement all contribute to an experience the audience will not soon forget. And just in case the audience does forget some details of the experience, they'll always have the handout.

If you plan to provide handouts, visit View, Notes Master and add your logo to the footer.

TIP 2: TRY OUT TOASTMASTERS

If you're not a member of a speaking club, you should be. Any speaker can benefit from attending a regular meeting with the sole purpose of learning and improving a full range of speaking skills. Toastmasters International, at *www.toastmasters.org*, is a good choice because it's inexpensive and all clubs are run by the volunteer efforts of their members. When you join, you'll participate in speaking exercises during meet-ings and give a series of prepared talks according to a sequence in a training manual.

The biggest benefits will likely come from simply attending regularly. As you're exposed to more speaking opportunities in a supportive environment, you'll develop skills to manage your nervousness, and your confidence will increase not just in public speaking but all aspects of communication.

Some clubs haven't yet embraced the use of presentation technologies. If your local club doesn't yet use PowerPoint, bring a data projector and introduce some of the ideas you've picked up in this book to blend projected media and solid speaking skills.

TIP 3: STRETCH YOURSELF

A live presentation draws on the full spectrum of communication skills, but almost no one is good at everything. You're probably better at one part of the BBP process—for example, writing your story, editing your headlines, distilling your ideas to their essence, checking your reasoning, creating visuals, or speaking and presenting. When you know your strength, pick a different area to work on improving because you'll still need to use all your skills when you create and deliver a presentation. For example, if you're good at writing, learn graphics, or if you're good at graphics, work on your public speaking.

TIP 4: INNOVATIVE HANDOUTS

Create an unconventional note-taking handout by including only the three Anchor slides on a single piece of paper. As the audience members see each Anchor slide on the screen, it will cue them to the corresponding image on the handout and reinforce the top-level, visual-verbal message you want to communicate.

TIP 5: GOT GOBO?

Many standard meeting rooms feature fluorescent lights and ordinary tables, but with inexpensive lighting tools, you can change the atmosphere of the room to remove the distractions of a shabby presentation environment. For example, a simple way to light up the presentation environment is with a *gobo*, which is a partial screen with the cut-out of a pattern that's placed over a light. When you turn on the light, it projects the image of the pattern onto a surface.

Use a gobo to project a subtle pattern to cover up an uneven wall or to add a soft color to make glaring lights less obvious. As with all the visuals you've prepared for the presentation, any visual effects should be transparent and never distract from the message. If you've "got gobo," or any other special lighting, keep in mind that people should remember the message and not the lighting.

TIP 6: VISUAL MNEMONICS

Having problems trying to remember what you want to say? Try using the graphics on your slides to trigger your memory. For example, if you display a particular image on a slide and you plan to make certain points when you narrate it, associate each point with an element on the photograph. When you use an image on a slide as a visual mnemonic, you make your ideas, as well as the presentation, memorable.

TIP 7: MAKE THE CONVERSATION HIGH VOLTAGE

In *Moving Mountains* (Crowell-Collier Press, 1989), Henry M. Boettinger wrote, "Presentation of ideas is conversation carried on at high voltage—at once more dangerous and more powerful." This is one of the best definitions of presentations because it packs so much meaning into a brief sentence:

- You're presenting *ideas*, not your ego.
- A presentation is a *conversation*. There are at least two people involved.
- A presentation is *high voltage*. It's not boring.
- A presentation is *dangerous*. It's risky.
- A presentation is *powerful*. It has strength.

The next time you speak, keep Boettinger's wise definition in mind to stay focused on the meaning you pack into your presentations.

TIP 8: MAGNIFY INTIMACY

One of the most powerful techniques in film is magnifying the face of an actor to give the audience a feeling of intimacy with that person. Although you won't see that technique in most presentations, new technologies continue to transform the presentation landscape.

For example, in some presentations, an IMAG image magnification camera will zoom in on a presenter's face while he or she is speaking at a live event. The image is often featured in a split-screen format next to the speaker's slides on a wide screen. If you have the chance to have your face magnified on a screen, embrace the opportunity because you're giving the audience a chance to see you up close. However, before you do, rehearse using a live camera similar to the one in the presentation along with the event producers, who may arrange for lighting and makeup to make sure that you look good on the big screen.

TIP 9: FLIP THROUGH FLIP CHARTS

If you use paper flip charts along with your screen presentation, when you walk over to the flip chart, write out a headline in a complete sentence that corresponds to the point you want to make on that slide in the storyboard. Writing out the headline on the flip chart keeps your point persistent because it stays visible to the audience, reminding them of the point and reinforcing it. The headline on the flip chart will stay visible after you return to the screen media, so make sure that it's a point you want to make visible through the rest of the presentation; otherwise, cover what you wrote with a blank sheet.

TIP 10: PREDESIGN YOUR MEDIA TOOLS

If you work with a touchscreen computer or flip charts, consider predesigning parts of the slides or printed pieces before you use them. For example, you might have the background scene of a slide set up and then write over it using a touchscreen computer with a stylus. Do this with scanned documents, screen captures, and just about any other type of media so that when you start sketching, you already have a visual beginning point.

PRESENT THIS, NOT THAT

In this chapter, you will:

- Review a range of presentation examples using a visual storytelling approach.
- See how the core visual storytelling principles look when applied to different topics.
- Get inspired by seeing how to apply new techniques to your presentation.

So far, this book has demonstrated how to apply visual storytelling in-depth to a single presentation example. Chapter 4 showed you how Act I of the story template helps you choose the specific ideas you'll present in the first five slides of a presentation, and Chapter 5 showed you how Act II guides you through the process of setting the priority and sequence of the rest of the slides. Chapter 6 offered instructions on how to set up your storyboard and narration, and Chapter 7 illustrated some of the many ways to sketch your storyboard. All of this came together in Chapter 8 as you added the specific graphics that are a good fit for you, your headlines, and your audience. Finally, Chapter 9 demonstrated how to deliver your presentation using your powerful new toolkit.

Although these chapters used a single presentation example, the same underlying process will unlock a clear visual story from any topic and guide your audience to clear and memorable understanding.

WHAT OTHER EXAMPLES CAN I SEE?

The types of presentations that are possible to create visual stories are endless. This chapter shows you more examples of BBP in action as it is applied to a wide range of topics and purposes, showing what a presentation might look if you were to:

- Introduce a case to jurors in an opening statement with The Trial.
- Keep your team on track toward completing a project with The Plan.
- Summarize your market research findings to your clients with The Analysis.
- Update and gain the support of your boss for your activities with The Report.
- Teach your students about a new topic with The Class.
- Sell the services of your company or organization to a client with The Pitch.

Because of space limitations, the examples in this chapter show selected portions of story templates, storyboards, and slides, focusing primarily on the critical Act I, map, and anchor slides rather than on the explanation and backup slides that will contain your own specific photos, charts, graphs, screen captures, and diagrams. Every presentation was built using the same process in this book, but each looks and feels very different. Likewise, your presentations will reflect your understanding of your specific audiences that determines the words you write in the story template, the graphics you add to the storyboard, and the way you deliver the experience.

As with the example of the transportation-related presentation in the earlier chapters of this book, the example presentations in this chapter adhere to the design constraint of a limited budget to show you what is possible with an inexpensive stock photography website and your own creativity—if you have a larger budget or work with a professional graphic designer, you probably can get even more polished results. If adding graphics is not your strength, work with others who can help.

EXAMPLE: PRESENTING IN COURT

This book began with the example of a headline-making visual story used in a courtroom in Chapter 1, and it's worth taking a quick peek under the hood to see what made the first slides of that presentation work so well. Although you may never present an opening statement in a trial, when you explore the thought process behind this example, think of how you will write your own clear and concise words in Act I of your story template and apply equally effective yet simple visual techniques to your storyboard.

ACT I: THE CLASSICAL STORYTELLING FOUNDATION

Chapter 4 explained that at the beginning of your presentation, you are faced with the formidable challenges not only of setting up the framework that will help the working memory of your audience understand what is to come but also of making an emotional connection. The attorney who presented the opening statement as described in Chapter 1 accomplished both goals by the way he structured his ideas in Act I of his story template, as shown in Figure 10-1, which established the story thread and pattern that would help the jurors sew up an understanding of the case.

Act I – The Compelling Setup	
The Hook	Bob Ernst is dead
The Relevance	You get to be like CSI detectives and follow the evidence
The Challenge	A mountain of evidence will lead you to a pharmaceutical company
The Desire	You'll hear two sides of the story and will get to weigh the facts and find justice
The Map	Follow the three parts of the case to find justice for Mrs. Ernst

Act II – The Engaging Action		
Theme	**Chronology**	**Evidence**

FIGURE 10-1

Act I of The Trial presentation example.

Although the specific words in Act I are brief, they're a good example of how a sequence of concise statements works dynamically to create the underpinnings for a compelling visual story. When you work on your Act I headlines, keep in mind the absolute importance of getting Act I right. If you know your audience well and you write the correct words, you'll hit your target, as the attorney did in this example.

NOTE Notice that the Act II category headings in Figure 10-1 have been changed in this example from "Anchors" to "Theme," from "Explanation" to "Chronology," and from "Backup" to "Evidence"—other examples in this chapter are also tailored to the presentation content, as described in the section "Tip 3: Tailor Your Act II Column Headings to Your Profession" in Chapter 5.

A PHOTOGRAPHIC HOOK SLIDE

The hook headline in the story template, "Bob Ernst is dead," quickly oriented the jurors to the context for the trial—Bob had died of a heart attack. As described in Chapter 1, this clear and direct statement is the foundation for the hook slide, which in this example included three variations of a single photograph, here presented across three slides in Figure 10-2. The headlines of all the Act I slides are hidden in this example and the rest of the examples in this chapter. Although you may likely keep the headlines visible through most of Act II because they guide understanding of the in-depth new information on your explanation and backup (evidence) slides, they are not essential in Act I because here you are primarily making an emotional impact. And, as always, your narration will supply the verbal information that synchronizes with your visual slides.

FIGURE 10-2

The hook slides introduced to the jurors a gripping story.

As Mark Lanier told an anecdote about Carol and Bob while the first photograph was on the screen, his spoken words packed the on-screen image with meaning. Here the jurors could connect emotionally with Bob and Carol because anyone could relate to the details of their life together and be happy for them. But the emotion that had been attached to the first slide was suddenly stripped away visually with the removal of the background in the second slide, signaling that something unexpected was about to happen. The third slide becomes deeply poignant when visually Carol is suddenly left alone, with only an empty outline defining the space where her husband once was. Although the photo sequence is very simple, it had a profound impact. When you think of writing and illustrating your hook headline, consider how to use a simple anecdote and photograph to quickly orient your audience in an equally savvy way.

REVIEWING THE ACT I SLIDES FOR THE TRIAL

Transitioning from the preceding photograph with a heavy black outline of Bob, shown on the upper left in Figure 10-3, Mark now "deputized" the jurors as crime scene detectives in the relevance slide (upper right) with the simple phrase *CSI: Angleton* illustrating the hidden headline "You get to be like CSI detectives and follow the evidence." Mark knew that this technique would connect with his audience because many of the jurors had indicated in questionnaires that the popular *CSI* television show was one of their favorites. Even if all the jurors had not seen *CSI*, they would know its premise because of the show's broad market awareness. As you write and illustrate your relevance headline, consider what words and images will instantly place your audience at the center of the action in an effective way like this.

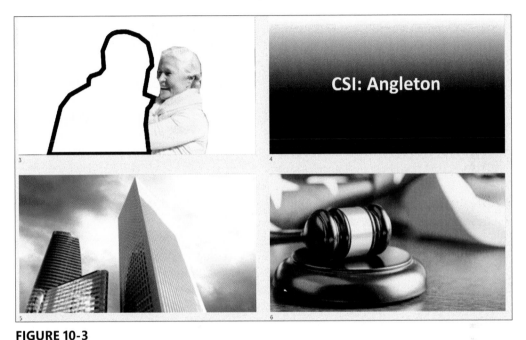

FIGURE 10-3

The hook, relevance, challenge, and desire slides of The Trial.

In keeping with the classical storytelling form described in Chapter 4, the lawyer's next step was to present the main characters with a challenge they face on the challenge slide—a large quantity of evidence that they are going to encounter in the upcoming trial. In this case, Mark defined the jurors' challenge in the hidden headline "A mountain of evidence will lead you to a pharmaceutical company," illustrated with an office building like the one shown on the lower left in Figure 10-3. In screenwriting terms, this introduced the challenge that is built into your challenge headline—an obstacle or an event that confronts the main character and begins the action that drives the story forward. Mark defined the obstacle as the evidence these "CSI detectives" would now need to follow.

However, for the problem to be fully defined, Mark needed to provide the jurors with a second crucial element—desire, or where the jurors wanted to be, which is defined in the story template with the headline "You'll hear two sides of the story and will get to weigh the facts and find justice." The image of a gavel (lower right in Figure 10-3) along with Mark's narration reinforced the problem the jurors faced: they will climb the mountain of evidence that leads them to the company (challenge), and when they have understood the evidence they must bring the situation to justice (desire).

The underlying structure of many conventional presentations often neglects to engage audiences at an emotional level, leaving them struggling to figure out why they should care. But with Act I of the story template, Mark's presentation efficiently adapted a story technique to make the topic personally engaging to his audience. By creating a gap between challenge where the jurors stood and desire where they wanted to be, Mark tapped into the core element of classical story structure—unre-solved tension. People do not sit comfortably with tension, and it is the quest to resolve the tension that compels the main character to action. By presenting the jurors with a problem, Mark engaged the jurors both emotionally and intellectually, and he answered the toughest audience question any presenter faces: "What's in it for me?"

REVIEWING THE MAP AND ANCHOR SLIDES FOR THE TRIAL

By using Act I of the story template, Mark would not leave his audience without a way to get from A to B. As described in more detail in Chapter 1, the map slide, shown on the upper left in Figure 10-4, distills the entire presentation into a single slide based on the hidden headline "Follow the three parts of the case to find justice for Mrs. Ernst." With the three-part formula of *motive + means = death*, Mark introduced the vast amount of new information to the jurors as being as simple as 1-2-3. Just as the murder-mystery motif is a familiar structure, the jurors would also know the phrase "as easy as 1-2-3." If the upcoming story would be that easy to understand, the jurors could relax their minds as they listened to the case.

Next, Mark had written Act II of his story template to divide the story of the case into three anchor (Case Theme) headlines that he would spend equal amounts of time explaining. Each corresponding anchor slide carried forward the 1-2-3 numbering system along with an enlarged version of each icon from the map slide. Each image used on these slides was carefully chosen to convey the visual essence of each anchor headline.

As illustrated simply yet powerfully here, the ideas and images and narration you use on your anchor slides are the most important ideas you want your audience to integrate into long-term memory. Similarly, you'll want to apply a blend of your best creative and intellectual thinking to design your Act I and anchor slides because they represent the verbal and visual essence of the most important information you want to communicate.

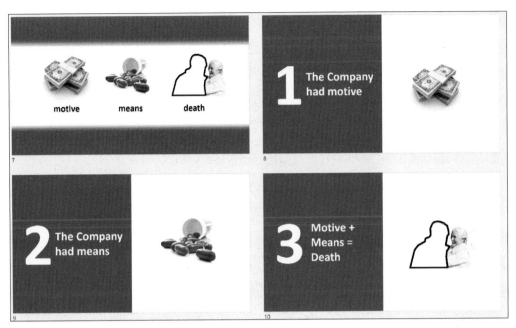

FIGURE 10-4

The map and anchor slides of The Trial.

With this familiar story structure in place on the map and anchor slides, Mark solved the toughest communication challenge any presenter faces—how to make it easier for an audience to understand new information. As described in Chapter 2, as much as you might hope otherwise, the reality is that you cannot pour information directly into your audience's minds and have them simply "get it." The working memory of your audience can become quickly overloaded when the audience is unfamiliar with the information or if the material otherwise is not presented properly. To overcome this problem and increase his audience's ability to understand his case, Mark related the new information of the case using a story framework through Acts I and II that the audience already knew—the murder-mystery motif.

The graphics used on these slides are created using stock photography, family photographs, or tools within PowerPoint. This presentation is a good example of how the simple visual surfaces of BBP presentations offer few clues that there is a sophisticated verbal strategy beneath them, yet the powerful impact of the approach is very real and profound. As you apply simple visual surfaces to your written story structures, you'll begin to tap into similar results in your presentations.

EXAMPLE: PRESENTING A PLAN

The Trial example showed a range of verbal and visual techniques to apply to your presentations even if you never set foot in a courtroom. The next example, named The Plan, might come in handy if you find yourself leading a team toward accomplishing a project. In this scenario, your group has a deadline to accomplish a task, but you're running into problems that might delay the project.

WRITING ACT I OF THE STORY TEMPLATE

As you start your story template, you've done your research with your audience and know that there is a shared sense of frustration with the delays on the project. As an experienced project manager, you know what the basic problems are and have a plan for how they can be resolved. The hook headline, shown in Figure 10-5, affirms "We've been racing to finish the project, but now we're running behind."

Act I – The Compelling Setup	
The Hook	We've been racing to finish the project but now we're running behind
The Relevance	We've got to get back on track to earn our incentives
The Challenge	What are some of the problems you think are standing in our way?
The Desire	We must solve the problems to reach the finish line
The Map	Let's overcome the obstacles by re-focusing on 3 areas

FIGURE 10-5

The Plan presentation with Act I completed.

In the storyboard sketches shown in Figure 10-6, the hook headline plays out as a photo of team project planning (left), and the relevance headline shows the photo of a contract that affirms, "We've got to get back on track to earn our incentives."

FIGURE 10-6

Sketches of the hook and relevance slides of The Plan presentation.

TIP: SET UP A LIGHTBOX A *lightbox*, available at some stock photography websites, is a very useful tool in your research for available graphics. Use a lightbox to temporarily collect photos in a single place, without committing to purchasing licenses until you are ready to use specific photos.

As described earlier, the challenge is a crucial slide on which you need to make sure that your audience feels emotionally connected to the challenge they face. To make sure that is the case, when you present the challenge slide, ask your audience, "What are some of the problems you think are standing in our way?" Then, if you have a touchscreen computer, write the responses directly on the screen, such as "lack of focus," "confusion," or "duplicated effort," as shown on the left in Figure 10-7. (If you don't have a touchscreen computer, write the responses on a flip chart instead.)

Asking your audiences questions will shift the dynamic of the presentation because you are not telling your team what their problems are; rather, they are telling you. Instead of risking that they will be alienated by feeling that you know it all, you give your audience a feeling of ownership. When you advance to the desire slide (right), you affirm that all the problems are valid, and "We must solve the problems to reach the finish line" while you use red ink to cross out each of the phrases you had written on the previous slide.

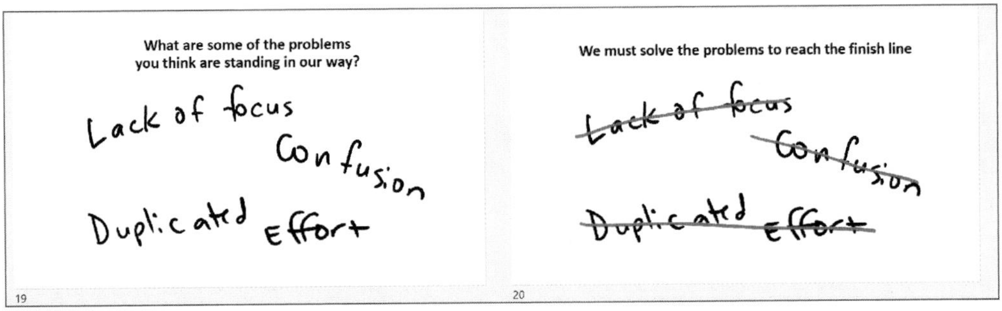

FIGURE 10-7

Sketches of the challenge and desire slides of The Plan presentation.

Figure 10-8 shows these four slides with formatting and graphics added. The hook and relevance slides (upper left and right) feature full-screen photographs with the headline hidden. The challenge slide (lower left) features a headline only and the desire slide (lower right) shows that sketching was done on the slide during the live presentation.

FIGURE 10-8

The hook, relevance, challenge, and desire slides with graphics added.

REVIEWING THE MAP AND ANCHOR SLIDES FOR THE PLAN

Although you opened the floor to a conversation with the audience on the challenge slide, you also know from research and your experience as a project manager that you need to address three primary problems, which you've spelled out in three anchor headlines in your story template, shown in Figure 10-9.

Act II – The Engaging Action
Anchors (5 minutes)

Overcome lack of focus by reviewing the plan each morning

Overcome confusion by talking to someone directly

Overcome duplicated effort by checking off completed items on the group app

FIGURE 10-9

Story template showing the three anchor headlines of The Plan example.

Next, when you create your map and anchor slides from the headlines as described in Chapter 7, read each headline, and consider what you can sketch to illustrate the main point of each headline. For example, as illustrated in Figure 10-10, the map slide has the headline "Let's overcome the obstacles by re-focusing on three areas," so the sketch is a simple 1-2-3 showing you'll cover the three areas. The three areas are then covered in the anchor headlines:

■ The first anchor headline, in the upper right, is "Overcome lack of focus by reviewing the plan each morning," and the sketch is a project plan.

■ The second anchor headline, lower left, reads "Overcome confusion by talking to someone directly," and has a sketch of two people talking to each other.

■ The third anchor headline, lower right, reads "Overcome duplicated effort by checking off completed items on the group app," and features a sketch of a smartphone with a group app on it.

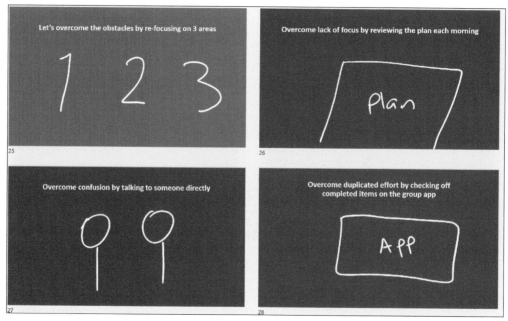

FIGURE 10-10

Sketches of the map and anchor slides.

Once you have the sketches in place, search for graphics for each of the slides. Figure 10-11 shows each of the anchor slides with a stock photograph that illustrates each point, and the map slide features the three anchor photographs side by side.

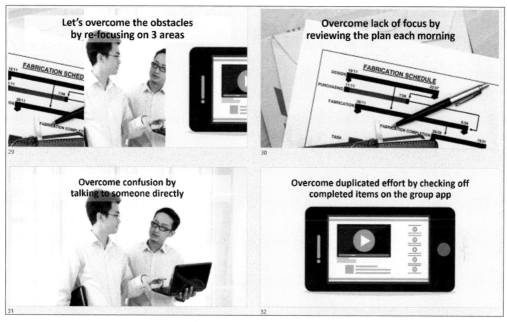

FIGURE 10-11

The map and anchor slides with graphics added.

As you sketch the rest of the explanation and backup slides, use the range of graphical possibilities as described in Chapter 7 to sketch the slide headlines and then to add graphics. As you saw in earlier chapters, these graphics might include photos, screen captures, diagrams, charts, or other media elements.

TIP Stock photography Websites usually offer different sizes of graphics for licensing. For example, the small size of a photograph with a resolution of 72 dpi is generally fine for on-screen presentations, which will fill a standard PowerPoint slide measuring 7.5 inches by 10 inches. Carefully read all licensing agreements and size specifications for graphics before purchasing to make sure you are covered for the appropriate use.

EXAMPLE: PRESENTING RESEARCH RESULTS

Now that you've had a taste of using visual storytelling as a way to present The Plan, the next example presents a new challenge—communicating the results of market research you conducted to your company's clients with The Analysis. Your client's sales have dropped, and the client has asked your market research firm to help.

This type of presentation featuring quantitative information is typically called a "data-driven" presentation. In spite of the research realities presented in Chapter 2, many data-driven presentations are designed using the myth that you can simply drive data into your audience's heads, and they will "get it." This approach doesn't take into account the importance of respecting the limits of working memory, synchronizing the visual and verbal channels, and guiding the attention of an audience in specific ways.

Visual storytelling, on the other hand, accepts these research realities and subscribes to the idea that there is no such thing as a data-driven presentation—there are only "cognitive-driven" presentations because ultimately the audience's minds will determine whether understanding happened, not the data.

Act I of The Analysis presentation, shown in Figure 10-12, is a good example of how dramatically different a formerly data-driven presentation looks when you restructure it using visual storytelling. In this example, the hook headline summarizes that your client has hired your market research firm because "Your sales dried up last year in your most lucrative market segment." Next, the relevance headline puts your clients in their proper place as the main character of this story as "You asked us to drill into the numbers and analyze the situation." The challenge headline explains the challenge you believe the client faces: "You have tapped out your existing revenue base." The desire then goes on to confirm to your client that "You need a strategy to get profits flowing again." Now, what should your audience do to get from the challenge to the desire? They should "Consider three innovative ways to reach new customers and increase revenues," according to your map slide.

Act I – The Compelling Setup	
The Hook	Your sales dried up last year in your most lucrative market segment
The Relevance	You asked us to drill into the numbers and analyze the situation
The Challenge	You have tapped out your existing revenue base
The Desire	You need a strategy to get profits flowing again
The Map	Consider three innovative ways to reach new customers and increase revenue

Act II – The Engaging Action		
Recommendation	**Explanation**	**Methodology/Data**

FIGURE 10-12

Act I of The Analysis presentation example.

If it's helpful to you, rename the Act II column headings for this type of presentation as shown in Figure 10-12 from "Anchor" to "Recommendation" and from "Backup" to "Methodology/Data." As always, you end Act I of the story template with the map headline and expand on it with the anchor (Recommendation) headlines in Act II. Then you flesh out each anchor (Recommendation) headline, as shown in Figure 10-13, with further explanation and backup (Methodology/Data). With this approach, you know that you have logically organized your thoughts and built-in scalability to present the same material in 5, 15, or 45 minutes (as described in Chapter 6) without losing the integrity or quality of your critical thinking.

Act II – The Engaging Action		
Recommendation	**Explanation**	**Methodology/Data**
Reach suburban commuters and increase share 22%	More than 64% of your customers travel at least one hour per day	We conducted a random survey in your three target geographies
		More than 4,000 respondents completed the survey
		An analysis found that two-thirds travel at least one hour daily
	The right mix of radio ads and podcast sponsorships will help you reach them	Your customers break out into three types of listeners
		You can reach them by allocating revenue based on their listening preferences
		Targeted buys like this produce consistent results
	A $5 million investment in advertising can produce at least a 10% increase in sales	Fabrikam faced a similar situation in Q1
		They invested $5 million in a similar ad buy
		The result was a 17% increase in sales

FIGURE 10-13

The first anchor (Recommendation) headline of The Analysis story template, with its accompanying explanation and backup headlines.

Although this structure might look straightforward and logical, it literally turns upside-down the most common structure of data-driven presentations. In the conventional structure, you normally jump right into the detailed data and the methodology and then you hold off on making your recommendations until the very last slides. It's natural to think of structuring a presentation this way because you might think that if you start from the beginning of a project and go one at a time through the detailed steps you took to arrive at a recommendation, your ideas will have more credibility.

However, the risk you take when you do that is that you overwhelm the limited capacity of working memory of your clients with so much new information, as shown in Figure 10-14, that they are disoriented and confused—which diminishes your credibility.

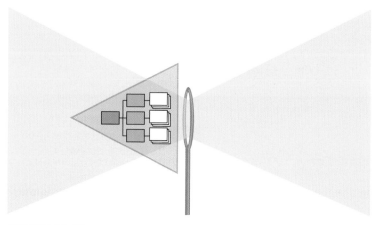

FIGURE 10-14

Presenting your methodology and data first—before your recommendations— can quickly overwhelm the working memory of your audience.

None of this is to say that you will not present detailed data or charts when you show the explanation and backup (Methodology/Data) slides. If your clients have prior knowledge of complex data structures, the slides can include those elements without overwhelming their working memory because the understanding of the structure of this information is already held in the audience's long-term memory. If the source of the data is important to have available for detailed discussion, provide that on paper or in an electronic document to accompany the presentation.

RESEARCHING AND ADDING AVAILABLE GRAPHICS FOR THE ANALYSIS

Now that you have addressed the data you will cover in the explanation and backup (Methodology/Data) columns and you have determined the priority and sequence of all the slides in Act II, free yourself up creatively to make the critical top level of the presentation as interesting, engaging, meaningful, and memorable to your clients as possible. Being visually creative in what is supposed to be a data-driven presentation might initially be perceived as intellectual fluff, but you know that your creative visual surfaces rest on a foundation built from a rigorous critical-thinking process. If your graphics are an aesthetic match with your audience, your clients will find the images refreshing, and the presentation itself will differentiate you from your competitors.

CREATING YOUR OWN GRAPHICS If you can't find the illustrations you need, create your own or hire someone to create them using a vector illustration software program. Aim for a simple, pared-down style for the illustrations. If you export these graphics in .emf, .wmf, or .svg file formats, you might be able to group, regroup, and recolor the elements using the PowerPoint graphics tools.

REVIEWING THE SLIDES FOR THE ANALYSIS

After creating slides from the headlines in the story template, start with sketching the map and anchor slides as shown in Figure 10-15.

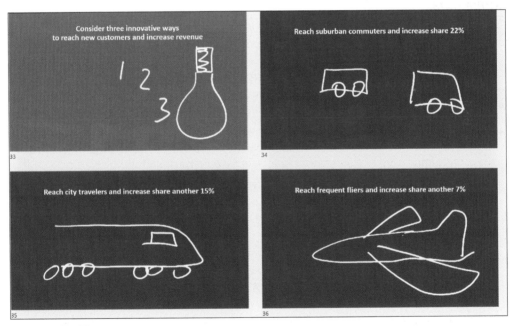

FIGURE 10-15

Sketches of the map and anchor slides of The Analysis presentation.

A sketch of light bulbs illustrates the headline "Consider three innovative ways to reach new customers and increase revenue." The first anchor slide, upper right, features a photograph of cars on a highway to illustrate the headline, "Reach suburban commuters and increase share 22%." The second anchor slide, lower left, features a photo of city traffic to illustrate the headline "Reach city travelers and increase share another 15%," and the third anchor slide, lower right, features a photo of an airplane to illustrate "Reach frequent fliers and increase share another 7%."

After photos were added to the slides as in Figure 10-16, the map and anchor slides create a compelling and interesting way to present the most important information your audience wants to know.

FIGURE 10-16

The map and anchor slides with graphics added.

The explanation and backup slides that follow, along with your backup printouts and spreadsheets, will go into the rigorous detail of quantitative-based reasoning that your client expects.

Much more than capturing the data on the slides, you have captured the imagination of your audience so that they can literally see what your abstract recommendations will mean to them. And in the process, you turned a data-driven presentation into a cognitive-driven presentation, with a visually appealing result.

EXAMPLE: PRESENTING A REPORT

The next example of a presentation is based on a scenario in which your team recently contributed to the successful launch of Product A, and you are now working on the launch of Product B. Your regional supervisor is paying you a visit, and you want to let her know how things are going, so you prepare a presentation for her—The Report. You see this supervisor only occasionally, so this is one of your few chances to meet with her in person.

Because this is just an update and not a set of recommendations, as in The Analysis, you initially plan to put together only an "informational" presentation to show her the facts. When you dig a little deeper into what people mean by this phrase, they usually say that they want to provide someone with lists of facts, typically in the form of bulleted lists of information. Without purpose or context, a list is just that—a list. If what you want to do is simply pass on facts for someone's reference, you don't need to go through the trouble of creating a presentation or having a meeting—just send the facts in an email message, document, or spreadsheet and save yourself and your audience the time.

However, if you and your audience go through the trouble of gathering together, it should always be for a purpose—to make information and facts *useful* in a way that helps make a decision.

When you do have a reason to meet beyond just passing on facts, completing Act I of your story template is a reliable place to start your presentation because the process of completing Act I always guides you to transform information into clear understanding that your audience finds meaningful and practical.

Generic informational presentations normally lack a structure with a beginning, middle, and end. However, with Act I as a structure for your introduction, you know that you will start strong and end strong every time. With Act II as a structure for the body of your presentation, you know that you will elevate the most important information to the top level of your audience's attention and cover the explanation and detail from there. Instead of listing every possible piece of information and showing *every* detail, you get right to the most important information and show only *the most important* details.

In this specific example, you might not be recommending or selling anything to your supervisor, but she does have something you need—her ongoing support. She wants to know you are on top of things so that she can focus on handling problems elsewhere. With this perspective in mind, Act I of your story template for The Report takes shape, as shown in Figure 10-17. In this example, the hook headline explains, "Product Launch A went like clockwork," and the relevance headline affirms, "You'd like to make sure Product Launch B goes just as smoothly."

Act I – The Compelling Setup			
The Hook	Product Launch A went like clockwork		
The Relevance	You'd like to make sure Product Launch B goes just as smoothly		
The Challenge	You haven't had a chance since last quarter to examine how things are working here		
The Desire	You'd like to be confident things are working smoothly		
The Map	Be assured we will meet our goals and launch Product B on time		
Act II – The Engaging Action			
Summary	**Breakdown**		**Details**

FIGURE 10-17

Act I of The Report presentation example.

The challenge headline summarizes the challenge your supervisor faces: "You haven't had a chance since last quarter to examine how things are working here." Where she wants to be at desire is, "You'd like to be confident things are working smoothly." To get from a state of uncertainty at the challenge to confidence at the desire, you'll present the map headline, "Be assured we will meet our goals and launch Product B on time." Instead of leaving your boss unclear about what she should do, you now have presented information in a way that ensures she can take action on it, even if that action is to believe something new or different—in this case, to be assured of your progress.

As shown in Figure 10-17, for this type of presentation change the Act II column headings from "Anchors" to "Summary," and from "Explanation" to "Breakdown," and from "Backup" to "Details." As you write your anchor (summary) headlines, you'll cover the three most important points that explain how your supervisor will be assured that you will meet your goals:

■ **Anchor 1** We accomplished what we said we would.

■ **Anchor 2** We are on track to accomplish our new goals.

■ **Anchor 3** We are prepared to overcome challenges that appear.

As you complete the rest of the story template, you'll cover the explanation (Breakdown) and backup (Details) slides that include the diagrams, charts, screen captures, photos, and anecdotes that back up your appeal for her support.

REVIEWING THE ACT I SLIDES FOR THE REPORT

Finding graphics for your slides doesn't have to be a time-consuming and elaborate process, as demonstrated in Figure 10-18. The hook, relevance, challenge, and desire headlines are all on these four slides in the standard sequence, except the font has been changed to white to match the background, so they are not visible. The hook slide (upper left) features a photo of a box to illustrate the hidden headline "Product Launch A went like clockwork." The relevance slide (upper right) features the same photo on the left and a duplicate photo on the right to refer to the headline "You'd like to make sure Product Launch B goes just as smoothly."

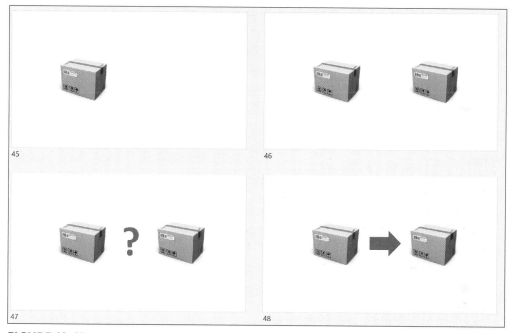

FIGURE 10-18

The hook, relevance, challenge, and desire slides of The Report.

The challenge slide (lower left) features the same two boxes and between them a text box with a question mark to illustrate the headline "You haven't had a chance since last quarter to examine how things are working here." On the desire slide (lower right), the same two boxes now have an arrow between them that illustrates "You'd like to be confident things are working smoothly."

The simplicity of using just a single photo of a box to tell a visual story across the four slides is a good example of how finding and using graphics can be simple and easy—but still have a sophisticated impact.

Because you are giving this presentation to such a small audience, deliver it on a lap-top screen or in a printed form using notes pages handouts. But whatever way you go, with a strong story foundation in place, you have transformed what normally might be an "informational" list of facts into a much more meaningful and useful story that you carry forward both visually and verbally.

EXAMPLE: PRESENTING IN A CLASSROOM

Beyond courtrooms and meeting rooms, visual storytelling has proven effective at structuring presentations used in classrooms and training rooms at every educational level. After all, the research realities described in Chapter 2 that inspire visual storytelling are being extensively tested and applied by educational psychologists interested in improving learning using multimedia. And just as with The Analysis example, applying visual storytelling to an educational presentation usually does not involve creating new material; rather, you restructure existing material in a new way to make the material easier for your students' working memory to handle.

In an educational presentation, the aim in the first few slides is to make the topic of your course emotionally relevant to your students and set the framework that will guide your students' understanding of the material to follow in the class. Instead of potentially losing students' interest and dampening their motivation to learn, you'll help them maintain interest from the first slide to the last.

In the example Act I shown in Figure 10-19 you are an instructor teaching a class on DNA. You introduce the hook as "DNA is one of the great scientific discoveries of all time" and then engage the students by placing them in the relevance as "In this class, you will get to play a role in discovering it for yourself." Next, the challenge the students face is "Without knowing how to approach it, DNA seems like an unsolvable puzzle," and desire is "You'd like to solve the puzzle to learn how to apply the knowledge of DNA." Students can resolve the tension between not knowing how to approach the puzzle of DNA and solving it by following your map, "Solve the DNA puzzle in three steps."

Act I – The Compelling Setup	
The Hook	DNA is one of the great scientific discoveries of all time
The Relevance	In this class, you will get to play a role in discovering it for yourself
The Challenge	Without knowing how to approach it, DNA seems like an unsolvable puzzle
The Desire	You'd like to solve the puzzle to learn how to apply the knowledge of DNA
The Map	Solve the DNA puzzle in three steps

FIGURE 10-19

Act I of The Class presentation example.

With an engaging start to the presentation in writing in Act I, the next step is to complete the Act II columns of the story template. Begin by renaming the anchor column heading to "Key Learning Objective." Often the biggest challenge for educators when completing Act II is not completing the explanation and backup slides because those usually already exist in some form. Rather the difficulty comes in distilling the explanation and backup columns into an even simpler set of three anchor (Key Learning Objective) headlines. It is essential that you provide students with only a few anchor headlines that they will certainly remember, which then will serve as long-term memory reference points to access your explanation and backup headlines. In this example, as you write your anchor (Key Learning Objective) headlines, you'll cover the three most important points you want your students to remember from the class:

■ **Anchor 1** Learn the theory.

■ **Anchor 2** Review the research.

■ **Anchor 3** Apply what you know.

Continue by completing the other two columns of the story template, and then create your Act II slides from these according to the process described in the other examples in this chapter.

REVIEWING THE MAP AND ANCHOR SLIDES FOR THE CLASS

After you've sketched your slides, create a simple slide layout for your map and anchor slides by adding the illustration of a DNA strand as in Figure 10-20, and place the headlines to the left. Abbreviate the map headline to read "Solve the puzzle," as shown on the upper left, then add the three anchor headlines to the other three slides. With this approach, you use a single image and four headlines to create these important slides for your presentation.

Create the rest of the slides from the headlines of the story template, using these anchor slides to guide you and your students through the engaging experience of solving the DNA puzzle.

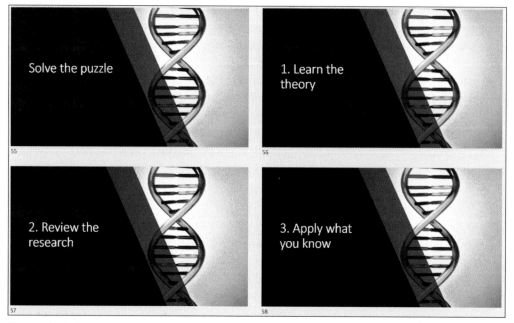

FIGURE 10-20

Map and anchor slides of The Class presentation.

EASING VISUAL STORYTELLING INTO YOUR ORGANIZATION

Although this presentation example of The Class is designed for a 45-minute presentation, you can use the story template to plan a much longer class or even a multiyear curriculum. Consider how much time you have—45 minutes, 2 hours, 3 days, or 3 years—and write in the anchor (Key Learning Objectives) column the three most important lessons you want someone to learn during that period. Then continue working in the story template from left to right—you'll add more columns to the right of the backup column depending on how deep you want to go into the material.

Together with your engaging story template structure, these slides add a visual dynamism and interest that increase the likelihood your students will remember and apply the most important information you want to teach.

EXAMPLE: PRESENTING A PITCH

In this example, you're an internet services firm making a sales pitch to a potential client. The most common outline in these types of presentations features a structure with category headings like Our Company, Our Team, Our Services, Our Differentiation, and Our Clients—the message would be essentially "All About Us." Each category heading is usually followed by list after list of facts, without a story to be found anywhere to tie them together.

Often the intention of this type of presentation is to create a single, uniform, consistent message that can be distributed to the sales team to deliver exactly as is. The only problem, though, is that the typical organizational process of making the presentation uniform also makes it canned, generic, and one-size-fits-all—in other words, boring. Not surprisingly, even though some companies spend millions of dollars and countless hours and untold energy in creating these presentations, many sales teams ignore them.

The problem is solved when the company gets the sales teams together in a room with marketing and other interested parties and puts a story template on the screen so that everyone can work on it together. Now, by viewing the first five headlines they write in Act I, everyone can agree that the salespeople in the field need to start strong every time with a story structure that puts the company's prospective clients in the starring role of the presentation. With your hook headline, you affirm to your client that "Your numbers have been off the mark" and in the relevance that "You're under pressure to improve your game." With these two simple headlines, as shown in Figure 10-21, suddenly the entire focus of the presentation has changed from "All About Us" to "All About You"—the salesperson's audience.

Act I – The Compelling Setup		
The Hook	Your numbers have been off the mark	
The Relevance	You're under pressure to improve your game	
The Challenge	Your current messages are not reaching your target	
The Desire	You'd like to hit the target more accurately and frequently	
The Map	Aim for three goals, and you'll hit the marks you want	
Act II – The Engaging Action		
Benefit	**Feature**	**Demonstration**

FIGURE 10-21

Act I of The Pitch presentation example.

Custom-tailoring this presentation to this specific audience continues in the challenge headline, which defines the client's challenge as "Your current messages are not reaching your target," and in the desire headline, which defines the client's goal as "You'd like to hit the target more accurately and frequently." How does the client get from A to B? The map headline provides direction in the form of the headline "Aim for three goals, and you'll hit the marks you want."

As your team moves to Act II to flesh out the rest of the presentation, you can change the Act II headings from "Anchor" to "Benefit," from "Explanation" to "Feature," and from "Backup" to "Demonstration." Now, in the anchor (Benefit) column, write headlines that explain how aiming for three goals will help your audience hit the marks they want. By choosing to answer the question *How?*, you make this an explanatory presentation rather than a persuasive one. This makes the presentation feel more like a consulting session than a stereotypical sales pitch. But even more importantly, this structure defines and elevates the three most important benefits as the client sees them from the context of Act I:

- ■ **Anchor 1** Hit better sales numbers with Service X.
- ■ **Anchor 2** Hit better margins with Service Y.
- ■ **Anchor 3** Hit better customer ratings with Service Z.

Here the benefits for the audience have been tightly integrated into the wording of the headlines to bring these benefits to the top level of the audience's attention. You'll definitely talk about your services throughout the rest of the Act II columns, but now the three anchor (Benefit) slides make it clear how any and all of the information in the presentation is important to the audience. This ensures that from the start, your audience is perfectly clear about the answer to the continuing question "What's in it for me?" If your service or product has more than three benefits, make the presentation modular by creating more anchor sections and hiding the slides that do not apply or interest a particular client.

PREPARING GRAPHICS FOR THE PITCH

The visual storytelling method described in this book is only one approach among many, and is intended to serve as the foundation for gaining skills you can continue to develop. The core principles work, and at the same time, feel free to improvise on them. For example, consider using a single image on the screen as you present the Act I headlines to your audience, as shown in Figure 10-22. Here a single slide of a dartboard appears on the screen, as your audience wonders what's going on—giving you the advantage of gaining their attention. As the image remains on the screen, begin talking to your hidden headline "Your numbers have been off the mark," then transition smoothly to your point in the relevance headline, "You're under pressure to improve your game." Then speak to the challenge headline, "Your messages are not reaching your target," then speak to the desire slide, explaining, "You'd like to hit the target more accurately and frequently."

Here with the economical use of a single image, you verbally relate the story of the first few headlines, making a memorable impact as you set up the Pitch to your audience.

FIGURE 10-22

A single slide that remains on the screen while the hook, relevance, challenge, and desire headlines are presented verbally.

You'll continue to show your Act II slides as usual, and when you reach the Demonstration (backup) slides, you'll switch over to another application on your desktop, as described in Chapters 7 and 8, to show sections of your live demonstration of Services X, Y, and Z at the appropriate places.

With the story template as a foundation, the BBP process produces a crisp package that is easy for any salesperson to tailor and customize, using custom layouts and placeholders that do not require the salesperson to have any graphical skill in creating layouts. But perhaps most importantly, because the sales force is involved in the creative conception and development of this story, they will feel they own it and this will be something they really use.

NOTE   As mentioned at the start of this chapter, the design constraints of the examples in this chapter include a limited budget, stock photography, and graphics that can be created within PowerPoint. With a larger budget, hire a professional presentation designer to create custom layouts and graphics especially for your presentation. Within your budget and time constraints, only your imagination and creativity will limit the possibilities.

HANDLING OBJECTIONS TO VISUAL STORYTELLING

As you begin the process of creating a visual story, keep in mind that every decision you make along the way can mean the difference between whether or not you hit the mark with your audience. Your success depends on the words you choose for your story template, the illustrations you sketch on the storyboard, the aesthetics you create across the slides with the graphics you add, and finally the way you deliver the presentation and engage your audience.

If you try visual storytelling and it doesn't work or is otherwise not received well, the most common reasons are because the story template, storyboard, graphics, aesthetics, or delivery need more work. Sometimes the content of the story template is an intellectual mismatch with the audience, or the wording is too simplistic—or not simple enough. At times the storyboard graphics are an aesthetic mismatch, or the delivery style does not connect with the audience. If any of these might be an issue, discuss the situation with your team—and with your audience, if possible—to figure out what happened, and then return to the story template, the storyboard, the guidelines, and your audience research.

However, you might present a perfectly good visual story and still find that the audience is resistant to your approach. For example, if you give your first visual story to a group where there is a strong bullet-point culture, their immediate response might be "Where are the bullet points that we expect?" or "This is too simplistic—where's the text?" If you expect you might get that reaction, prepare the audience in advance for what is about to come. Bring handouts of the notes pages, and pass them out while you verbally assure your audience that the detailed information is available here in printed format instead of on the slides. Assure them that you respect their time so much that you've done a great deal of advance work to identify only the most important information they need to know.

EASING VISUAL STORYTELLING INTO YOUR ORGANIZATION

It takes leadership to ensure that visual storytelling works, especially when working with teams and within organizations. It's not a matter of simply having an effective approach because even the best approach in the world can be stifled by an entrenched bullet-point culture. If your organization's culture cannot stray outside the narrow bounds of the conventional approach, it will take an organization-wide commitment from senior leadership that gives everyone permission and the resources to make a successful transition to a more effective approach. This has happened at the board of directors level of major organizations that have decided to move beyond a conventional approach that no longer works for them.

If you expect you might get these types of reactions, listen to the comments. If they are valid concerns, accept them and reply that you'll take them into account while you prepare your next presentation. But if the comments are more about politics than the presentation, defend your story foundation and explain how and why visual storytelling works effectively to increase the audience's understanding of your material. Explain the research realities from Chapter 2, the classical story structure of Act I from Chapter 4, the logical critical-thinking structure of Act II from Chapter 5, and the way the storyboard balances verbal and visual channels from Chapters 6 through 8. If appropriate, set up a separate meeting at your organization where you use the Chapter 2 research realities to compare the old way and the visual storytelling side by side. When you are confident you have effectively prepared your visual story, you can be confident that you present a clear case for how and why your new way of communicating works.

BBP GUIDELINES

Beyond Bullet Points (BBP) includes sets of guidelines for the processes described in this book—here, they are compiled in one place for easy reference.

THE BBP GUIDELINES

The BBP Guidelines cover the fundamentals you should follow through each of the key phases of developing a BBP presentation.

THREE GUIDELINES FOR WRITING HEADLINES

Your BBP Story Template depends on a special writing style that boils down your story to its essence. Follow these three ground rules to keep your writing concise:

- Write concise, complete sentences with a subject and a verb in active tense.
- Be clear, direct, specific, and conversational.
- Link your ideas across cells.

THREE GUIDELINES FOR STORYBOARDING

Inspired by a filmmaker's storyboard, your Microsoft PowerPoint storyboard helps you manage both the words you speak and the images you show. Follow these three ground rules to keep your storyboard coherent:

■ Be visually concise, clear, direct, and specific.

■ In Act II, sketch consistency within columns and variety across columns.

■ Sketch outside the screen, too.

THREE GUIDELINES FOR ADDING GRAPHICS

Adding graphics is the crucial last step in designing the storyboard. Follow these three ground rules to make sure you get the graphics right:

■ See it in seconds.

■ Align the aesthetics with the audience.

■ Defend your foundation!

THREE GUIDELINES FOR DELIVERING YOUR PRESENTATION

Your single storyboard helps you manage your spoken words, projected visuals, and printed handouts. Follow these three ground rules to ensure that the rest of the live presentation experience is engaging:

■ Step into the screen.

■ Remove the distractions.

■ Manage the flow.

Appendix B

STARTING YOUR CHALLENGE AND DESIRE HEADLINES

As you write your Challenge and Desire headlines in Act I of your story template, you might find it helpful to review a range of phrases that provide the words you can use to start each headline.

To use this table, look down the Challenge column, and when you find a challenge phrase that matches the challenge faced by your audience, look across at the Desire column to see a corresponding desire phrase. When you've found one of each, refer to Appendix C to fill in the space between challenge and desire with a Map headline.

CHALLENGE (WHAT CHALLENGE DO I FACE?)	DESIRE (WHERE DO I WANT TO BE?)
You're overwhelmed about x.	You'd like to gain control.
You're unclear about x.	You'd like to be clear.
You're uncertain about x.	You'd like to be certain.
You don't know what to do about x.	You'd like to know what to do.
People don't appreciate your value.	You'd like people to appreciate what you do.
You have an unsolved problem with x.	You'd like to solve the problem.
Situation x is in disarray.	You'd like to bring the situation into order.
You don't suspect you have a problem with x.	You'd like to know if there is a problem.
Situation x is bad and getting worse.	You'd like to turn things around before it's too late.
Situation x is stagnating.	You'd like to stir things up.
There's a great new idea out there.	You'd like to incorporate it into what you're doing now.
There's a bad idea out there.	You'd like to avoid it and stick with what you're doing.
You're uncertain whether you should support x.	You're certain you'd like to give your support.
You don't know yet about x.	You'd like to know about it.
There is confusion about x.	You'd like to clear up the confusion.
There is ambiguity about x.	You'd like clarity.
You're feeling frustrated about x.	You'd like to feel better about it.
You feel like you're not earning enough.	You'd like to improve your earnings.
You're not sure if we're a good match.	You'd like to know more so you can decide.
You don't know us.	You'd like to know us.
You don't know how to begin x.	You'd like to know how to begin.
You don't know how you can help.	You'd like to know how you can help.
You're unclear how all the pieces fit together.	You'd like to be clear how the pieces fit together.
You're not sure where you should go.	You'd like to know where to go.
You're unsure how we've been doing.	You'd like to know how we've been doing.
You're frustrated with x.	You'd like to remove the frustration.
The odds are against you.	You'd like to find a way to beat the odds.
You're dissatisfied with x.	You'd like to be satisfied.
You see a negative trend regarding x.	You'd like to see a positive trend.
Your numbers are down.	You'd like to bring your numbers up.

CHALLENGE (WHAT CHALLENGE DO I FACE?)	DESIRE (WHERE DO I WANT TO BE?)
You face obstacles.	You'd like to overcome the obstacles.
You have several options.	You'd like to choose the best option.
You've been dealt a bad hand.	You'd like to figure out how to win the game.
You feel out of control.	You'd like to gain control.
You don't know how x happened.	You'd like to know how x happened.
You've heard one side of the story.	You'd like to hear the other side of the story.
You're concerned about x.	You'd like to resolve your concern.
You don't know what to do in a new situation.	You'd like to know what to do.
You don't know the topic.	You'd like to know the topic.
You're overwhelmed.	You'd like to gain control.
You see injustice.	You'd like to find justice.
The truth has been hidden.	You'd like to reveal the truth.
Something is irritating you.	You'd like to remove the irritation.

Appendix C

STARTING YOUR MAP HEADLINES

Once you have written your Challenge and Desire headlines, you'll need a Map headline to close the gap between the two headlines. As you consider what to write, review a range of phrases that provide the words you can use to start each headline.

To use the following table, look down the middle column to review words and phrases to begin your Map headline, and then look at the range of phrases in the right column to complete the headline. You'll find a range of Map headline possibilities, including themes to integrate through the rest of the story template. This is only a partial list to get you started—feel free to keep building the table with your own headlines.

EXPLANATION	■ Understand ■ Observe ■ See	■ How this works ■ The way this is structured ■ The three components ■ The three sections
RECOMMENDATION	■ Partner with ■ Work with ■ Hire ■ Join ■ Ask ■ Make use of ■ Tell ■ Support	■ Us ■ Our people ■ Our team ■ Our organization ■ Our network
	■ Approve ■ Accept ■ Permit ■ Adopt ■ Buy ■ Support ■ Facilitate ■ Be assured of	■ The idea ■ The efforts ■ The proposal ■ The budget ■ The product ■ The service ■ The initiative
	■ Disapprove ■ Reject ■ Prevent ■ Don't adopt ■ Don't buy ■ Don't support ■ Question ■ Doubt	■ The idea ■ The efforts ■ The proposal ■ The budget ■ The product ■ The service ■ The initiative
	■ Adjust ■ Change ■ Transform	■ Your strategy ■ Your course ■ Your situation

RECOMMENDATION (CONTINUED)	■ Share	■ Your ideas
		■ Responsibility
		■ The burden
		■ The risk
	■ Grow	■ More market share
		■ Better relationships
		■ Profits
THE CHECKLIST MOTIF	■ Check off	■ Three items from the list
		■ Three things you need to do
	■ Follow	■ Three simple steps
		■ The formula (A+B=C; 1+2=3)
	■ Do ■ Think	■ Three things
THE JOURNEY MOTIF	■ Follow	■ The three road signs
		■ The roadmap
	■ Look for ■ Avoid	■ The three pitfalls
		■ The three dangers
		■ The three missed signals
	■ Discover ■ Find ■ Uncover	■ The three elements
		■ The hidden treasure
		■ The three secrets
		■ A new route
		■ What has been hidden from you
THE GAME MOTIF	■ Put together the puzzle ■ Solve the puzzle	■ In three steps
		■ To reveal the big picture
		■ To discover what happened
	■ Score	■ A touchdown
		■ A goal
		■ A run
	■ Win	■ A goal
		■ The game

THE GAME MOTIF (CONTINUED)	■ Watch	■ How the shell game was played ■ How the house of cards was built ■ How the hand is played ■ How the cards were dealt
	■ Hit ■ Aim for	■ The target ■ The bull's eye ■ A home run
THE PROJECT MOTIF	■ Build	■ The structure in three steps ■ The three parts of a strong foundation ■ A solid base
	■ Tap into	■ Three undiscovered wells ■ Three new opportunities
	■ Remove ■ Avoid ■ Overcome	■ The three barriers ■ The three obstacles ■ The three hurdles
	■ Build a bridge ■ Cross the chasm	■ To get to the other side ■ To get what you want ■ To avoid pitfalls
	■ Turn it around	■ In three stages ■ In three steps
THE STORY MOTIF	■ Watch ■ Follow ■ Pay attention to	■ How the story unfolds ■ Motive + means = death ■ The three parts of the story
	■ Find ■ Interpret ■ Follow	■ The three clues

INDEX